THE CLASSLESS SOCIETY

DATE DUE

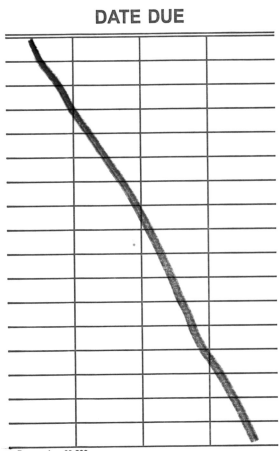

THE CLASSLESS SOCIETY

Paul W. Kingston

STANFORD UNIVERSITY PRESS
STANFORD, CALIFORNIA
2000

Stanford University Press
Stanford, California

© 2000 by the Board of Trustees of the Leland Stanford Junior
University

Printed in the United States of America on acid-free, archival-quality paper.

Library of Congress Cataloging-in-Publication Data

Kingston, Paul W.
  The classless society / Paul W. Kingston.
      p.   cm. — (Studies in social inequality)
  Includes bibliographical references and index.
    ISBN 0-8047-3804-1 (cloth : alk. paper)—ISBN 0-8047-3806-8 (pbk. : alk.
paper)
    1. Social classes—United States.   2. Social mobility—United States.
I. Title. II. Series.
HN90.S6 K56 2000
305.5—dc21   00-023556

Original printing 2000

Last figure below indicates the year of this printing:
09   08   07   06   05   04   03   02   01   00

Typeset by G & S Typesetters in 10/14 Sabon

For Jane

CONTENTS

Tables

Figure

As the opening paragraph of Chapter 1 clearly indicates, I stake out a strong position on a controversial topic in this book. No suspense is called for: I argue that the United States is now a classless society, not a novel conclusion. Nor, of course, is it generally accepted; indeed, in many quarters it amounts to academic (and political) heresy. But it is the conclusion, I'll argue in fine detail, that good evidence compels.

What distinguishes my no-classes argument, I believe, is that it is based on an unusually systematic, wide-ranging synthesis of the findings of empirical social science. Because I want to persuade skeptics, I make the case by relating in fairly substantial detail what the best research has established. I think it unlikely that skeptics can be convinced by a book that follows the conventional "Research shows . . . (Some Scholar 19xx; Some Other Scholar 19xx)"—and then pronounces the validity of its conclusion. Here you'll get details of the best relevant research so that you can judge for yourselves whether I draw reasonable inferences. My strategy is based on the premise that the force of data, confronted firsthand, can be persuasive.

But, emphatically, this strategy is not based on any sense that "facts" somehow speak for themselves. Any convincing assessment of the question "Are there classes?" must be embedded in a reasonable conceptual framework. Too often proponents of each side talk past each other because they don't rigorously address the question, "How would you recognize a class if you saw one?" To answer this theoretically loaded question, it is essential to define class and stipulate the analytical criteria and kinds of evidence that should be used to establish whether classes exist.

My answer to the above question draws directly on long-standing, common tenets of class theory, broadly conceived to include disparate arguments. By treating class structuration as a multidimensional variable, I make explicit and precise what is often implicit in the realist traditions of class theory. I try to establish clear, reasonable grounds for engaging the issue. These conceptual grounds are as essential to my argument as the empirical findings that support it.

So, despite the preponderance of empirical material in the following pages, my effort is not a matter of pitting theory *versus* empirical research—much less implying that the latter is intellectually preferable to the former. Rather, I'm motivated by the premise that theoretical propositions should be empirically validated. That should be pretty uncontroversial, but I feel compelled to state it because some class theorists seem reluctant to consider the relevance of empirical research. I focus on the empirical side because class theorists have promulgated many abstract statements, conceptual distinctions, and speculative propositions with relatively little attention to developing empirical support. What is needed is an intensive empirical assessment of all these ideas.

Fortunately, many good analyses can be used to make this assessment. But didn't I just say that there has been relatively little empirical testing of class theory? The point is that many analyses bear directly or indirectly on limited aspects of class theory. What's missing is a suitable synthesis of these studies oriented to the large general question about the extent of class structuration.

My debt to the efforts of numerous scholars will be readily evident. In many cases, I summarize key findings and integrate the author's own limited anticlass conclusion into a larger framework; in other cases I summarize findings and make inferences that counter the author's own. Regardless, this book is possible only because so much good work preceded it. There is an implicit message in this synthetic approach: that sociologists have conducted lots of good research and that we should believe the results of our collective enterprise. True, not all the claims of class theorists can be subject to equally rigorous tests, but we have more than enough good evidence to cast very serious doubt on the essence of class theory.

The fact that I wrote this book surprises me. If you'd asked me in my undergraduate or graduate days, or even in my early professional career, whether classes exist, I'd surely have said yes. As a college sophomore, the first quantitatively grounded social science that I ever read was Goldthorpe's *The*

Affluent Worker. I was persuaded by its central message: no embourgeoisement; the working class lives. In graduate school I was taken by Burawoy's
class-based critique of status-attainment research, and Giddens's *The Class
Structure of the Advanced Societies* was my favorite book. I myself wrote
about upper class elite education. As an instructor of introductory sociology,
I lectured on the reality of classes in explicit contrast to gradational analysis. I came out for Fitzgerald in the famous Fitzgerald-Hemingway debate on
the rich (see Chapter 9).

So what happened? Perhaps my memory strives unduly for a moment of
epiphany, but I do recall how a question in Sociology 101 activated nagging
doubts. We were looking at a basic mobility table with both outflows and
inflows. I made the obvious point about unequal chances of getting ahead,
but I recall a student saying (roughly), "But the people in all the categories
have pretty diverse backgrounds." So much for the demographic cohesion of
classes. About the same time (the mid-eighties), I read James Davis's (1982)
devastating empirical critique of the class culture argument (see Chapter 7
for a lengthier discussion). After that, more and more analyses seemed to
support the idea that class simply didn't matter in the way people (at least,
sociologists) thought it did. Steven Brint's (1984) skeptical analysis of "new
class" theories was also a particularly influential model for the kind of analysis that I thought was important to conduct.

In other words, as far as I can tell, my conversion to a "no-classes" argument wasn't motivated by any personal experience or political change of
heart. Crudely put, the data made me do it.

Yet, plainly enough, class theory is hardly politically innocent, and my
argument is unlikely to be evaluated on purely analytical grounds. (Neither
my critics nor those who agree with me are exempt from this charge.) Therefore, at both the beginning and the end of this book I consider the relationship between class theory and political commitment. I do this not to inocu-
late my argument from criticism ("Of course that ideologue won't agree
with me"), but rather to encourage a reflexive reading, leading to an intellectual engagement in which concerns for objective evidence at least have a
relatively prominent role.

Although textual citations indicate my gratitude to many other scholars,
a number of people provided direct assistance and support that deserve special acknowledgment.

This book has had a long birth, and therefore I must thank some who offered advice many years ago as well as those whose help was more recent: Bethany Bryson, Ted Caplow, Sarah Corse, Steve Finkel, William Form, Thomas Guterbock, Lionel Lewis, Mark Lupher, and Murray Milner. Ryan Hubbard, Ann Kingston, Amy O'Leary, and Kevin Schanning provided valuable research assistance. My enjoyable collaboration with Simon Langlois, Yannick Lemel, and Heinz Herbert Noll on a related project prompted me to develop an international perspective and sharpen my thinking. I gratefully draw on our joint labors. I also give special thanks to Erik Olin Wright, who graciously provided unpublished data from his own research project. As will be evident, I take strong exception to Wright's position, but I greatly admire his sustained and sophisticated commitment to testing class theory—and his ability to express it so clearly. David Grusky, one of Stanford's series editors, was always kindly encouraging, and his "friendly" criticisms prompted me, more than the reactions of any other, to rethink and eventually revise my argument.

My colleague and great friend Steve Nock gave me many useful scholarly comments and, much more significantly, kept me emotionally on track throughout the project. That help was invaluable. And, quite literally, without Joan Snapp this book would never have been completed. With matchless patience and good cheer, she somehow turned my hand-scribbled pages into coherent text—and always denied for herself the credit that she so richly deserved. Jane Kingston, my wife, contributed three words to the book—its title—and countless expressions of support and prodding that led to its completion. And, of course, I dedicate the book to her because she's such a great partner in life.

THE CLASSLESS SOCIETY

CHAPTER ONE

Framing the Issue

Are there classes in America? No—at least not significantly so in light of a meaningful, realist conception of class.

My qualification is important and will be elaborated. Yet it is not a qualification that follows from an idiosyncratic sense of class, nor from an unusual method of analysis. My answer is a frontal and fundamental challenge to class theory. Very directly, my thesis is that groups of people having a common economic position—what are commonly designated as "classes"—do not significantly share distinct, life-defining experiences. I advance this thesis on the record of many sophisticated empirical analyses. If we take this record seriously, it indicates that class theories misrepresent the structure of inequality in contemporary American society.

I am acutely aware that in taking this position I risk being labeled a social ostrich, or worse. Everyone can see the reality of rich and poor and the many gradations of material comfort that exist between these extremes. And if class is our "dirty secret," as the prominent literary critic Benjamin Demott has claimed, it is not very well kept. What American is surprised by the claim that the children of rich people have a much better chance of getting ahead than the children of others? That certainly comes across as a "class analysis" even if the public discussion doesn't neatly fit the conceptual frameworks favored by scholars. Also, haven't Americans repeatedly been exposed to an "underclass" in television specials and journalistic accounts? The empirical referents of this group may be less than clear in the public mind, partly because the term triggers such a range of ideological responses. Yet whether this ill-defined group is an object of compassion or scorn, the reality of an underclass is commonly accepted. At the same time, self-designated "middle-class" people bemoan a collective fate—for example, being "squeezed out" of higher education by rising tuitions and financial aid programs that favor lower-status families. Few politicians can resist proclaiming that they represent this group.

What these references to popular "class analysis" suggest, however, is that Americans recognize the reality and significance of economic *inequalities* in our society. Though used with some ambivalence, the language of class is a convenient shorthand for describing these inequalities. Beyond question, huge inequalities exist and Americans recognize them. But this use of class language is not analytically rigorous or precise. The crucial point is that the reality of economic inequality, even substantial degrees of it, does not necessarily imply the existence of classes. As I will argue, these inequalities generally reflect multirunged ladders of gradation, not differences in how a few discrete groups—that is, classes—actually live. This distinction is vital, even if it is unlikely to inform how most people talk. As I will also elaborate, *how* inequality is structured—specifically whether there are divisions between bounded classes—fundamentally affects the nature of our political life and the likely trajectory of social change.

Indeed, this is why class analysis generates such scholarly contention. The stakes are overtly and ineluctably political. Class theory is energized, both as an analytical concern and as a political enterprise, by the resonance of Marx's famous aphorism "All history is the history of class struggle." This is so whether analysts accept, modify, or reject the proposition. In claiming to have identified *the* key driving force of history, Marx established the terms of the debate: Does class structure fundamentally undergird collective life? And relatedly, is class conflict the main determinant of social trajectories? How scholars have answered these questions has often had more to do with their ideological concerns—hopes and fears about social transformations—than empirical evidence.

Like others who have confronted the issue, then, I must anticipate that my answer—typically deemed a conservative one—will be judged on ideological grounds. I will dispute in a later discussion that a "no-classes" answer necessarily has conservative implications, but my concern here is not to advance any particular political agenda. My straightforward hope is that you will accept the possibility of adjudicating the issue on empirical grounds and evaluate the quality of the evidence presented. (Yes, in that very general sense, you must be a positivist.)

My answer challenges a long-standing intellectual tradition that has been recently revitalized: class *theory* is alive and prominent. In the last decade or two, it has been revived by a new openness in Marxist thought, distinctive emphases within the Weberian tradition, and some empirical work that employs class as a central concept. Theoretical dispute reigns on very important questions about class. But it is impossible to overlook the scholarly prominence of these arguments, much less their common insistence that class is the fundamental stratifying force—or at least one that intersects with race and gender in defining the system of inequality.

Unfortunately, class theorists tend to be long on abstract statements and conceptual distinctions and short on empirical support. Of course some gap between theory and research is a normal part of the scholarly enterprise. I argue, however, that class theory not only has been developed with little empirical validation, but has been advanced in the face of much disconfirming research. The task of the following pages is to marshal evidence for this indictment. Obviously the force of my argument hinges on how I address the question "Are there classes?" Two issues are paramount: (1) the definition of class and, relatedly, the defining characteristics of class theory; and (2) the analytical criteria and kinds of evidence that should be used to establish whether classes exist.

I can summarize my position by saying that classes exist to the extent that class location—an objective position within the economic order—significantly shapes the fundamental content of social lives. To employ the well-known analytical distinction, I thereby take a realist rather than a nominalist approach. To be useful, class theory can't merely define specific social divisions as consequential; it must show that these divisions correspond to the collective realities that people experience and perceive. In advocating this realist approach, I follow the lead of such disparate thinkers as Marx (in much of his writing), Weber, Schumpeter, Warner, and Fussell. As Dennis Wrong (1988: 441) has written, " all of the major nineteenth- and twentieth-century theorists of class were unmistakably 'realists,' regardless of whether they thought classes were based on economic interests, shared values, or common access to power."

The key organizing concept in my analysis is what Anthony Giddens (1973: 105) calls structuration, "the modes in which 'economic relationships' become translated into 'non-economic' social structures." In this perspective, it is not a yes/no definitional matter of whether classes exist. The concept of structuration suggests that the stratifying force of class can be variable and that its reality can be discerned only in how people carry out their lives. And so, in brief, my qualification to the "no" means that class structuration in America is weak: for the most part, groups of people having a common economic position do not share distinct, life-defining experiences.

Because I use a very inclusive definition of class theory, the above indictment applies to a wide range of arguments.[1] Despite all the analytical and political disputes among class theorists, they share basic premises about social structure. The defining premise is that the *stratification system most fundamentally consists of a small set of distinct groups—classes—defined and ordered by their economic position.* In this view, the number of these groups is small; the size of most groups is large. Even if theorists disagree about how to define economic position, the common claim is that the class system is most basically an economically rooted phenomenon.

The related premise of all class theories is that *class positions and relations are greatly consequential, in both individual and collective life.* The impact, so class theorists claim, extends to crucial realms of life: notably, how people live in material terms, what opportunities they have for emotionally satisfying lives, how political life is structured and social goods are distributed, and how technologies are used and economic change is managed. That is, the impact of class is felt in both the micro and macro aspects of social life. Class theorists generally make strong claims: in their view, class is either the main axis of stratification around which fundamental aspects of society are structured, or it is at least one of the main axes. Although the latter, more modest view seems to have greater currency among contemporary theorists, the distinctive analytical power of class theory derives from the claim that classes are a central, enduring feature of social organization.

Let me stress that my definition of class theory covers more than all the Marxian and neo-Marxian variants. It incorporates as well the recent developments in neo-Weberian analysis (e.g., Goldthorpe 1987) and Marxian-Weberian hybrids (e.g., Giddens 1973). Some of these analysts equivocate about using the term "class" and their work has been labeled "closure theory" (Murphy 1988). Yet in each case, these theories emphasize the distinctiveness and social consequence of large socioeconomic groups. Relatedly, they reject conceptualizing the stratification system as multirunged ladders of continuous gradation—the premise of the most thoroughly developed theoretical alternative (outlined in the next section).

To be sure, differences *within* class theory are significant, but important common claims have too often become obscured in all the debates, often arcane, about these differences. Indeed, some of the disputes between Marxian and Weberian class theories are less substantive than the theorists often claim. Erik Olin Wright, for example, is the leading figure in neo-Marxist class theory. In attempting to resolve the "problem of the middle class"—a large group that is not readily accommodated in Marx's abstract dichotomous class model—Wright (1985) argues that, in addition to property, skill and organizational position are systemic sources of exploitation. Whatever the merits of this viewpoint, it does have more than a slight Weberian tinge. Indeed, Wright himself has recently argued that "posing Marx and Weber as polar opposites is a bit misleading because in many ways Weber is speaking in his most Marxian voice when he talks about class" (1996: 694). By the same token, Anthony Giddens claims primary theoretical allegiance to Weber and some inspiration from Marx; but his emphasis on the role of property in defining the class system makes him seem more Marxist than many self-professed Marxists may be willing to concede. Furthermore, as I detail in Chapter 3, theorists who disagree about the underlying basis of the class structure end up depicting the major lines of cleavage in remarkably similar ways.

This is not the place to dissect the conceptual distinctions among all varieties of class theory, nor to assess their concordance with classic traditions. Much more to the point here is to emphasize that seemingly divergent theorists have commonly claimed that economically rooted cleavages in the stratification system fundamentally shape social life. The burden of my argument, then, is to show that they are all wrong.

But Differences . . .

Class theorists have answered important questions in different ways. Some brief attention to these differences is in order.

1. What is the fundamental stratifying factor or set of factors within the economy? The Marxist answer, in brief, is property: classes are defined by relations of production, and thus the fundamental divide is between capital-

ists and the proletariat. Weberians stress labor-market capacities, the differential rewards that accrue to property, organizational authority, and skills. Hence, in the Weberian view, differences in the sphere of distribution define classes. At issue is the primacy of production-based versus distribution-based differences in defining classes.

2. What is the nature of class relations? In Marxist metatheory, classes are a constitutive feature of capitalist society—a form of economic organization that inherently exploits the propertyless. By definition, the objective interests of classes are fundamentally in opposition, and class conflict is the expected eventual consequence. In contrast, theories of class that emphasize people's location within the distributive sphere are more apt to portray class relations as potentially antagonistic, not necessarily conflictual. In this latter view, class relations are open to compromise and subject to historical contingencies. In short, the issue turns on the inevitability and severity of class conflict.

3. What impact does the class system have on the trajectory of social change? Again, the larger Marxist metatheory sets the terms of debate. The Marxist perspective is deterministic, even teleological: contradictions in a mode of production are expressed in class conflict, and in an ongoing process the resolution of this conflict ushers in a new, more advanced mode and eventually human emancipation. The anti-Marxist dissent expresses a much more open sense of history. In varying ways, it suggests that the class structure shapes the range of social possibilities but does not determine the course of history.

4. What is the scope of theoretical claims? The range of scope varies from the entire sweep of history ("All history is the history of class conflict") to the particulars of a specific contemporary society. Between these extremes of inclusive and restrictive scope, class theories have been applied to conceptually defined social orders like capitalist societies, modern welfare states, and postindustrial societies. In general, the greater the scope of the theoretical argument, the more abstract it tends to be.

Each of these questions has prompted volumes of controversy, often about the internal logic of conceptual statements. For example: Is exploitation a feature of production or of distribution? What is an objective class interest? Questions such as these tend to be addressed by advancing definitions, drawing conceptual distinctions, and making abstract claims about the internal logic of a system—claims often without obvious empirical referents. Implicitly and explicitly, controversies about these matters are also fueled by ideological differences. Some answers make social transformation seem more or less likely (or possible) and are valued for that reason.

I argue, however, that differences on these issues are worth debating only if it can be shown that conceptually defined classes identify social entities that have distinctive, characteristic experiences. Class theory can make a compelling case only if it meets this challenge. For instance, why debate the significance of class conflict within the logic of capitalistic development unless identifiable groups defined as classes actually struggle with each other? Why try to decide on conceptual grounds whether capitalism creates basic fissures with attendant objective interests when there is an historical record to consider? My argument, in other words, is that these differences within class theory are salient insofar as class structuration exists—a criterion elaborated in Chapter 2.

THE THEORETICAL ALTERNATIVE

To sharpen the sense of what is distinctive about class theory, it is useful to briefly outline the main theoretical alternative, so-called stratification theory. I say "so-called" deliberately because there is no definitive text that comprehensively represents this general perspective. Nor is there any towering intellectual figure with which to associate this argument: there is no Marx or Weber of stratification theory. Even so, a general orientation has emerged in the writings of many sociologists, predominantly American (see Curtis and Jackson 1977 for a prime example).

Three related propositions define this perspective:

1. There are at least several critical dimensions of social hierarchy—e.g., income, occupational prestige, cultural valuation.
2. Each of these dimensions has many levels of rank; the hierarchies reflect multirung ladders of continuous gradation.
3. A person's rank position on one dimension is not necessarily linked to rank position on other dimensions, and indeed some discrepancies are likely.

Thus, in contrast to class theory, the stratification perspective contends that individuals do not "cluster" as large stratified groups; rather, they experience multiple hierarchical distinctions of degree, with some variation in their relative position across hierarchies. Like class theory, this perspective recognizes the reality of inequality (even though it may be cast in a more benign light). What distinguishes these two theories are their claims about the distributional patterns of these inequalities.

At the same time, the distinction between class theory and stratification theory shouldn't be drawn too sharply. The absence of class doesn't mean that all distributional matters are entirely gradational, even as they relate to the organization of work. Most notably, the occupational hierarchy isn't simply a range of jobs distributed across continua of prestige, authority, and the like. The characteristics of some specific occupations, especially in the professions and skilled crafts, seem to create limited social solidarities. Still, to the extent that such solidarities exist, they represent clusters of limited scope within a largely gradational hierarchy, not the large stratified groups envisioned by class theory.

My point in the following pages is not to defend or elaborate any particular stratification theory, though my critique suggests the need for work in this direction. Rather, as a way to highlight the deficiencies of class theory, I will note how many findings generally support the stratification model.

If the contrast between class theory and stratification theory largely turns on different views of how economic resources are distributed, the more fundamental critique of class theory is that economic distinctions have become largely irrelevant. Culture is much in vogue. The common argument of many postmodern accounts is that the economic realm has become fundamentally destructured, and that cultural distinctions—decoupled from economic differences—are ever more significant. These distinctions include gender, race, religious identity, lifestyle commitments, and "choice" politics (e.g., ecological activism).

Surely any full account of the distinctions that matter in our social and political life must incorporate a wide range of cultural groups. But postmodernists are better at contending with the disputes of the political arena than explaining the nature of the economic realm. That realm is too self-evidently crucial in people's lives to dismiss as outmoded. The postmodernists, however, draw attention to the important issue of how economic position is connected to cultural and political commitment.

SO WHAT?

Class theory and stratification theory have very different political implications. Consider what stratification theory suggests: individuals are often subject to cross-cutting pressures (should she, say, act on the basis of her status as a modestly paid librarian? Or as a well-educated consumer of "high" culture?); individuals can perceive the possibility of "moving up," if only a little, no matter where they stand in the social hierarchy; and individuals with limited prospects in one realm of life have chances to realize their aspirations in other realms. To the extent that social arrangements are thus, large groups of individuals are unlikely to develop overarching collective senses of "we-ness" and "they-ness." Hence, there are fewer prospects of collective political action, especially for egalitarian concerns.

Of course, this implication is comforting to those who essentially favor the status quo or desire only minor reform. Conversely, and just as obviously, those on the left—with faith in the liberating potential of class conflict—will want to deny the validity of stratification theory. After all, the potential strength of underdogs lies in their numbers, but this potential can be realized only if they present a united front. The hope for a "revolution from below," then, rests on the assumption that classes, especially the working class, can be vital historical agents.

At the same time, I suggest, the stratification model doesn't necessarily imply positive sentiments about social arrangements. Your sense of justice may be deeply offended by, say, the fact that one-tenth of households has more than two-thirds of all net worth, or by the fact that socioeconomic status (a continuous measure) is strongly related to educational attainment. Both facts are consistent with the stratification model, and neither can be taken as evidence that classes—relatively bounded social groups defined by common economic positions—exist.

Nor does the general validity of stratification theory imply acceptance of a functional model of society. In analyzing the history of the concept of social class in American sociology, Michael Grimes (1991) has effectively argued that stratification theory, with its emphasis on multiple dimensions of finely gradated inequality, developed as part of a more encompassing functional paradigm. Denying the reality of antagonistic classes, this portrayal of social hierarchies is readily compatible with the functionalist vision of society as a well-integrated, consensually based, and meritocratic arrangement. Indeed, in this general vision, inequalities have been portrayed as functional—and thus, at least implicitly, a good thing. Yet, whatever their common ideological and analytical roots, stratification theory and the functional model are not *necessarily* coupled. Each of the three core propositions in stratification theory can be true without any implication that inequalities are necessary, meritocratically based, functional, or desirable.

AN ANTICLASS ORTHODOXY?

If I asked readers, at this stage of the book, to register their opinion on my basic thesis, what way would the vote go? Some might opt out on the grounds that I haven't suitably conceptualized the issue or that I have misguided epistemological commitments. But what of those who grant that this is a legitimate inquiry? I don't think it's at all clear how the vote would go—an uncertainty that shows how intellectually alive (perhaps increasingly so) the issue is.

Class theorists may be inclined to dismiss my thesis as merely repeating the reigning anticlass orthodoxy in American stratification research. (The term "stratification" in itself has been viewed as reflecting this perspective.) Undeniably, class theory has not had a prominent role in American sociology, certainly in comparison with British and Continental sociology, where the intellectual ghost of Marx has been more conspicuous. This neglect is not surprising in the context of American culture. Although the actual extent of American "exceptionalism" is surely in doubt, widespread belief in it created an inhospitable climate for theories of class. The very notion of class appears to contradict American ideals of equality and opportunity. It has seemed much "too European," and with its inexorable links to the Marxian legacy, much too radical in its political implications. Yet class theorists seem to attribute greater intellectual closure within the academic mainstream than actually exists (cf. Knottnerus 1987).

Perhaps the most commonly cited example of anticlass analysis is Robert Nisbet's (1959) essay "The Decline and Fall of the Concept of Social Class." In uncompromising language he pronounced the death of class as a useful sociological concept: it is "nearly useless for the classification of data of wealth, power, and social status in contemporary United States and much of Western society in general." Strong words indeed, but it is worth recalling that they appeared in a seven-page essay, more than three decades ago, in an unprestigious journal.

Only very recently has the death-of-class thesis been advanced with any rigor, and much of that criticism is from non-American scholars. Jan Pakulski and Malcom Waters (1996), two Australian scholars, effectively argue that class theory stands or falls on the demonstration that alleged class divisions correspond to matters like mobility patterns and political behavior. However, their indictment—though largely correct, I believe—primarily consists of general assertions about the empirical record. They largely presuppose the conclusion, and seek to explain how and why it happened. The skeptic or fence-sitter may well demand more careful scrutiny of the relevant evidence. These same skeptics may also find Clark and Lipset's (1991) brief (and partially qualified) critique of class theory less than convincing because it relies on a limited range of data. Certainly Clark and Lipset's critics (e.g., Hout, Brooks, and Manza 1993) think the evidence supports the ongoing reality of class, but the debate is inconclusive partly because the distinction between inequality and class is not sharply maintained. At the same time, prominent class theorists such as John Goldthorpe and Erik Wright have mounted vigorous defenses (even if they seem to defend ever less ambitious versions of class theory). The prominence of their research is enviable.

Class theorists can rightly note that American stratification researchers have often implicitly denied the significance of class by not including class-rooted perspectives in their analyses. Their bias, in other words, is largely one of exclusion, not explicit denial. The obvious case in point is the status-attainment approach that has involved ever more sophisticated retests and elaborations of Blau and Duncan's (1967) work. Clearly, individual-level continuous measures of hierarchy have held privileged position within this approach, though the conditioning effects of structural context have been added to the basic model. But in light of debates about the limits of this approach, it is not settled whether the methodological tail (i.e., the general linear model) wagged the substantive dog, or whether it embodied implicit, undeveloped theory. Whatever the case, it is surely obvious that status-attainment researchers gave much more attention to reporting regression coefficients than to testing, much less refuting, class theory.

In a similar way, all the research on the impact of continuous measures of stratification (like years of education or occupational prestige) on various dimensions of social life has largely had a life of its own, divorced from the concerns of class theory. A typical concern, for example, is whether occupational prestige is associated with an index of social tolerance or political ideology. A researcher can then specify the size of "effects," meaning the average increase in the dependent variable corresponding to a unit change in the stratification measure. As informative as such findings may be, they say nothing about the reality of classes. Whether discrete "classes" of workers have distinctive views has received far less attention, especially since the advent of regression-based techniques. The upshot is that class theory was not so much challenged as ignored.

At the same time it is worth recalling that prominent American sociologists have used class as their central referent for analyzing the system of inequality. The Lynds (1929, 1937)—the esteemed chroniclers of life in Middletown—portrayed a class-ridden society. Though not rooted in Marxian theory, they initially described a two-class society: a business and working class sharply divided by income, consumption and leisure styles, political attitudes, and personal values. Subsequent visits convinced them that a six-class division better captured the emerging complexity of an industrializing society. Warner's account of "classes" in Yankee City (Warner and Lunt 1941) was probably even more influential. For Warner, "classes" were prestige groupings, essentially consensual judgments about social standing based on a vaguely determined mixture of income, wealth, and occupation, but also based on interaction patterns and lifestyle. Obviously, for the Lynds and Warner, the conceptual underpinning of class was quite different, but their shared presumption was that the system of inequality was comprised of relatively discrete, hierarchically ordered groups. And C. W. Mills (1951, 1956), the contemporary of Nisbet, had no doubt about the ongoing existence of a class system—although it was one that was being transformed with the emergence of midlevel bureaucrats and technicians.

There is no point here in detailing the history of the concept of class in American sociology, but this brief recital of a few prominent statements should be sufficient to indicate that the concept of class (primarily in non-Marxist terms) has long had considerable scholarly standing. In recent years, as I have already noted, far from withering away, class theory is alive and well. Indeed, the American Sociological Association recently created a professional section called Race, Class, and Gender, an action suggesting that class-based scholarship enjoys current vitality within the discipline.

Ironically enough, for all the allegations of anticlass orthodoxy, our students' texts now discuss class structures as the received wisdom of our discipline. That is the inescapable message of Kerbo (1996), Gilbert and Kahl (1993), Rossides (1990), and Rothman (1993)—four well-respected, commonly used stratification texts, none written from a Marxist orientation. Introductory texts, even those self-labeled as "balanced," routinely consider alternative ways of measuring "class" and typically present "class profiles," summary statements about the conditions of life within particular classes. Reports of distinctive class cultures and family patterns are standard fare in marriage and the family texts as well.

To be sure, the coverage of class in these texts is neither conceptually rigorous nor consistent. Many appear to consider diverse aspects of stratification (e.g., income and educational categories) under the rubric of class with little attention to the conceptual and empirical problems of doing so. These discussions also do not typically resolve important issues like whether classes are distributional groupings or relational forces linked in some system of privilege and oppression. One recent review (Lucal 1994) convincingly indicates that the former is at least implicitly the much more common view. Even so, the reality of classes is not at issue.

Class theorists should recognize, then, that their case has not been summarily dismissed after receiving a full hearing. And for their part, the critics of class theory should also recognize that they have not conducted this hearing. The issues that class theorists raise are alive because they have been only fragmentarily addressed. As suggested in the Preface, I believe that the accumulated weight of many diverse studies argues against claims of substantial class structuration, but the challenge of synthetically interpreting these results is before us. Whatever the merits of my assessment of class theories, I am not defending a well-established theoretical orthodoxy.

At the outset, however, I should note an important limitation in the scope of this analysis. My focus is on the current extent of class structuration, not its history. I am strongly inclined to believe—as Pakulski and Waters contend in their aptly titled book, *The Death of Class*—that class was very significant in the early industrial order but now has been supplanted by other forms of differentiation. That history is surely fascinating in its own right, but it doesn't need to be understood in order to grapple with the large issue of the current vitality of class. The current situation is sufficiently contentious and complex to warrant its own sustained analysis. Even so, in the concluding chapter I point to social developments that fostered contemporary classlessness and deny the possibility of any future for class.

OUTLINE OF THE BOOK

A brief outline of the layout of my argument may usefully guide the reader through the ensuing chapters.

In Chapter 2, "The Case for Realism," I explain and defend a realist conception of class—a perspective which is crucial to my whole argument. Relatedly, I elaborate on Giddens's notion of structuration, which treats "class-ness" as a multidimensional variable. I discuss the five dimensions of structuration: inter- and intragenerational mobility, social interaction patterns, cultural orientations, subjective class sentiment, and political action.

Chapter 3, "Class Maps and Inequality," sets out the contours of the class system—what I call class maps—as depicted in various theoretical schemas. The question to be addressed in later chapters is the extent to which the class divisions identified in these maps correspond to differences in the way people live. This chapter also sharpens the conceptual distinction between class and economic inequality and reports data on the latter.

Chapters 4 through 8 constitute the empirical heart of the book; they separately consider each dimension of structuration. In "Mobility" (Chapter 4) I reassess well-known facts about inter- and intragenerational mobility to make the case that classes are not intergenerationally reproduced social groups and that the considerable mobility within careers also undermines structuration. All this mobility is the great solvent of classes. In "Class Sentiment" (Chapter 5) I detail the weak connection between objective class location and subjective senses of class—that is, the virtual absence of "us and them" sentiments among people in particular classes. In "The Politics of Class" (Chapter 6) I turn to the matter that so energizes debates about class. Even if you don't accept the Marxian conceit that all history is the history of class conflict, the potential significance of class—as explained earlier—is rooted in its political implications. The resonance of class in our political life is slight. "Class Culture" (Chapter 7) confronts the fashionable "culture-fication" of class theory, largely prompted by Pierre Bourdieu's work. This effort, I argue, doesn't salvage class theory so much as damn it. I construe "culture" broadly to include such matters as family life, artistic and entertainment tastes, and metaphysical commitments. In "Friends, Residences, and Families" (Chapter 8) I review the limited evidence about class-based interactions outside the workplace. I also consider the bearing of the feminist critique of class theory for the larger question of whether there are classes. Obviously, just under half of the labor force cannot be ignored.

"Lives of the Rich and Poor" (Chapter 9) focuses on the extremes of the economic hierarchy. The rich (an upper class?) and poor (an underclass?) receive separate attention because they largely escape the gaze of the standard survey-based studies that form the basis for Chapters 4–8. The so-called new class (essentially a professional elite) and a service-sector proletariat are not incorporated in standard, full-fledged class maps (Chapter 3), but because they figure so prominently in many discussions of the new class system, they also warrant separate attention (Chapter 10, "The Postindustrial Effect").

"American Unexceptionalism: A Comparative Perspective" (Chapter 11) asks whether the conclusions that hold for the United States are also appropriate for other countries. The empirical evidence cited in the previous chapters relates almost exclusively to the United States—an interesting case in its own right and the one for which relevant evidence is most fully and readily available. Yet, of course, only comparative research can establish the extent to which the United States is a model for class structuration in other societies.

The final chapter, "Beyond Class," summarizes this critique, seeks to decouple the no-classes argument from ideological commitments, and considers its implications for the analysis of stratification and the future of our political life. History continues despite the death of class.

CHAPTER TWO

The Case for Realism

A realist orientation to class analysis is crucial to my whole argument; in this perspective, classes exist only if it can be shown that there are relatively discrete, hierarchically ordered social groups, each with distinctive common experiences. A realist conception of class must rest on empirical demonstration that social life is patterned in this way. Of course this general commitment to the possibility of falsification still leaves open very important issues like deciding on what kinds of experiences are to be assessed. And even with agreement on this matter, analysts may still disagree about how distinctive a group must be before it can be called a class. Yet, in any case, the realist accepts the challenge of an empirical test. The ensuing debates can then turn on assessing whether there is sufficient evidence to make the case for the reality of distinct economically defined groups.

As a matter of logic, I can't argue that this realist approach is inherently superior to a nominalist approach. Ultimately, definitions and concepts must be judged on their usefulness in generating insights and making the world comprehensible. My judgment is that the most useful sociological concepts tend to be tied—in direct, observable ways—to the lives of specific individuals. Even if most class theorists share this view, it is not universal.

Keep in mind, however, the implication of the nominalist alternative: classes are real because they are *defined* as real. One nominalist might posit the existence of a two-class system because it is presumably inherent in the nature of capitalism: the owners of the means of production and those who sell their labor to these owners. This dichotomy is likely to be portrayed as a simplifying assumption that lays bare the fundamental dynamics of a complex situation. Another nominalist, however, might posit the existence of a twelve-class system based on differential possession of resources that can be used to exploit others. Again, the correspondence between conceptual category and actual groups is not necessarily tight, but the presumption is that this more elaborated conceptual schema makes better sense of social complexity than dichotomous models. Who's right? This can't be definitively known, of course, because definitions are not right or wrong, just more or less useful.

The justification for any nominal definition of class is that it conceptually illuminates the underlying logic of the social system, what holds it together and drives its trajectory. But why get mired at the level of definition and simply presume that classes are socially significant? After all, a nominalist perspective is useful only if it eventually helps us make sense of what actually happens in the lives of particular people. Ultimately, that has to be the aim of any social-scientific approach to class. Real people shouldn't get lost in abstract discussions. All class theorists—realists and nominalists alike—suggest that class has great social consequence in the most concrete aspects of people's lives. My argument is that there is no reason to postpone any longer the task of testing this claim. Lots of good relevant evidence is available, certainly enough to move intellectual debates beyond competing assertions. Of course data don't speak for themselves. The necessary preliminary task is to establish the criteria by which to decide whether distinctive classes exist.

THE CRITERIA OF STRUCTURATION

In crude terms, the issue here is how to recognize a class or a class system if you saw one. As I have mentioned, Anthony Giddens's concept of structuration provides a useful way to frame the issue because it encapsulates the basic idea that underlies all class theories in the realist tradition. When Giddens writes about "the modes in which economic relationships become translated into 'non- economic' social structures," he simply means that the nature of people's economic lives is systematically connected to how they live outside of the workplace. In Giddens's judgment, this "translation" is apparent in matters like intergenerational mobility patterns, social networks, and group orientations in politics. *Because* groups with roughly similar economic positions have distinctive experiences in these and other matters, he believes, classes exist as social entities. These groups are "structured" in class terms.

Drawing on the broad legacy of class theory, Giddens indicates that this structuration has multiple dimensions so that each class is marked by economic, social, cultural, and political similarities. Structuration—the reality of classes—doesn't hinge on any one social pattern; rather, it reflects a constellation of experiences forging group unity. So when Giddens outlines the class system, he is saying that at least several important within-group similarities reinforce each other, creating fundamental divisions within society.

As should become very plain, I don't agree with Giddens's conclusion, but his analytical perspective shapes my inquiry. First, it suggests that "class-ness" is a variable: structuration can in principle exist to varying degrees, and the task of the analyst is to specify the extent to which structuration does exist. Societies can differ in their level of class structuration, and the amount of structuration within any society may also vary over time. Thus, my opening question in Chapter 1 may have some rhetorical value, but it is not analytically precise. It would be better to ask: *To what extent* do classes exist?[1]

Secondly, this more precise question suggests that classness may be more pronounced in some dimensions than others. Intergenerational life chances, for instance, may be significantly "structured" by class position—strong structuration in this dimension of classness. But people may not feel a corresponding sense of "we-ness" with those in a similar position—low structuration in this dimension. How strongly the dimensions of structuration are interconnected should be empirically tested.

I largely follow Giddens's lead in suggesting five primary dimensions of class structuration. These five dimensions encompass the main features of social life that theorists have used to depict the reality of classes.

The pattern of inter- and intragenerational economic mobility. As a foundational point, most class theories contend that class is a persistent feature of life, shaping what occurs throughout people's own lifetimes and what occurs in the lives of their offspring. For that reason patterns of occupational mobility are crucial for assessing structuration: class position is significant to the extent that it delimits economic life chances. More than anything else, a person's job usually determines material well-being and, in turn, material resources have all kinds of social ramifications. Classes have real structure, then, if mobility—both intra- and intergenerational—*within* certain large occupational categories (in effect, within classes) is relatively easy and regular, and mobility *out* of these categories is difficult and infrequent.

It should be easy to see why mobility patterns are so significant. Imagine that workers do have the same types of jobs throughout their careers. As a result, their actual work experiences are likely to stay relatively constant. It's therefore meaningful to talk about a person's class—an enduring condition of life. Conversely, if people have different *types* of jobs throughout their careers, their "class location" may often appear to change as well. Thus many occupationally mobile workers may be seen as part of one class at one time, in a different class some years later, and perhaps a still different class at another time. With such occupational mobility a person's class is hard, if not impossible, to discern.

The same logic applies to intergenerational mobility patterns. Class is usually portrayed as an enduring *family* matter, a condition that is both inherited and passed on to future generations. To the extent that parental occupations are linked to the occupations of their offspring, basic features of economic inequality are transmitted through families—and, relatedly, the impress of class is felt from childhood through adult life. In many lights, the patterns of intergenerational mobility may be the most decisive consideration in assessing class structuration; indeed, Weber gave it greatest emphasis in discussing the constitution of social classes.

Mobility patterns also have important implications for the sociocultural dimensions of class. Any class effects on what people think and do are more likely if people have a fixed location within the class system—that is, if their childhood and adult class locations are the same, and if their different jobs are within the same class throughout their career. The reasoning here is very simple: the longer and more consistent the influence of class-rooted experiences in people's lives, the more likely these experiences are to shape activity and consciousness. In short, mobility patterns are both a critical dimension of class structuration and an important determinant of other dimensions of structuration.

Interaction patterns. To state the obvious sociological premise, patterns of interaction are the fundamental basis of social life. Social groups emerge out of recurrent interaction, and those we interact with have the greatest impact on our lives. Applied to the issue of structuration, this general point suggests that class is socially significant if people engaged in similar types of work tend to interact socially with each other in their out-of-work lives. If so, classes exist as *communal* groups—that is, groups bound together by interaction and a sense of togetherness rooted in sociable contact. Thus class structuration is more pronounced to the extent that "class members" live near each other, choose friends from the same class, belong to community groups with others of their class, and marry within their class. These are the most concrete and decisive expressions of social interaction.

Like occupational mobility, then, interaction patterns are in themselves an important indicator of structuration, but they also directly influence the extent of structuration in other dimensions. This is especially so as they reflect the subjective side of life.

Cultural orientations.   Cultural life is rooted in interaction patterns and significantly reinforces them. It involves collective sentiments about matters like truth, justice, beauty, and pleasure, as well as the accompanying social practices and norms. Culture is, indeed, a broad and diffuse concern. Yet discussions of distinctive class cultures have tended to focus on lifestyles, valued personal characteristics, attitudes about social issues, and the nature of family life. Within-class similarities on these matters is thought to create emotional bonds that hold classes together as cohesive communal groups. Thus, we can use Giddens's logic once again: to the extent that class categories distinguish distinctive patterns of social behavior and attitudes, class structuration is more fully established.

Claims about distinctive class cultures in family life seem especially decisive in assessing this dimension of structuration. Class theorists often argue that the "lessons" of common socialization in the family are a key mechanism furthering class reproduction. Presumably children learn the dispositions and personal styles that either maintain their economic privilege or their acquiescence to the privilege of others. This dimension of structuration is therefore directly linked to interaction patterns and that most economic dimension, occupational mobility.

Class sentiment.   This dimension broadly refers to the extent that class members—defined by common, objective location—share a feeling of "we-ness" with other class members and a corresponding sense of "they-ness" about others. Like the previous two dimensions, this involves assessing classes as communal groups. What I call class sentiment, however, deserves separate attention if for no other reason than it has figured so prominently in many discussions of class.

Indeed, by invoking class sentiment as a dimension of structuration, I inevitably raise an underlying issue in class theory: the relationship between objective and subjective factors in the *definition* of class. Class is usually defined as an objective matter, related in some way to location within the economic hierarchy. In this light, even if objectively defined class positions tend to be connected to some subjective expressions of class consciousness, that connection is viewed as a consequence of class, not a defining feature of it. In contrast, some theorists largely define classes in subjective terms. This means that those who have some sense of economically related kinship with each other are members of the same class; therefore, class divisions correspond to the economic divisions that people collectively perceive.

The objective/subjective debate has generated considerable controversy, but it's not very productive for determining whether classes represent important social divisions. However theorists specify the significance of objective and subjective factors in the definition of class, they should all agree that society is *more* structured in class terms if objective and subjective cleavages reinforce each other. Like most class theorists, I take an objective starting point, but class sentiment can then be treated as a critical subjective dimension of structuration with important political implications. Class-rooted activism is likely only if people have a sense of collective fate with those in similar economic circumstances.

Political action. Since so much of the debate in class theory turns on the *relationship* between class and political action, it is problematic to include class-rooted political action as *constituent* of class structuration. Again, definitional disputes intrude. Most class theorists explicitly exclude political considerations in their definition of class and look to analyze the contingent relation between "economic" class and political consciousness and action (e.g., Wright 1985). Yet others make the formation of a politically coherent or even mobilized collectivity part of their class definition (Przeworski 1977). In this perspective, a class includes those who pursue its "interests." This conceptual impasse can be sidestepped by simply asking to what extent proposed class cleavages—objectively defined divisions in the economic order—correspond to patterns of political activity. For example, to what extent is there "class voting"? Political mobilization can be seen as one more factor that simultaneously reinforces class structuration and indicates its significance.

Think what strong structuration on each of these dimensions would imply:

1. People would largely inherit the economic position of the families in which they were raised and be destined to that position throughout their own lives.

2. As a result, they would generally marry, befriend, and live near those in similar economic circumstances.

3. As a result of both numbers 1 and 2, they and their economic counterparts would share distinctive lifestyles, worldviews, and ways of dealing with family members.

4. They would feel emotionally bonded (as a specific aspect of number 3) to those of like economic station, and perhaps antagonistic to others.

5. They would be involved in the political arena, pursuing the collective interests generated by their economic positions.

If all these conditions were so, no one would have difficulty saying classes exist. Classes would clearly represent decisive fissures in the social fabric. The case for class theory would be closed in its favor.

Obviously enough, however, reality is not like this imagined condition. But this divergence doesn't mean that classes aren't real; lesser structuration can still represent very significant social divisions in class terms. The imagined condition of strong structuration across dimensions provides a useful analytical reference point for my central question: *to what extent* do groups of people having a common economic position share distinct, life-defining experiences? In later sections of this chapter, especially "Methodological Considerations," I propose how this question should be addressed.

As my discussion of the separate dimensions suggests, the class structuration of society reflects the intertwined, mutually reinforcing impact of economic, social, cultural, and political patterns. Although some aspect of "classness" may be slighted here, these five dimensions seem to encompass the primary considerations that many theorists have invoked in making claims about the impress of class in everyday lives. Considered together, they represent a composite variable of classness.

The likely objection is not that these dimensions exclude important considerations, but rather that they include too much. To be sure, not all class theorists see each of these dimensions as decisive or even significant in evaluating the merits of their argument. And certainly no serious analyst claims that there is strong structuration on each of these dimensions. That is a high hurdle, rightly rejected as a standard for the existence of classes. Even so, I believe that it is fair to say that classes are *more* "real" as social entities to the extent that structuration is apparent in each of these terms. By the same token, as I have mentioned, an analyst could make a persuasive argument for the significance of classes even if structuration is less than strong on one or even several dimensions. In any case, a broad view seems preferable to a view that has been limited from the start.

Which dimensions should be accorded the greatest weight in assessing the overall level of structuration? That you can decide for yourself. My intentions are simply to report evidence relating to the level of structuration on each dimension without any predetermined weighting system.

STRUCTURE VS. FORMATION?

This emphasis on class as collective experiences means that little is gained by asserting the analytical priority of class *structure* over class *formation*—or, indeed, even attempting to maintain the distinction. Wright (1985: 9–10) distinguishes these two concepts in a fairly conventional way:

> Class structure refers to the structure of social relations into which individuals (or in some cases, families) enter which determine their class interests. . . . [It] defines a set of empty places or positions . . . [and it] exists independently of the specific people who occupy specific positions. . . . Class formation, on the other hand, refers to the formation of organized collectivities within that class structure on the basis of the interests shaped by that class structure.

Thus, in this formulation class structure represents the cleavages arising from the unequal distribution of some fundamental stratifying factor(s)—property, authority, or labor-market capacities, for example. These structurally defined collectivities may or may not have common experiences (e.g., mobility chances or patterns of sociable interaction), and they may or may not be organized to act on their imputed common interests. That is, class formation is variable, ultimately limited by structural constraints but shaped as well by social factors and historical contingencies.

The problem with insisting on this distinction between class structure and formation is formidable. It amounts to saying, "I know the innermost logic of the system, the immanent force underlying social hierarchy, and I'm right even if it is not recognizable in individual or collective life." The obvious rejoinder is that the impact of a fundamental stratifying force should be evident in people's lives. Its significance cannot be granted by conceptual fiat. Any depiction of class structure—with typically related imputations of exploitation, domination, alienation, and the like—becomes meaningful only if it reflects concrete class formations. All the conceptual argumentation about the logic of the class system loses force if class positions are not systematically linked to variations in life-defining matters like the kinds of jobs people get, what they value, whom they marry and befriend, and how they act politically.

Having heard that, class theorists could still rejoin that the current lack of class formation doesn't preclude its eventual emergence. That is, the class structure creates the potential for class formation to emerge. This is especially so if the theoretical depiction of the class structure, such as Wright's, involves imputed conflicts of objective interests, creating incentives for collective action to change that structure. Of course the historical record can't be used to disprove a potentiality, but it can be used to suggest whether that potentiality is likely to be realized. Even so, in the next chapter on class maps I'll outline Wright's theory about the exploitive nature of the class structure and use that discussion in the concluding chapter to argue that some new emergence of classes is very unlikely.

In the pages ahead I will detail *how* these five dimensions of structuration will be analytically employed. Essentially this will involve assessing whether prominent schemas of class categorizations—what I call "class maps"— distinguish social groups in terms of these dimensions. That is, to what extent do individuals categorized as, say, "working class" share distinct class-related experiences and outlooks that differ from the experiences and outlooks of individuals categorized in other classes? Yet before turning to the methodological concerns involved in answering such a question, I must first address a vital theoretical issue. I have deliberately stressed here the *individualistic* underpinnings of my inquiry. Because this theoretical commitment is controversial within class theory, it deserves explicit justification.

INDIVIDUALS AND THE SIGNIFICANCE OF BOUNDARIES

Classes are composed of people: that's the bedrock meaning of my commitment to an individualistic approach in analyzing class. If classes are real, you should be able to identify their "members" and show that these people have distinctive experiences. I argue that you can meaningfully talk about, say, "working-class culture" only if significant numbers of people, defined by some criteria as "members" of the working class, actually do share particular cultural orientations. Similarly, it's reasonable to say something like "the capitalist class pursued its interests" only if identifiable "members" of this class actually did something in concert.

I recognize, of course, that some class theorists would argue that this emphasis on locating individuals within the class system and examining their personal experiences misses what's important about class. As I uncontroversially asserted, class theory is energized by the Marxian legacy. That long and well-elaborated legacy emphasizes *macro*sociological concerns—most significantly, the centrality of class conflict in determining the course of history.

Why not evaluate, then, macrolevel claims of class theory as a distinct argument? To be sure, macrolevel theorizing can be a valuable enterprise, but it should rest on suitable microlevel foundations. Without these foundations, macroanalysis can be an empty exercise. This general point applies to both Marxist and non-Marxist class theory, but because a distinctive macrolevel concern figures so prominently in the Marxist literature, I'll focus my remarks on its limits. Let me stress that this is not a brief for microanalysis *instead* of macroanalysis. Rather, my argument is that, at least for the issue of class, macroanalysis can be fruitful only if it rests on a solid base of microanalysis.

Very often, class theory, especially in its Marxian variants, lacks that base. To explain the historical trajectory, Marxists may consider historical particularities, but most basically they evoke the structure of social relations and conflicting class interests generated by capitalism. Relations between "labor" and "capital" are central to the social dynamic. So, for instance, why did the welfare state emerge? The Marxist answer: It was the systemic response to the struggle—the class conflict—between capital and labor.

At this level of analysis, then, it may seem unimportant to demarcate class boundaries and place individuals within particular classes—and, relatedly, to consider the implication of this location for their lives. What's important, presumably, is that the class system is a macrolevel phenomenon with macrolevel consequences. The class system can thus be studied as an emergent phenomenon.

But it is important to recognize that the macrolevel significance of class emerges here only because class (and class conflict) is definitionally constituent of capitalism. The very fact that the means of production are privately owned is presumed to establish the existence of classes with objectively opposed interests, thus making class conflict endemic. Now, at a very abstract level, you could perhaps analytically summarize imputed divisions of interest as a division between "capital" and "labor." But it's a very long reach from such an abstraction to explaining, say, the welfare state as the result of a specifically class-based dynamic. If all social forces involved in shaping the welfare state are simply defined as class forces ("capital" or "labor"), the analysis is unassailable. But, more importantly, the analysis is largely uninformative.

This sort of macrolevel class analysis doesn't tell us what we want to know: which social groups were decisive and how did their actions have concrete effects? If it could be shown that even a small proportion of owners (call them "capitalists," if you want) did actually band together and press for welfare-state measures with an eye toward some general interests of owners, and that other owners at least agreed with this effort, then you would have the beginnings of a genuine class-based explanation of political events. In this case you could say a class exists—a perception of shared fate, a unity of political beliefs—and that the mobilization of a segment of this class was politically significant. But such an argument can be compelling only because it is grounded in the circumstances of people who earn their livings in a distinctive way. Specific segments of some putative class can act on "behalf" of their class only if there is a class to begin with. Historical actors shouldn't get lost in the conceptual abstractions of "capital" and "labor." The challenge to class theory is to establish that some members of real classes have acted as a collectivity.

Indeed, take away the problematic Marxian metatheory of capitalism, and the case for a necessarily distinctive macrolevel understanding of class dissolves. Instead, consider the implications of a less freighted, common understanding of capitalism: that it is an economic system that essentially involves private ownership of most enterprises, a pervasive drive for profits, and a relatively free market for goods and services, including labor. To varying degrees, individuals are "winners" and "losers" in the operation of this system, but the centrality of capital and labor as factors of production doesn't necessarily mean that there are "capitalists" and a "working class." Whether capitalism operates with or without classes—that is, relatively distinct economically rooted groups—can and should be an open question.

If classes are to be seen as history makers, they must represent groups of people sharing distinct life experiences. Otherwise, classes become little more than supra-individual, quasi-metaphysical social forces—conceptual products whose reality can never be demonstrated. To put the matter baldly, history is not experienced and made by abstract collective entities but by actual people. Of course what people collectively do shapes the social trajectory, but whether class dynamics shapes this trajectory depends on whether individuals have aligned themselves in class terms. That means we must categorize people—set "class boundaries"—and see how designated "class members" act. This individualistic approach doesn't mean a neglect of macrosociological concerns; it underscores the fact that macrolevel phenomena are inevitably rooted in individual lives.

In short, establishing the reality of classes at the individual level is the essential prerequisite for macrolevel class theory. Failing to do so, the analyst must in effect say, "Class forces structure society despite no evidence that people live class-defined lives." The hollow force of that position strongly suggests that the microlevel foundations of macrolevel phenomenon must be given their due accord. So I follow the methodological dictum: first things first.

METHODOLOGICAL CONSIDERATIONS

To test class theory, the empirical analysis essentially pivots on whether the distributions of values for the factors related to structuration "break" at designated class boundaries so that there is substantial internal consistency *within* classes and substantial differences *across* classes. This means taking theoretically specified class maps—schemas that locate individuals/families within a class system—and seeing whether they identify social divisions in

terms of the dimensions of structuration. For example, do blue-collar workers (often designated "working class") have largely similar socializing patterns that differ notably from the socializing patterns among all white-collar
workers (often designated in the same class map as "middle class")? If
so, the finding would support a class map that designates class boundaries
in these occupational terms. Or, do blue-collar and lower white-collar workers have largely similar patterns, both differing from upper white-collar
workers—support for an alternative class map? And, of course, socializing
patterns may not correspond to the boundaries designated in any map—a
finding that undercuts class theory. As conceptually straightforward as this
task may appear, it faces some practical and theoretical difficulties.

Many Tests

As the example about socializing suggests, it's impossible to have *a* test of
class theory because theorists propose varied maps. To make an overall judgment about class structuration, it's necessary to see whether any of the theoretical maps identify significant social divisions. This diversity within class
theory makes the analytical burden both complex and cumbersome, and inevitably because of data availability, some maps can be subject to greater
scrutiny than others.

Because these maps frame the whole analysis, I detail their common features and important differences in the next chapter. I will postpone discussing
the methodological difficulties in operationalizing specific class schemas until Chapter 3. As will be evident, however, the operational specifications of
class position in each of the maps tend to be imprecise, and the potentially
relevant research is not always designed to test specific class theories.

Appropriate Data

A second difficulty involves deciding what kinds of evidence are most compelling and what particular studies should receive the most attention. In the
pages ahead, I favor quantitative research, especially survey-based studies,
over qualitative research. For matters like occupational mobility the reasons
should be obvious. Yet one might rightly question whether survey items about
matters like political ideology or affective relationships really get at what's
going on. Even the most ardent proponent of survey research must concede
that nuances, ambivalences, and "deep structures" of meanings are not well

represented in computer printouts of these data. Sure, but at the same time let's not overlook the virtues of well-conducted survey research. What may be lost in subtlety can be gained in having results that generalize to the entire population (and specific segments of it) and can be readily checked by others. And, it's worth reemphasizing here, the claims of class theory are rarely subtle: as a presumed major axis of differentiation, class divisions should be apparent even with crude methods. Rather than making a wholesale, uncritical defense of survey methods, then, I simply urge you to be a critical consumer of the cited survey data, recognizing the strengths and limits of particular studies, as well as the overall pattern of results across studies.

For matters like communal attachment or marital relations, there's no denying the distinctive insights of ethnographic research. I will selectively refer to some of the more provocative and well-recognized studies as I discuss specific dimensions of structuration. Even so, it should be recognized from the outset that their results are difficult to incorporate in an assessment of *general* patterns of structuration. There are always inherent concerns about representativeness.

Consider, for example, David Halle's *America's Working Man* (1984), a richly evocative account of the lives of some workers who would frequently be labeled "working class." The obvious question: are these male, blue-collar workers in a New Jersey chemical plant typical of the working class? Halle can't be expected to answer that question. Moreover, because qualitative research usually focuses on one group alone, it's hard to determine whether the studied group systematically differs from other groups. Although Halle seems to do a superb job of detailing what these blue-collar workers' lives are like, it is impossible to tell from the presented evidence whether this group is like or unlike other types of employees. In the terms of my analysis, this is the crucial consideration in deciding whether classes exist.

For some matters there is simply not enough good information to offer fully conclusive judgments about structuration. I will duly note when provisional conclusions are in order. On other matters, however, I face an oversupply of potentially relevant studies (for example, all the occupational mobility studies). Rather than exhaustively cite this literature—often uneven in quality or repetitive in its findings—I will selectively assess the implications of recent, well-conducted studies as well as report some of my own research that addresses understudied concerns. Undoubtedly, there are uncited "counterfindings" that I'm unaware of, but my argument rests on the claim that the cited studies exemplify the general thrust of the best empirical analyses.

Finding Class

Perhaps the greatest difficulty is determining whether structuration exists. This issue involves intertwined methodological and theoretical concerns. Recall the challenge to class theory: it must be shown that, for relevant dimensions of life, classes are internally consistent (to some nontrivial degree) and are distinct from other classes (also to a nontrivial degree). The obvious question is: *how* consistent and distinct?

At least some minor association between class location and some aspects of a dimension of structuration is expectable, but that can hardly be taken as confirmation of the claim that class represents a major axis of differentiation. Given the ambition of its claims, the case for class theory must rest on the finding that class has fairly strong and pervasive impacts. No one can claim, however, that there is a crucial test for this matter, nor that there is a fixed, a priori criterion for establishing whether a "class break" is sufficiently large to indicate class structuration. Necessarily, each of us must make judgments about the magnitude of any apparent class structuration.

To do this, it is most directly relevant to consider bivariate analyses, the simple relationship between class location and pertinent variables (e.g., political orientations and cultural tastes). Bivariate analyses, especially in crosstabular form, clearly indicate whether class theorists have identified significant social divisions. Of course, bivariate analyses can say nothing about the causal significance of class. For example, are apparent "class effects" on political attitudes spurious, that is, attributable to the mutual association between class and political attitudes and other variables? What the bivariate associations show is whether class-based differences do exist, whatever their cause.

Forgoing the language of independent and dependent variables, with its loose implication of causality, would be helpful here. Rather than thinking about classes as the *cause* of some practice or attitude, it is more revealing to look at the distribution of values related to this or that practice as indicating the *identity* of a class, its structuration. If structuration is evident, the case can be made that classes represent meaningful social divisions.

In the absence of a bivariate relationship (or the finding of a trivial one) the inference is straightforward: class theory falls short. For some matters, however, analysts have established a modest, statistically significant association (gamma coefficients, say, in the .10–.25 range) between class and some measure of a dimension of structuration. How should coefficients of this size be interpreted?

Consider, for example, an analysis (Wallace and Jepperson 1986) that I cite in Chapter 5 on the relationship between class location and class self-identification. (I've chosen here an analysis that makes one of the strongest cases for class theory.) This study indicates a modest correlation (gamma = .22): the higher the class, the higher the rate of middle-class identification. A good majority of white-collar workers consider themselves "middle class" instead of "working class"—but so do a *majority*, somewhat smaller, of blue-collar workers. That is, despite the correlation, it can't be said that the white-collar/blue-collar divide represents a distinct division between white-collar "middle class" identifiers and blue-collar "working class" identifiers.

To further see the limits of correlational statistics, consider the modest relation between class location and voting orientation. As you probably know, those in higher classes tend (often slightly) to have a greater probability of voting Republican. Thus, it might be said, class voting is consequential for electoral outcomes. However, classes aren't structured by common, *distinct* political orientations: a majority of every class has leaned to the Republicans from 1972 to 1990 (De Graaf, Nieuwbeerta, and Heath 1995; see Chapter 6). In short, while there are class-related degrees of political "leaning," there's nothing approaching a "middle class" party versus a "working class" party.

Now, consider whether classes are distinguished by their trust in fellow citizens, a value plausibly related to class cultures. (Again, I've chosen an example that makes a relatively strong case for class theory.) It might be expected that the circumstances of life among the higher classes would be conducive to trustful attitudes—after all, life has worked out relatively well for them. And, indeed, that's what we find (see Table 2.1). The gamma between a five-category measure of class and trust is .2: managers and professionals are the most trustful. But note as well that in each class there are substantial numbers of trustful and distrustful people. No class is united by a *common* attitudinal orientation, though the level of distrust is fairly high among all those below the managerial professional ranks.

What these three examples are meant to show is that it is highly illumi-

TABLE 2.1
Attitudes About Trustworthiness by Omnibus Measure of Class*

Trust	Lower Blue Collar	Skilled Blue Collar	Routine White Collar	Lower Managerial Professional	Elite Managerial Professional	Row Total
Most can be trusted	27.5%	30.6%	33.4%	42.8%	57.1%	33.6%
Depends	4.6	2.8	2.6	6.9	8.6	4.3
Can't be too careful	67.9	66.7	64.0	50.3	34.3	62.1
Total	100% (567)	100% (216)	100% (572)	100% (376)	100% (35)	100% (1,766)

NOTE: *1994 General Social Survey: "Generally speaking, would you say that most people can be trusted or that you can't be too careful in dealing with people?"

nating to look *within* class distributions and at *absolute* class differences, not just at relative class differences—as seems more common. Perhaps class is modestly related to the frequency of some social practice or disposition, but if large proportions of all classes do the same, then it can't be said that classes are structured by common, *distinct* orientations. And, just as significantly, if class is related to some practice but only a small proportion of any class engages in it, then classes aren't structured by *common*, distinct orientations.

So, when possible, in cases of modest association between class and relevant outcomes I'll provide detail about within-class distributions and absolute class differences. In this way you can directly assess the extent of class structuration and form your own judgment. Of course, statistical coefficients summarizing the association between class and other variables can be noteworthy only if there are substantial absolute class differences (and they are convenient to report), but the specific distributions that produced the coefficients most clearly indicate the extent of structuration.

This means that what is small to me may be big to you (or vice versa), but if we interpret results differently, at least the basis of our disagreement should be clear. To anticipate the charge that I may see a half-empty glass where proponents of class theory would see a half-full glass, I suggest that correlations in the .2 or less range indicate that there is very little in the glass. Also, statistical significance should not be confused with substantive consequence.

Using these joint criteria of within-class similarity and across-class difference doesn't mean structuration exists only if large majorities within a class share some practice and large proportions of other classes engage in some "opposite" practice. It does mean, however, that the case for class structuration is undermined to the extent that members of a particular class are divided among themselves on relevant matters or that classes are not differentiated from each other.

The Multivariate Perspective

I have argued that the case for class theory should largely stand or fall on the simple patterns of association between class location and variables related to the five dimensions of structuration. However, many who have previously tested aspects of class theory may think that analyzing bivariate associations is too simple-minded, making it too easy for class theory to be validated.[2] After all, class location is related to (essentially) continuous stratification variables, like education and income, that are also often associated with indicators of structuration. So what may appear to be a "class effect" on some issue is often spurious, and thus the case for class theory is undermined. By this logic, class theory would be convincing only if it was shown that class effects are independent of factors related to different axes of stratification.

I must confess to considerable sympathy for this argument, especially insofar as analysts insist that the independent effects of education and other stratification variables can't be subsumed under some gross aggregate—"the class effect." Class theory shouldn't be saved by claiming its competitors' explanatory power as its own. And, surely, to the extent that apparent class "effects" are shown to be spurious, the case for class theory is diminished. If class is a life-defining force, it should, in itself, have notable consequences for how people live; but the significant fact is that class generally lacks this *causal* force. I will therefore relate the results of multivariate analyses in subsequent chapters; indeed, multivariate analyses receive considerable attention, in part because so many analysts have thought they are essential to assessing the claims of class theory.

Even so, I look on multivariate analyses as complementary and secondary to the results of bivariate analyses. What's most critical, I believe, is whether classes are marked by the within-group similarity / across-group differences that indicate structuration. It's hard to imagine that many people go through some mental "partialing" exercise and then conclude that class doesn't matter, that their education and other factors really explain what they do. In any case, the reality of classes is independent of the statistical adroitness of the general population. Structuration is fundamentally determined by the sheer fact of whether there are class-associated differences in key realms of life.

The complementary value of multivariate analyses is in showing whether any class-related differences can be attributed to the causal force of class per se. In the light of these analyses it's useful to think of class as a specific independent variable whose explanatory power may be compared to that of other independent variables. What, for example, are the relative net effects of class and race on political orientations?

Another specific value of multivariate analyses is that they point, at least indirectly, to the merits of stratification theory—in Chapter 1 described as the main theoretical alternative to class theory. In multivariate models, education and other nonclass stratification factors like income generally have linear, additive effects on many outcomes, and categorical measures of class account for little or no additional variance. This relational form is difficult to reconcile with class theory, which claims that the economic hierarchy is marked by distinctive social groups. Findings of linear, additive effects support a multidimensional, multigradated version of stratification theory.

About Education

In assessing the independent input of class in multivariate models, it is especially crucial to recognize that education is conceptually distinct from class. Nor can "education effects" be construed, except possibly in very partial terms, as indirect class effects. Some class theorists may disagree: an individual's education and income are the *result* of class, and thus any effects of these factors really reflect indirect class effects. However, this argument falters on both conceptual and empirical grounds.

Here is the general pattern of results that must be interpreted: (1) parental class is related to their offsprings' education; (2) children's education is related to their own subsequent class position; and (3) in multivariate models their education is related to numerous social and political outcomes, but their own class position is not related or is only weakly so.

The first point to keep in mind that measures of class and education are substantially but not tightly linked. The correlation between parental occupational status and educational attainment is about .4, between educational attainment and occupation status about .6 (Jencks et al. 1979). Occupational status (the underpinning of class) and education are therefore not empirical proxies. And the correlation between occupational status and income is also moderate, less than .5 (Jencks et al. 1979). In path analytic terms, because the regression of educational attainment on class origins yields a large, dominant residual term, we know that education must mainly shape outcomes quite independently of origins.

Moreover, even if current class location partially reflects the impact of prior education, current class rarely *causes* educational attainment, which of course typically occurs before people reach their position in the class system. Therefore, if in adulthood education is independently related to some variable and current class location is not, it obscures matters to aggregate all stratification effects as class effects. Recognize what such a pattern of results indicates: (1) the more educated, on average, differ from the less educated on this variable, no matter what their class; but (2) any bivariate relationship between class and that variable only reflects the fact that class and education are related.

Perhaps the strongest argument for seeing education as a class variable is the claim that particular levels of educational attainment essentially represent certification of different sorts of class-rooted cultural capital. Thus, at elite schools, privileged children learn the personal styles and cultural dispositions that "fit" elite occupational positions—and having acquired the "right" academic credentials, they are slotted to top positions. And, conversely, the lesser privileged are excluded from top positions because they lack these credentials and related cultural orientations. Instead, their education slots them into lower-status positions. Thus it is presumed that schools instill or at least reinforce class cultures and act as mechanisms for class reproduction.

This is not the place for an extended critique of the cultural capital/credentialist argument about education. I will just briefly note important limitations. Arguments for the *general* class-reproduction component of education are undermined by the fact that many of those favored in the labor market by virtue of their education do not have the benefits of privileged birth, and even more fundamentally by the fact (detailed in Chapter 4) that the overall connection between class origins and destinations is modest. Furthermore, even if some part of the payoff to education represents this kind of credentialing process, the credentialist argument surely misses an important part of the story. Other explanations of why education is economically rewarded are much too plausible to ignore. In particular, you don't have to accept all the tenets of human capital theory to acknowledge that more educated people tend to be more capable people in truly productive ways—and tend to be better rewarded for that reason. (This is so whether schools create this competence or merely certify it.) No one can claim that schools consistently instill intellectual skills and thus enhance productive ability, but the content of what is learned in schools certainly encompasses much more than class-rooted cultural distinctions. Think of the general analytical and practical utility of algebra; it involves more than an arbitrary cultural "taste." And within schools, by far the best predictor of success is general analytical ability, not class.

These considerations all suggest that education represents a decisive axis of stratification in its own right, not reducible to the force of class. The intellectual challenge is to explain its distinctive, pervasive consequence, rather than attempting to save class theory by conflating education and class.

In justifying my approach to assessing class theory, I have necessarily only alluded to the variety of class schemas or maps—in effect, theoretical statements about the number and composition of classes within the class system. In the next chapter I show how class cartographers have drawn their maps. And to further sharpen my no-classes argument, I'll also consider the conceptual meaning and actual extent of economic inequality in contemporary American society.

CHAPTER THREE

Class Maps and Inequality

The composition of Adam Smith's world in *The Wealth of Nations* was very simple: pin makers and the owners of pin-making factories. So, too, was Marx's abstract view of capitalism in *Capital*: the struggle between two all-encompassing groups, the capitalists and the proletariat, was its defining feature. Such dichotomies may represent a useful premise in a highly abstract model of the social system. Yet neither Marx nor Smith claimed that these dichotomies represented the actual social divisions in a particular society in a specific historical moment. Nor do any contemporary theorists who take a realist approach to class. The early industrial factory system cannot be taken as the model for the social divisions in the complex economy of contemporary time.

Consider, in broad brush, some of the realities that theorists must incorporate in their depictions of the class system:

"Ownership" is widely distributed throughout the population through pension funds and personal investments.

The "owners" don't really run most large corporations. Cadres of highly paid workers (managers), often with some ownership stakes, usually control these institutions.

A professional elite commands a high proportion of the best paid positions and wields great influence in important economic sectors.

The labor force is highly differentiated in pay, terms of employment, physical work conditions, authority, and technical/knowledge requirements. Fast-food counter workers, lathe operators, dental hygienists, claims adjusters, administrative assistants, sales representatives, teachers, department managers, VP's for human resources—all are formally alike as salaried workers, and share little else in their economic lives.

The public sector is a large employer, and the not-for-profit sector is a significant one.

Most women are employed, and the occupational structure is substantially segregated by gender.

These facts are not in dispute, despite some ongoing scholarly debates about the precise magnitude of the "managerial revolution" or the recent net effect of "de-skilling/upgrading" developments in the workplace. Considered together, they suggest the great diversity of economic circumstances— and, hence, the formidable challenge of meaningfully categorizing workers into discrete classes. This challenge has been summarized as the "problem of the middle class," but it may be even more apt to refer to it as the problem of the middle class*es*. That is, what are the class circumstances of all those people who don't really own the means of production but, to highly varying degrees, have more favorable economic circumstances than unskilled and marginally skilled industrial workers—those long regarded, that is, as the core of the working class?

Of course, for Marxists, the "problem"—what Wright calls an "embarrassment"—has been particularly vexing because of their theoretical allegiance to a dichotomous model of class relations. Marxist "solutions" have varied: defining it away (all sellers of labor power *are* workers); projecting the demise of intermediate strata; and conceptualizing new "class" locations, even if the resulting groups are labeled class "factions" or "strata" and the division between the capitalist and working class is still deemed most fundamental. This last solution has attracted increasing attention. To cite a prominent example, Wright (Wright et al. 1989: 270) has written, "My conviction was that conceptually clarifying the structural location of the middle class was essential for understanding the process of class formation in contemporary capitalism." Not all Marxists share his conviction, much less his particular solution, but without some effort in this direction Marxists condemn themselves to empirical irrelevance.

For non-Marxist class theorists, the middle class(es) are not as problematic because their depictions of the class system are generally not rooted in a larger metatheoretical argument about capitalism and the historical trajectory. Neither the number of classes nor the relations between them are fixed by a priori theoretical commitments. Even so, the great diversity in the contemporary work force poses a daunting challenge. On what basis can this work force be categorized into relatively discrete groups that capture the "middle" nature of so many lives? And what is the resulting class system?

Non-Marxists, then, may be relatively open to incorporating the middle class(es) in their theoretical arguments, but they also lack any clear theoretical guide about how to do so. Predictably, their models of the class system differ in conceptual coherence and empirical specification.

As I noted earlier, class theorists intensely debate the underlying basis of class distinctions. For Marxists, it is relations to the means of production: your position in the sphere of *production* determines your class. For most other class theorists (shorthand: neo-Weberians), it is primarily a common location in the sphere of *distribution*: how well you materially live, because of your labor-market capacity, determines your class, though some neo-Weberians (e.g., Erikson and Goldthorpe 1993) also incorporate a concern for the nature of experiences in the realm of production. In theoretical disputes these differences assume enormous significance: production-based or distribution-based? The answer has obvious implications for the presumed "interests" of classes and, relatedly, the potential role of classes as agents of change. The production-based argument lends itself to a view of classes as inherently and fundamentally antagonistic. By contrast, the distribution-based (labor market capacity) argument allows for multiple divisions of interest of varying intensity.

Yet, to reiterate my point in Chapter 1, these conceptual disputes about the presumed bases of the class system are largely irrelevant unless real classes—relatively discrete groups—can be identified. The decisive issue is whether theorists have identified major fault lines or cleavages within the stratification system that demarcate groups with distinct common experiences. Without classes there can't be a class system.

At this juncture, let me repeat two points about this analytical approach. First, it totally ignores any concern for the *process* of class formation. Class theorists such as Przeworski (1977) and Parkin (1974), for example, emphasize the role of group struggles in *creating* class boundaries. In this view, class structure is not so much a "given" feature of the social system as it is the creation of social action. Parkin highlights the role of social closure: the process by which groups attempt to maintain their control of valuable resources and to limit the access of other groups to them. Class boundaries, then, reflect the result of competing group strategies of exclusion (e.g., credentialism) by the favored and usurpation (e.g., unionism) by the underdogs. In no way do I deny the significance or interest of analyzing these processes;

however, at issue here is whether the *outcome* of these processes represents closure in class terms. In effect, I look at the various class maps as a set of propositions about where closure was realized and then test to see whether these propositions can be supported.

Secondly, this approach eschews any presumptions about class "interests"—either objective or subjective. For instance, I make no assumptions about whether highly paid managers share inherent (objective) interests with owners or even whether they perceive common interests. Class theorists have advanced divided views on both matters. I simply advocate seeing whether this group expresses distinct common perspectives, especially about the division of social resources—no matter what the content of these views. The result of this analysis helps determine where—if anywhere—class boundaries should be drawn.

THE CARTOGRAPHY OF CLASS

My task now is to review some prominent examples of what I'll call class maps. By no means do I consider all efforts to map the class system, nor do I want to claim that the included analyses represent equal levels of theoretical sophistication. Rather, I have selected a wide range of maps that typify prominent contemporary arguments. Considered together, I contend, these maps suggest both the important commonalities and key differences in theoretical depictions of the class system.

Table 3.1 summarizes the main features of contemporary class maps. Included are the maps of two explicitly neo-Marxist class cartographers—Erik Olin Wright (1985) and Nicholas Poulantzas (1975); and five others who may be broadly categorized as neo-Weberians (though they varyingly incorporate Marxian concerns for ownership): Anthony Giddens (1973), John Goldthorpe (1987; also Erikson and Goldthorpe 1993), as well as the American text writers Daniel Rossides (1990), Dennis Gilbert and Joseph Kahl (1993), and Harold Kerbo (1996). These latter three cartographers may lack the scholarly prominence of the others, but their work represents a convenient summary of the main competing views within non-Marxist American class analysis.

Because of their prominence (and complexity), I also include greater detail about Erikson and Goldthorpe's and Wright's schemas in tabular form (Tables 3.1a and 3.1b). These two schemas seem to have emerged as primary

TABLE 3.1

Class Maps

Class Divisions	Relation to Occupation/Property Categories	Est. Size* (Percentage)	Conceptual Basis
Giddens (1973)			
Upper	Large property owners/top executives	1	Shared market capacity shaped by ownership, skill, and manual-labor power—reinforced as distributive and sociocultural groupings
Middle	White-collar position	54–59	
old	small proprietors		
upper	managers, professionals		
lower	routine office, sales		
Working	Blue-collar positions	40–45	
upper	skilled		
lower	unskilled		
Goldthorpe (1987)			
Service Class (Class I)	Higher-grade professionals, high-level managers, large proprietors	28 (I & II)	Broadly shared market and work situations: sources and amount of income, job security, and location within systems of authority and control
"Cadet" Service Class (Class II)	Lower-grade professionals and administrators, higher-grade technicians, small business managers, supervisors of nonmanual workers		
Routine Nonmanual (Class III)	Routine administration; routine sales, service	11	
Petty Bourgeoisie (Class IV)	Small proprietors, self-employed artisans	7	
Farmers (Class IVc)	Farmers and other self-employed in primary production	3	
Skilled Workers (Class V, VI)	Skilled manual, lower technicians, supervisors, supervisors of manual workers	24	
Nonskilled Workers (Class VIIa)	Semi- and unskilled manual workers	26	
Agricultural Laborers (Class VIIb)	Agricultural and other workers in primary production	1	

TABLE 3.1
(continued)

Class Divisions	Relation to Occupation/ Property Categories	Est. Size* (Percentage)	Conceptual Basis
Gilbert and Kahl (1993)			
Capitalist	Large owners	1	Clusters of shared status defined by source of income, occupation, and education, plus related processes of symbolization
Upper Middle	High-level managers, professionals, medium owners	14	
Middle	Lower managers, semiprofessionals, sales (nonretail), craftsmen, foremen	60	
Working	Operatives, low paid craftsmen, clerical, retail sales		
Working Poor	Service, laborers, low paid operatives	25	
Underclass	Unemployed, welfare recipients		
Rossides (1990)			
Upper	Large owners	1–3	Shared levels of benefits across dimensions of economic standing, prestige, and power
Upper Middle	Substantial proprietors, upper-level managers and professionals	10–25	
Lower Middle	Smaller proprietors, marginal and semiprofessionals, middle management, sales, clerical	30–35	
Working	All blue-collar	40–45	
Lower	Economic marginality/poverty	20–25	
Kerbo (1996)			
Upper	Large owners	0.5	Groups with common interests with respect to occupational, bureaucratic, and property structures
corporate	Very high-level managers (nonowners)	0.5	
Middle	All other nonmanual positions	43	
upper	unspecified distinctions of income and authority		
lower			
Working	Manual positions	43	
upper	skilled blue-collar		
lower	unskilled blue-collar		
Lower	Poverty	13	

Poulantzas (1975)			Groupings of social agents defined mostly by place in the productive process, but also by political and ideological considerations
Bourgeoisie	Owners, upper and middle managers	6	
Traditional Petty Bourgeoisie	Small owners	14	
New Petty Bourgeoisis	All other white-collar and "unproductive" workers	53	
Working class	Blue-collar (material "productive" work)	27	
Wright (1985)			Location determined by relations of exploitation—i.e., ownership—and secondarily by expertise (education) and organizational assets (authority)
(a) Capitalist	(a–c) Owners distinguished by size	1.8	
(b) Small Employer		6.0	
(c) Petty Bourgeoisie		6.8	
(d) Expert Manager	(d–k) Primarily managers and professionals with varying levels of education and authority	5.5	
(e) Expert Supervisor		3.1	
(f) Expert (Nonmanager)		2.9	
(g) Skilled Manager		3.7	
(h) Skilled Supervisor		6.3	
(i) Skilled Worker		13.1	
(j) Nonskilled Manager		2.8	
(k) Nonskilled Supervisor		7.2	
(l) Nonskilled Worker	Low-level office workers (no authority or expertise), blue-collar workers	40.6	

NOTE: *Estimated sizes taken from the cited sources, except Poulantzas from Johnston and Ornstein (1985) (Canadian data), Giddens (my estimates), and Goldthorpe (Erikson and Goldthorpe 1993).

See Tables 3.1a and 3.1b for details on the Goldthorpe and Wright (1985) class schemas.

TABLE 3.1A

Goldthorpe's Class Schema

FULL VERSION		Seven-Class*	Five-Class	Three-Class
		COLLAPSED VERSIONS		
I	Higher-grade professionals, administrators and officials; managers in large industrial establishments; large proprietors	I + II	I–III White-collar workers	Nonmanual workers
II	Lower-grade professionals, administrators, and officials; higher-grade technicians; managers in small industrial establishments; supervisors of nonmanual employees			
IIIa	Routine nonmanual employees, higher grade (administration and commerce)	III		
IIIb	Routine nonmanual employees, lower grade (sales and services)			
IVa	Small proprietors, artisans, etc., with employees	IV a + b	IVa + b Petty bourgeoisie	
IVb	Small proprietors, artisans, etc., without employees			
IVc	Farmers and smallholders; other self-employed workers in primary production	IVc	IVc + VIIb Farm workers	Farm workers
V	Lower-grade technicians; supervisors of manual workers	V + VI	V + VI Skilled workers	Manual workers
VI	Skilled manual workers			
VIIa	Semi- and unskilled manual workers (not in agriculture, etc.)	VIIa	VIIa Nonskilled workers	
VIIb	Agricultural and other workers in primary production	VIIb		

SOURCE: Erikson and Goldthorpe 1993: 38–39, table 2.1.

NOTE: *The seven-class version is used in the comparative mobility studies and most other analyses.

TABLE 3.1B
Wright's Class Schema

Relation to the Means of Production

	OWNER		EMPLOYEE		
10 +	Capitalists	Expert managers	Skilled managers	Nonskilled managers	Manager
2–9	Small employers	Expert supervisors	Skilled supervisors	Nonskilled supervisors	Supervisor
0–1	Petty bourgeoisie	Experts	Skilled workers	Nonskilled workers	No authority
		EXPERT	SKILLED	NONSKILLED	

Number of Employees (left vertical axis)

Relation to Authority (right vertical axis)

Relation to Scarce Skills

SOURCE: Wright (1997): 47, fig. 2.1.

competitors—a battle between Marxist and Weberian versions of class theory. Following a general discussion of the main commonalities and disagreements among class theorists about the cartography, I've inserted a discursus on Wright's logic. As I've argued, the presumed underlying logic of the class structure doesn't directly bear on whether classes exist as real entities, but it does have implications for whether forces promoting class structuration might be activated.

In broad outline, all class theorists solve the "problem" of many middle-level people by drawing a basic three-class division—even if most of the theorists make finer distinctions as well and locate class boundaries at somewhat different places.

At the top is a small upper class. This elite is varyingly defined by substantial ownership or some combination of ownership, high managerial/professional position, and high income. No more than a percent or two of the population has this privilege.

Below this small elite stands a substantial middle class, in almost all schemas roughly equal in size to the working class below it. (Thus, the neo-Marxists recognize intermediate-level people as a distinct class, even if they may want to retain Marx's abstract dichotomous model for other theoretical concerns.) In all of the theories this middle class is *largely* identified as white-collar workers who lack elite levels of ownership, workplace authority, or labor-market capacity. To varying degrees, these theories recognize distinctions within the middle class. White-collar employees with varying levels of skill, credentials, and pay are categorized into upper and lower segments of the middle class. Small owners, too, are sometimes recognized as a separate segment. These differences, however, appear much less fundamental than differences separating the broad middle class from the upper and working classes.

All theories recognize a large working class; no one claims that this class has withered away or been fully "bourgeoisified" into some middle mass. The *core* of this working class is the (nonowner) manual worker, even if the inclusion of routine white-collar workers in this class is strenuously contested. In some formulations the distinction between skilled and other blue-collar workers is portrayed as a class divide, though one seemingly less fundamental than the middle/working class cleavage (Form 1985).

Notwithstanding these broad commonalities, there are important points of contention as well:

1. The composition of the upper class. Some theorists strictly consider only substantial owners as upper class; they relegate high-level managers and professionals to a supportive, upper-middle-class position because they lack the prerogatives of property (e.g., Wright 1985, and Gilbert and Kahl 1993). Others merge owners and high-level managers into a single class, at least implicitly suggesting that ownership per se is not the bedrock stratifying force (e.g., Goldthorpe 1987; Kerbo 1996; and even a neo-Marxist, Poulantzas 1975).

2. The class location of lower-level white collar workers, particularly clerks, salespeople, technicians, and semi-professionals. Some theorists maintain the long-standing shirt-collar distinction (blue/white) in separating the middle and working classes (e.g., Rossides 1990, and Giddens 1973). Others believe that the conditions of much lower-level white-collar work have been sufficiently "proletarianized" to warrant placing many of these workers in the working class (Gilbert and Kahl 1993, and Wright 1985).

3. The existence of a lower class. I have suggested that all theories employ a basic three-class model, though some also identify a separate lower class often called an underclass. If employment conditions define class position,

this group is largely *outside* the class system. However, some theorists view the large numbers of poor people with a common experience of chronic unemployment or marginal labor force attachment as a distinct class—in effect, Weberians resurrecting the Marxist notion of the *lumpenproletariat*.

Each of these maps cannot be fully and similarly assessed in light of all five dimensions of structuration (discussed in the previous chapter). The direct comparison of competing class maps has not been a major concern of empirical research. However, this cartographic survey does direct attention to the most commonly proposed fault lines. These related questions will therefore focus the inquiry in the following chapters:

> To what extent do blue-collar workers *or* blue-collar workers and lower-level white-collar workers represent a distinct working class?
>
> To what extent do all white-collar workers represent a distinct middle class? Or, to what extent do managers and professionals share a class position, either as a middle class "above" a blue-collar/lower-white-collar working class or as an upper middle class "above" a lower middle class composed of routine office workers?
>
> To what extent is there an elite class, composed of either business owners or owners plus very high-level managers and professionals?

I awkwardly preface these questions with "to what extent" as an important reminder that class structuration is variable. I will apply the same logic to assessing the reality of a class divide between unskilled and skilled blue-collar workers, as well as the reality of an underclass.

A DISCURSUS ON WRIGHT'S LOGIC

Erik Olin Wright's prolific contribution to class theory is distinguished by two commitments: to incorporate the existence of "middle class" lives into a realistic understanding of the contemporary class system; and to do so in a way that retains the Marxist conception that class divisions represent systemically rooted, objective conflicts of interest. Wright's elaborate class map (see Table 3.1b), then, is intended to indicate locations within the class structure in which incumbents, because of their differential control of assets that are valuable in production, are presumed to share interests in either defending or challenging the system of exploitive relationships. The incumbents of particular locations may not act on or even recognize their common incentives to address their systematically imposed exploitation, but it nonetheless exists. The implication is that at some point the exploitive relationship will be challenged because rational actors can't be supposed to indefinitely tolerate lesser material comfort than they otherwise might have.

As any reader of Wright's work will recognize, his theoretical arguments about the underlying basis of the divisions of objective interest have evolved—and so too, accordingly, in modest ways have his depictions of the class structure. (Wright himself explicitly underscores how his positions have changed.) However, his current exploitation-based theory reflects the general commitments of his sustained effort to revise class theory within a Marxist framework.

For Wright, exploitation has a fairly specific and complex analytical meaning—and a readily acknowledged normative connotation. It involves "antagonistic interdependence of material interests of actors within economic relations." Class exploitation is defined by these criteria:

> (a) The material welfare of our group causally depends on the material deprivations of another.
> (b) The causal relation in (a) involves the asymmetrical exclusion of the exploited from access to certain productive resources. . . .
> (c) The causal mechanism which translates exclusion (b) into differential welfare (a) involves the appropriation of the fruits of labor of the exploited by those who control the relevant productive resources (Wright 1997: 10).

Thus the exploiter depends on the effort of the exploited.

Following the Marxist tradition, Wright defines the relationship between owners and employees as exploitive—hence, the division between them is a class division. To differentiate the class locations of those within the disparate ranks of the employed, he divides the class of employees along two dimensions: their relationship to authority within production, and their possession of skills or expertise (ibid.: 19). Authority is a dimension of class relations, Wright argues, because it involves domination. Managers and supervisors exercise domination—"delegated capitalist powers"—by forcing workers to produce efficiently. While dominating workers, they also are controlled by capitalists and thus have "contradictory locations within class relations" (20). Moreover, for their distinctive service, managers are rewarded with high earnings; they command a "loyalty rent" and have what Wright calls a "privileged appropriation location within exploitation relations" (22).

Employees with high-level skills are also in a privileged appropriation location; they may receive a "skill rent." But to an extent like managers, they may command a "loyalty rent" as well because their labor is hard to monitor, and as controllers of knowledge they have a strategic location within the production process. Thus they are differentiated from regular workers who receive neither form of rent, as well as from managers who have a somewhat different "contradictory location" within class relations.

Wright has elaborately embedded his analysis of exploitation in abstract game theory, but his argument comes down to the claim that each of the non-capitalist classes would be better off if they negated the form(s) of exploitation which they were subject to. That's the basis of his previously cited claim that "class structure refers to the structure of social relations into which individuals . . . enter which determines their class interests" (1985: 9–10).

Thus the depiction of class locations in Table 3.1a represents, to use Wright's language, a mix of contradictory locations within class relations, privileged appropriation locations within class relations, and polarized locations within capitalist property relations. We are enjoined not to refer to these locations as classes—a usage that may be hard to avoid because the typology is so central to his analyses in books called *Class* and *Class Counts*.

The construction of this typology involved creating categories of the skill and authority involved in a job and cross-tabulating the categorical scores on these two dimensions. Wright is well aware that concepts can underdetermine operational indicators, but a conceptual problem is immediately apparent: authority and skill aren't readily represented in a few discrete categories. In effect, he has said there's a high, medium, and absent category for each. "Loyalty" and "skill rents," however, would seem to have a relatively continuous distribution, with associated degrees of objective "interest" in their nature, magnitude, and perpetuation.

Be that as it may, the primary challenge still confronting Wright's schema of "locations" is to show that it identifies socially meaningful groups. Wright accepts this challenge, and indeed even argues that the usefulness of empirical analyses based on his categorizations can be assessed without accepting the exploitation-based theoretical framework. *Could* the incumbents of these structural "locations" coalesce into meaningful social classes? The answer depends on your judgment about whether those similarly located can collectively perceive the common exploitive aspects of their situation and act together on that basis. I give my own judgment in the concluding chapter of this book.

OCCUPATIONS AND CLASS

Frank Parkin's oft-cited comment is worth repeating: "The backbone of the class structure, and indeed of the entire reward system of modern Western society, is the occupational order" (1971: 18). In directly obvious ways, occupations shape individual experiences in the realms of production and consumption, and as I will argue, occupational categories can be usefully employed to construct class categorizations.

Yet, however aggregated, the occupational categories commonly employed in government reports and most large-scale surveys are *not* class categories in any rigorous theoretical sense. For example, in 1990 the Census Bureau distinguished 503 "detailed" occupations, which represent an untheorized judgment that a sufficient number of workers perform sufficiently similar tasks to warrant a separate label. The presumption is that some commonality of job *tasks* defines an occupation. Armed with a set of criteria about these tasks, analysts are then supposedly able to allocate all specific jobs to a particular occupational category.

What a person does on a job is surely central to most senses of class, but it doesn't capture the full theoretical meaning of class. Not only can workers with similar occupational titles have greatly different labor-market capacities and wealth, but they may have highly varying levels of workplace authority, and also be divided between owners and employees. These latter two concerns are particularly pertinent to the Marxian emphasis on the social relations of production. And, of course, because a significant segment of the adult population—the retired, housewives, the disabled—is not economically active, a person's own current occupation can't always be the defining criterion of class location. For these people, unless they are dubiously deemed classless, some derivative measure such as former occupation or supporting relative's occupation must be employed.

Moreover, all theories of class involve, at least implicitly, some sense of hierarchy, but occupational categories per se are not inherently ranked. They represent differentiation, not hierarchy, even if they are correlated with hierarchical criteria like income. In short, there are clear disjunctures between the concepts "class" and "occupation," especially so for complex schemas like Wright's that employ multiple criteria in designating class locations.

The objection that occupational categories are not class categories is incontestable, but its significance should not be exaggerated. The force of this objection is generally much more conceptual than empirical: the primary operational indicator of class is usually broad occupational type, with some subsidiary concerns for ownership status. (Wright's schema is a partial exception; see below). As Table 3.1 indicates, the primary class boundaries are substantially defined in operational terms by conventional occupational categories. For example, the "working class" is defined as all manual workers (Giddens 1973), or as most manual workers plus clerical/sales workers (Gilbert and Kahl 1993). And, similarly, the "upper middle class" is often defined as managers, professionals, and most proprietors. With varying considerations in mind, then, theorists have imposed their own hierarchical ranking on the occupational structure and thus created their models of the class system.

With necessary caution, I argue, occupational data (e.g., in mobility tables) can be aggregated into most of the relevant class categories. Not all distinctions (especially the upper class) can be so measured, nor can all theories be equally well represented by occupational data. The fully elaborated Wright schema may be a particular case in point, but fortunately his schema has been subject to an unusual number of direct tests. Moreover, "collapsed" versions of his schema, used by Wright and others, appear to correspond roughly to conventional occupational categories. All of this is not to deny measurement problems in using occupational data to operationalize class distinctions; however, I argue that they are not so severe as to prevent finding notable class structuration if it exists.

An Omnibus Measure

In a number of the subsequent chapters I report analyses based on the General Social Survey. To conduct these analyses, I constructed an occupation-based measure of class that for convenience I'll refer to as the Omnibus Measure of Class. Within the limits imposed by the items included in the GSS, this measure is intended to reflect the main distinctions incorporated in a number of the class maps represented in Table 3.1. The five categories are: (1) unskilled and low-skilled blue collar and service workers and farm workers (approximately 29 percent); (2) skilled blue-collar workers and supervisors of blue-collar work (approximately 11 percent); (3) clerical, sales, and technical workers (approximately 27 percent); (4) lower-paid managers and nonelite professionals (approximately 25 percent); and (5) well-paid managers and elite professionals (approximately 3 percent). To be placed in category 5, the respondent must have a managerial position and have an individual income of at least seventy-five thousand dollars (the top category in the GSS income question), or be a physician, veterinarian, lawyer, judge, or architect. All other managers and professionals are in category 4.

Admittedly, the distinction, as measured, between lower-paid managers and nonelite professionals (4) and higher-paid managers and elite professionals (5) isn't common. However, because the material rewards of managerial and professional positions are so disparate, it seems sensible to distinguish an elite group that reflects a common sense of an *upper* middle class, roughly approximating Goldthorpe's "service class." If there is class structuration, the top end of hierarchy is its most likely location and deserves separate scrutiny for that reason. Obviously this income cutoff doesn't identify a distinct level of authority or work conditions; direct measures of these would be desirable. But because income is generally correlated with organizational position, the cutoff does probably tend to identify the higher level people within the disparate ranks of managers. Of course, these two categories can be "collapsed" into a larger upper middle class composed of all managers and professionals, just as other categories can be combined to more closely correspond to the divisions of particular schemas (e.g., the clerical-sales-technical category can be placed in a larger "working class" with blue-collar workers or designated as part of a larger white-collar "middle class"). The virtue of the Omnibus Measure is the analytical flexibility that it offers, not its own conceptual precision.

Whatever the disputes about how and where to locate the boundaries of the class system, all of these schemas share a common presumption: there are relatively large, hierarchically ordered groups with distinct life experiences. To sharpen the meaning of this claim, it is useful to directly confront the substantial inequality in the division of economic goods.

THE CONTOURS OF INEQUALITY

My no-classes argument may appear difficult to sustain, or even bizarre, in light of the oft-cited data about the highly unequal distribution of income and wealth in American society. Sure, sociologists might debate the location of class boundaries and the degree of class structuration, but isn't the demonstrable reality of rich and poor overwhelming evidence in itself of a class society? And isn't the reality of *increasing* inequality evidence of increasing class structuration? My answer, in short, is no.

This statement may appear paradoxical because inequality is inherent in the notion of classes and class systems: some groups have more economic advantages than others. For all the debates about the meanings and structure of class systems, that much is agreed upon. Yet, as noted in Chapter 1, we misrepresent the nature of contemporary stratification systems if we simply presume that the reality of inequality necessarily entails a class system. Analytically, the degree of economic inequality and the degree of class structuration are separate matters; and empirically, the link between the two may be quite variable.

Bear in mind my minimalist definition of a class: a substantial group having common economic circumstances and relatively distinct life experiences. Obviously some degree of economic inequality is necessary for a class system to exist. Yet inequality is only a necessary, but by no means a sufficient, condition for class structuration. At least hypothetically, any particular level of inequality can be accompanied by varying levels of class structuration.

Economic inequality, to be clear, refers to the division of material rewards—how the pie is divided among individuals or families. It can be adequately measured by indicators of dispersion like Gini coefficients related to income and wealth. (To be sure, all such measures emphasize some parts of the distribution over others and therefore produce somewhat different depictions of the degree of inequality.) Conceivably, there could be as many ranks in the economic hierarchy as there are individuals or families. Of course, in actual distributions, many individuals are at similar economic levels, but the general point remains that there are many ranks that can't be self-evidently grouped as a small set of classes.

In stressing this distinction between class structuration and inequality, I am not blazing a novel analytical path. Theodore Caplow (forthcoming) distinguishes four dimensions of stratification: *inequality*—essentially the conventional meaning I use; *consistency*—the degree to which rank on various dimensions of inequality are correlated; *compartmentation*—"the separation of strata in a system of stratification by barriers that effectively inhibit interaction or mobility between categories"; and *persistence*—the degree to which the three other features of the stratification system are maintained over time. Class theory primarily makes a claim about compartmentation: strata (large groupings) are hierarchically separated as social entities. The further common argument is that class systems are marked by relatively high levels of consistency (the working class lacks money, power, *and* prestige) and persistence. Yet Caplow argues that class theorists assume what is to be demonstrated: inequality doesn't necessarily imply compartmentation with accompanying consistency and persistence.

Jonathan Turner (1984), in his insufficiently appreciated book *Social Stratification: A Theoretical Analysis*, also cautions against conflating notions of inequality and class. For Turner, the analog of class structuration is the ranked "differentiation of homogenous subpopulations"—that is, "the degree and extent to which subsets of members in a society reveal common behavioral tendencies and similar attitudes so that they can be distinguished from other subsets of members in a society" (147). In this formulation, classes are homogenous subpopulations, but the "classness" of a society is properly treated as a variable, not the inevitable result of its level of inequality. Like Caplow, Turner argues that not only *can* class and inequality be analytically distinguished, but that they *should* be. Failure to do so may well create a misleading depiction of a stratification system.

The meaning of this crucial distinction—whatever terms are used—can be sharpened by seeing it in concrete terms. Imagine that the offspring of the spectacularly rich have slightly better life chances than the offspring of the very rich, who in turn have slightly better chances than the offspring of the merely rich, who in turn have slight better chances than . . . and so on down the many rungs of the income ladder. In this case, inequality is plainly evident and life chances are related to economic standing, but there is no evidence of class structuration—or compartmentation, or ranked homogenous subpopulations.

For the most part this distinction isn't so much denied as ignored for reasons of rhetorical convenience. Many analysts—most prominently economists—have imposed various "cutoff" figures on the distributions of income to define "classes." However, these are statistical contrivances, revealing in their own way, but they are not sociologically meaningful designations. Should the upper cutoff for the middle class, be, say, some multiple of the median income? If so, how do you decide what multiple to use? Or say if you prefer to impose some specific dollar amount as the upper bound, how do you choose that figure? Or say if you prefer to take a relative approach, defining all those in specific quintiles of the income distribution as "middle class," the questions are again obvious: Which quintiles? Why quintiles?

Obviously none of these questions has a right answer. The variety of responses, evident in myriad publications, suggests the problems with such statistical definitions of class. Whatever the cutoff used, can the analyst claim that those who fall below it have distinctly different lives from those above it—that is, that they have different class experiences? Of course no serious class theorist makes such a claim, but the language of class still remains misleadingly attached to the income distribution, especially now in all the references to the declining middle class.

Yet, as noted, analyses of "income classes" are revealing in their own ways about the stratification system. They make dramatically apparent that material resources are very unequally distributed and that this inequality has worsened. (Of course words like "very" and "worsened" are not innocent of normative implications, but some kind of normative implication is almost impossible to avoid in describing inequality.) The details of this inequality need not be rehearsed here, but a brief summary can usefully set the context for later discussions of class structuration.

Income

To specify the contours of income inequality is not a cut-and-dry statistical exercise. Gross income or disposable income? The individual, the family, or the household as the unit of analysis? (In recent years a little less than a third of all households are not families by the Census Bureau definition—that is, two or more individuals related by birth or marriage.) Adjustments for family size, geographic differences in purchasing power, and so on? This is not the place to dissect such issues; I'll simply rely on the most commonly used methods of presenting the data.

Table 3.2 indicates the household- and family-income distributions, and the changes in these distributions from 1970 to 1995. For 1970 the median household income (in 1995 dollars) was $32,229; by 1995 it had increased, only slightly, to $34,076. In the same period, median family income increased from $36,410 to $40,611. In short, the "average household" and the "average family" lived just slightly better over these years (not accounting for the declining size of the living units). This represented a momentous departure from the historical record of rather steady, substantial increases in

TABLE 3.2

Money Income: Percent Distribution, in 1970 and 1995,
in Constant (1995) Dollars

	Under $10,000	*$10,000– 14,999*	*$15,000– 24,999*	*$25,000– 34,999*	*$35,000– 49,999*	*$50,000– 74,999*	*$75,000– and over*
				HOUSEHOLDS			
1970	14.3%	8.0%	15.8%	16.9%	21.3%	16.3%	7.5%
1995	12.3	8.7	15.9	14.2	16.9	17.1	14.8
				FAMILIES			
1970	7.7%	6.7%	15.4%	18.0%	24.5%	19.0%	8.8%
1995	7.5	6.5	14.4	14.1	18.5	20.4	18.6

SOURCE: U.S. Bureau of the Census, *Current Population Reports*, P-60-193.

affluence. The dashed expectations of a continually better future may have
fueled the common perception that average people have lesser chances than
they used to.

In both years, households and families tended to cluster in the income
brackets near the median figure. About 31 percent of households had incomes between $25,000 and $50,000 in 1995; a notably higher proportion
(38.2 percent) did so in 1970. At the same time, a significant proportion of
households had low incomes, below $15,000: 22.3 percent in 1970, 21 per-
cent in 1995. And a significant and increasing proportion topped the $75,000
level: 7.5 percent in 1970, 14.8 percent in 1992. Inequality increased, then,
because the upper tail increased faster than the lower tail declined.

These changes in household inequality have been driven by less equal
earnings and changes in living arrangements. Economists attribute about
three-fifths of the increase in inequality to less equal individual earnings and
the remainder to declining proportions of families among households.

The distribution of income among families also shows ongoing concentration in the middle brackets but increasing proportions at the top end and,
to a much lesser extent, at the bottom end. Most dramatically, the propor-

tion with income above $75,000 more than doubled (8.8 percent to 18.6 percent). Correspondingly, the proportions of middle-income earners dropped: 42.5 percent made $25,000–$50,000 in 1970, only 32.6 percent did so in 1995. This pattern holds as well for the incomes of families with a "head" aged 25–54—those in prime earning years—though the overall degree of inequality is substantially less.

Looking at changes in the distributions across *absolute* income categories, then, indicates some "hollowing out" of the middle. This is the solid basis for the claim of a *declining* "middle class." However, the often exaggerated nature of this claim should also be recognized. We have some decline in the middle brackets, not the emergence of a bipolar society. Families are not moving in great numbers to both extremes, the poor and the rich. The increasing inequality reflects relatively constant proportions at the low end and increasing proportions at the top end.

Another way of getting perspective on our current inequality is to look at the Gini coefficients for family inequality over four decades. Here are the Census Bureau computations:

1949	.378	1969	.349	1989	.401
1959	.361	1979	.365	1991	.397

No long-term trend is evident, though the increase in the eighties was the most pronounced change. The degree of inequality in 1991 is not "radically larger" than in 1949, to use Frank Levy's understated words (1995: 25).

Still another way to depict inequality is to see the distribution in percentile shares—in effect, the way the total economic pie is sliced. Table 3.3 shows in 1995 that the bottom fifth of families accounted for 4.4 percent of all income, while the top quintile accounted for 46.5 percent. That means the middle three quintiles—often labeled the middle class—had almost half the pie. Obviously the fact that the top fifth's piece was about ten times the size of the lowest fifth's piece is dramatic testimony to current inequality.

The share of the top groups has long been substantial, but it has increased. Commensurately, the share of the middle three quintiles has dropped slightly, from somewhat more than half (53.6 percent) to less than half (49.1 percent). Like the data for absolute income levels, then, these data on income shares also point to some decline in the "middle class." But neither perspective suggests a major transformation.

TABLE 3.3
Share of Aggregate Income Received by Each Fifth
and Top 5 Percent of Families, 1970 and 1995

	Lowest 5th	Second 5th	Third 5th	Fourth 5th	Highest 5th	Top 5 percent
1970	5.4%	12.2%	17.6%	23.8%	40.9%	15.6%
1995	4.4	10.1	15.8	23.2	46.5	20.0

SOURCE: U.S. Bureau of the Census, *Current Population Reports*, P-60-193.

Wealth

Analyzing the distribution of wealth is beset by problems of definition (what to count) and data (e.g., response biases), even more so than income. Again, this is not the place to delve into the accountants' realm; suffice it to say that different procedures and data sets yield somewhat different results. Yet we can be confident of two general conclusions: (1) the distribution of wealth is highly unequal, much more so than the distribution of income, and (2) the distribution of wealth has become more unequal in recent years.

Edward Wolff (1995), perhaps the leading student of wealth distribution, has assembled illuminating data (see Table 3.4). In 1989 the top 1 percent had 39 percent of all net worth, and just less than half of all financial wealth. Plainly, wealth is not widely distributed through the population: the lower four-fifths hold a trivial share of financial wealth (6 percent) and a very modest share (15 percent) of all net worth. The "wealth pie" is much more unequally sliced than the "income pie."

Table 3.4 also makes evident that the distribution of wealth shifted dramatically in just a short time—in the direction of substantially greater inequality—with the top 1 percent being especially favored. This unusually sharp increase of inequality reflected the run-up in the stock market, where many of the wealthiest families had their assets concentrated. This increase countered the generally slight and often arrested trend toward greater equality since the Great Depression.

This barrage of numbers related to the division of the economic pie

TABLE 3.4

Percentage Shares of Total Wealth and Income, 1983 and 1989

	NET WORTH		FINANCIAL WEALTH		INCOME	
	1983	*1989*	*1983*	*1989*	*1983*	*1989*
Top 1%	33.75%	38.93%	42.89%	48.17%	12.84%	16.47%
Next 19%	47.58%	45.64%	48.39%	45.76%	39.03%	39.02%
Bottom 80%	18.67%	15.43%	8.72%	6.07%	48.13%	44.52%

SOURCE: Adapted from Wolff (1995), fig. 3.3.

doesn't tell a new story: the persistent and substantial inequality in American society is well recognized. What is not sufficiently acknowledged or noticed is that this inequality does not imply the existence of classes. Indeed, as the next four chapters show, inequality has substantially increased within a society marked by low class structuration.

CHAPTER FOUR

Mobility

In America, Marx wrote in *The Eighteenth Brumaire*, "classes are not yet fixed, but in continual flux, with a persistent interchange of their elements." Two current neo-Weberians, Robert Erikson and John Goldthorpe, draw out the implications of this observation:

> Most obviously, the degree of permanence or impermanence with which individuals are associated with different positions, and their rates and patterns of movement among them, may be expected to condition both the formation of identities and the recognition of interests and, in turn, to determine where, and with what degree of sharpness, lines of cultural, social, and political, as well as economic division are drawn. (1993: 2)

Both of these statements suggest the fundamental significance of mobility patterns for class structuration—and, more generally, underscore that classes exist *in* the lives of particular individuals.

Quite differently, some theorists have argued that the class structure only represents a set of fixed positions—without regard for their incumbents' life histories, or for the impact of these positions on how they and their progeny live. Thus the structure persists even if people's positions in the economic hierarchy differ from that of their parents, or if they have different sorts of positions within their own careers.[1] Yet that is a peculiarly "depeopled" sense of class and how it may be sociologically significant. How is there structure unless the incumbents of class positions have sustained interaction with each other—the necessary basis for developing a shared sense of interests and for cultivating common practices and orientations? And if classes are sociologically significant, shouldn't we see *lasting* impact in people's lives, affecting how they and their families make their living and, relatedly, how well they live?

Surely, most common usage, as well as most sociological thinking, indicates that mobility is a central concern here. The impact of the Weberian legacy is clear. Recall Weber's oft-quoted words, "the 'social class' structure is composed of the plurality of class situations between which an interchange of individuals on a personal basis over the course of generations is readily possible and typically observable." The proposition is straightforward: classes exist because economic mobility is low. This individual-level persistence in economic position is the necessary grounds for the formation of classes and a key indicator of their social impact. And, to emphasize the point, the converse is true too: mobility, inter- and intragenerational, is the great solvent of class structuration. A critically decisive issue for class theory, then, is the extent and pattern of socioeconomic mobility.

These prefatory comments may seem unnecessary. After all, in explaining why mobility patterns are relevant to class analysis, Erikson and Goldthorpe see fit to preface their justification with the words "most obviously." Yet what is obvious to them and many others has not been universally perceived in the world of class theory, especially some Marxian variants. Perhaps Marxian scholars have been turned off to mobility studies because of their identification with the Weberian legacy, notwithstanding Marx's own (admittedly, implied) receptivity. Whatever the motivation, however, there has been a fairly strong indifference, if not hostility, to mobility studies among contemporary Marxists. For that reason I quoted Marx himself to suggest that an aversion to analyzing mobility isn't inherent in the Marxist legacy. Of course, theorists may still claim that there are more interesting or fundamental issues than the bearing of mobility on class structuration. Yet to maintain this indifference to mobility studies is to maintain that class analysis should be disconnected from a concern with how people actually live.

As I contended in Chapter 2, a realist approach to class analysis is grounded in this concern. And I take up mobility as the first indicator of structuration because it is the most decisive one, shaping other aspects of people's collective lives. To affect how people live, class location must be at least relatively persistent. More specifically, people can have a sense of "we-ness" with others in their "class" only if they see that they have had similar experiences and are likely to continue to do so. That sense is unlikely to develop if class is transient, a temporary position in life for people with diverse backgrounds and futures. Similarly, distinctive class cultural practices are likely to emerge only if they are reinforced through the impress of relatively constant work experiences and sustained interaction with others who have had similar experiences. These concerns about class consciousness and culture are relevant, in their own right, to a full assessment of class structuration, but we should expect to see marked structuration in these terms only when class immobility is low. My point here echoes Goldthorpe's (1987: 20) argument: "Class formation at the demographic level, *in which the effect of mobility is crucial* [my emphasis], is *prior to* class formation at other levels. Classes, that is to say, must have some degree of demographic identity before they can acquire a socio-cultural identity or provide a basis for collective action."

EXAMINING MOBILITY

The following discussion focuses on *absolute* rates of mobility, the actual movement of people from particular origins to particular destinations. This analysis involves looking at two sides of the same process—what are called outflows and inflows. Thus we can see where people end up given a particular starting point (outflow)—for instance, what percentage of children raised in skilled blue-collar families have a similar job themselves and what percentage of them have other types of jobs. We can also see the family background composition of particular classes (inflows)—for example, what percentage of current skilled blue-collar workers were raised in skilled blue-collar families, and what percentage were raised in families in other classes. In short, absolute rates are what determine (1) how life chances are distributed by social class, and (2) how diverse the origins are of those in particular classes.

This focus on absolute rates is both simple to comprehend and most directly relevant to the issue of class structuration. Examining the simple relationship between class origins and destination is, moreover, consistent with my general point (Chapter 2) that structuration is most directly revealed in bivariate analysis. But what about relative rates, social fluidity, those versed in current mobility research might ask? As informative as these analyses are, I argue, they don't bear on the issue of structuration—that is, whether classes are demographically cohesive groups. Because the distinction between absolute and relative rates may not be clear to all readers, a brief clarification may be in order.

Analysis of social fluidity reflects the fact that much social mobility is attributable to large changes in the occupational structure. With the massive movement off the farm and the great growth of the managerial and professional ranks, lots of mobility was in effect structurally induced. That is, because the relatively privileged didn't produce enough offspring to fill the expanded number of positions at the top of the occupational hierarchy, the offspring of the lesser privileged had opportunities for upward mobility that they were more than willing to take. Technological change, not some democratic opening up of the system, was the prime instigator of social mobility.

This process is captured in analyses of relative mobility (see, for example, Erikson and Goldthorpe 1993). These analyses show the connection between class origins and destination, *net* the effects of the changed occupational structure (i.e., the changes that are apparent in the marginals of the mobility table). An indicator of social fluidity, these rates crucially point to the "openness" of the system, the processes underlying the mobility regime. Analyses of relative rates clearly indicate that class still matters in a particular sense: class origins are notably linked to destination, discounting the impact of structural transformation. An important implication of this research is that Americans can't congratulate themselves on creating much opportunity beyond what was systematically demanded by economic transformation. Were it not for the unintended consequences of technological change, social mobility—the sine qua non of opportunity—would be much lower than the actual rates that we experienced.

Yet this fact doesn't tell us whether classes are demographically cohesive groups. My argument here about class structuration follows that of Walter Muller (1990: 313), a leading class analyst: "If problems of class formation are at issue, the proper reference is to the *absolute* amounts of mobility or immobility as measured, for instance, by the total proportion of mobile persons or by indicators of the composition of given classes in terms of the class origins of their members." Whatever the causal mechanisms affecting mobility patterns—whether technological change, democratization of opportunity, or demographic factors—it is the total gross mobility, indicated by absolute rates, that bears on structuration. Most directly, the actual extent of flow from specified origins to destinations indicates whether the class system is reproduced across generations, as class theory suggests.

What matters is the outcome, not the cause of mobility. Socially mobile workers simply recognize that their own position differs from their origins, as it does for many others. Mobility is real in their lives, undiminished in their experience because it can be attributed to structural effects. By the same token, workers in particular types of jobs can recognize that many others with similar jobs didn't come from families like theirs. Is this fact the result of structural mobility or social fluidity? The distinction couldn't be less material to their lives—or to the demographic identity of classes.

THE EVIDENCE

Counter to the implications of class theory, the reality is that mobility across generations and within careers is commonplace. Social critics have often characterized social mobility as a myth, a belief perpetuated by ideology, not fact. Yet the evidence that I'll marshal in the following pages of this chapter plainly indicates that many Americans have had lives that sustain this "myth." With respect to mobility, in brief, class structuration is quite weak.

The evidence for this conclusion has long been available, but the immensely significant implications of mobility research for class structuration have either been ignored or insufficiently stressed. The actual patterns of inter- and intragenerational mobility are worth attending to in some detail because they are so concretely revealing about the nature of the class system. And yet, though the relevant statistical details are many, no technical expertise is required to recognize that these patterns are inconsistent with the implications of class theory.[2]

Intergenerational Mobility

A useful place to start is the standard mobility table constructed from a 17×17 matrix of father's occupation by son's current occupation, based on the 1973 Occupational Change in a Generation (OCG) that Featherman and Hauser (1978) and almost countless other stratification researchers have relied on. This relatively fine-tuned categorization is primarily based on Census Bureau major occupation groups, with some additional distinctions based on employment status (self-employed or not) and industry. As illuminating as this matrix turns out to be, some limitations should be acknowledged.

First, this categorization of occupation was not designed to represent any particular theoretical statement about the class structure. It is essentially a rough-and-ready expression of common understandings of the occupational hierarchy. But as I argued in Chapter 3, the correspondence between conventional occupational categories and theoretically specified class boundaries is usually fairly tight—sufficiently so that occupationally defined categories are clearly useful for testing class theory. With some judicious collapsing of categories, then, this occupational categorization can be used to roughly reflect most of the class distinctions identified in mappings of the class structure. (Wright's schema cannot be represented by such data and receives separate attention in a subsequent section.) A notable exception: it is not well suited to trace the lives of the upper class as that group has commonly been defined because it aggregates all owners (called "proprietors"), whatever the size of their enterprise.

Another limitation is that occupational position is measured at only two points—the son's adult memory of what his father did when the son was about sixteen and the son's current position. We know that job mobility within a career is common, and thus each data point may not reflect a person's typical, or at least most common, class location. With the possibility of such measurement error on each side of the relationship, the mobility table may misrepresent the extent to which class origins and destinations are linked.

And, of course, the story of only half of the population is told. Women have had a very secondary place in the development of class theory and related empirical research. Some similar data, however, can be used to examine their class mobility, though as will become clear, this analysis has its own distinctive difficulties.

Although they must be acknowledged, these limitations should not obscure the powerful inferences that may be readily drawn from the standard issue mobility table. The crucial and general implications are evident no matter how the seventeen occupational categories are grouped into classes. For simplicity, then, consider the results of using a five-category aggregation (Table 4.1) that taps common class distinctions—upper nonmanual (managers, professionals, nonretail sales), lower nonmanual (proprietors and clerical, retail sales), upper manual (foremen and craftsmen), lower manual (service, operatives laborers), and farm (owners and workers).

Inflows. First look at what the inflow table (top panel of Table 4.1) reveals about the social composition of classes. Within each of the nonfarm "classes," a *substantial majority* of the men had *different* class origins from

TABLE 4.1
Inflow and Outflow Mobility: Son's Current Occupational Group (1973)
by Father's Broad Occupational Group

| | SON'S CURRENT OCCUPATION | | | | | |
FATHER'S OCCUPATION	Upper Nonmanual	Lower Nonmanual	Upper Manual	Lower Manual	Farm	Total
A. *Inflow*						
Upper Nonmanual	29.3%	14.8%	9.0%	7.7%	3.2%	15.4%
Lower Nonmanual	16.7	16.2	8.6	7.7	3.3	11.5
Upper Manual	20.2	21.0	25.8	18.5	5.8	20.4
Lower Manual	21.8	30.5	32.6	38.5	7.0	29.7
Farm	12.1	17.5	24.0	27.5	80.7	22.9
Total	100.0	100.0	100.0	100.0	100.0	100.0
B. *Outflow*						
Upper Nonmanual	59.4	11.4	12.8	15.5	0.9	100.0
Lower Nonmanual	45.1	16.6	16.4	20.7	1.2	100.0
Upper Manual	30.9	12.2	27.7	28.1	1.2	100.0
Lower Manual	22.9	12.1	23.9	40.1	1.0	100.0
Farm	16.4	9.0	22.9	37.1	14.5	100.0
Total	31.2	11.8	21.9	31.0	4.1	100.0

SOURCE: Adapted from Featherman and Hauser (1978), tables 3.15 and 3.14.

their own eventual station in life. Men in the upper nonmanual/"upper middle class" had particularly diverse origins. Among *both* the upper and lower middle classes, most men could look back to family roots in blue-collar or farming life. The prime recruiting ground for the middle class, then, has been the blue-collar working class and farmers (a group that does not readily fit into most class schemas). And at the bottom end, although relatively few of the lower manual workers fell from middle class status, even this group is far from monolithic in occupational origins.

Aggregate the occupational categories in different ways, recompute the percentages, and the conclusion is still unmistakable: classes are *not* intergenerationally reproduced social groups. Social closure is minimal; the "members" of any class have diverse origins.

This conclusion also notably holds for the broad capitalist class if that can be defined as all proprietors. Just under 13 percent of them had capitalist fathers; 45 percent had blue-collar fathers. In short, few American capitalists were the beneficiaries of birth into a capitalist family. Of course the category "proprietor" is highly diverse, including the one-man odd-jobs operator, the owner of a neighborhood store, and (not very many) the captain of industry. Because the financial rewards of ownership are often small, some proprietors' sons may have opted for another life, and others may have not had the choice to take over the family business or be set up in one of their own. Even so, however these factors played out, the capitalist/ownership class is marked by a distinct lack of social closure.

Outflows. Now it is useful to consider an outflow table (see the lower panel of Table 4.1); I will again use a five-category classification as a basic point of reference. Of course the prevalence of class inheritance is a function of what class schema is used in the cross-tabular exercise, but the results of other aggregations also suggest that class immobility is far from the norm.

Overall, more than two-thirds of the men moved from their father's occupational stratum—51 percent upward, 17 percent downward. Only the sons of upper nonmanual fathers had notable occupational inheritance, but nonetheless, more than four-tenths of them were downwardly mobile. This high rate of intergenerational mobility does not represent minor changes in status—and, indeed, the mobility often represents a change in class location, especially if the manual/nonmanual distinction is seen to divide the working and middle classes. Thus, in light of class maps that employ this distinction, working-class sons *commonly* become middle class themselves—43 percent of upper manual sons and 35 percent of the lower manual sons. And, more generally, because the nonfarm occupational categories in Table 4.1 roughly correspond to class categories in Giddens (1973), Rossides (1990), and Kerbo (1996), all of the "movers" have in effect crossed a class boundary in these terms.

It is especially relevant to highlight that mobility from the manual working class to the nonmanual middle class was not just a matter of moving from blue-collar origins to what has arguably become a "proletarianized" lower nonmanual job (recall that Gilbert and Kahl [1993] and Wright [1985] locate lower-level nonmanual workers in the working class). To detail, 31 percent of the sons from the upper-manual stratum ended up with *upper* nonmanual jobs, as did 23 percent of those from the lower-manual stratum.

In short, the outflows show that the odds of attaining a higher class position favor those advantaged by family circumstances, but their chances are just relatively good, never a matter they can count on. Relatedly, substantial proportions of sons from the lower classes attained higher class positions; intergenerational class mobility was common. And because most of this mobility was upward, many men could say that they did realize the American dream of doing "better" than their fathers.

Mobility patterns. Table 4.1 shows a modest relation between origins and destination. Yet this fact, in itself, does not establish that life chances are structured by class. To reiterate, class theory implies that class location affects mobility patterns so that mobility within a class is relatively regular and mobility out of a class is relatively uncommon. That is, class theory is supported if there are "clusters" of positions in the economic hierarchy that delimit mobility patterns. Conversely, nonclass gradational stratification theories presume that each step up the socioeconomic ladder has roughly equal consequences for mobility.

Are there such clusters? This issue is unresolved, despite all the statistical sophistication brought to bear on it. Different methods have provided very different answers: (1) Blau and Duncan (1967) identified the blue-collar/white-collar and farm/nonfarm divisions as the only class boundaries shaping mobility; (2) Vanneman (1977) found a different "class break," one between blue-collar/clerical workers and all other white-collar workers; (3) Featherman and Hauser (1978: 177) concluded that their "analyses of interstratum occupational mobility between and within the generations provide no support for Blau and Duncan's interpretation of the relative permeability of 'class' boundaries with respect to upward and downward mobility"; (4) Breiger (1981) claimed support for an eight-class clustering, with self-employed professionals as the most "classlike" group; and (5) Kerckhoff, Campbell, and Winfield-Laird (1985) detected the greatest intergenerational continuity among professionals and farmers (thus making them the most "classlike"), greater fluidity within blue- and white-collar categories than across, and greater than expected intercategory flows for entrepreneurial occupations, though the size of these discontinuities is difficult to assess. In the face of these contradictory claims, the safe conclusion may be that we do not know whether specific class boundaries shape intergenerational mobility patterns.

Structural effects. All this mobility, as I previously noted, reflects massive changes in the occupational structure. The marginals in Table 4.1 indicate that farm workers dropped from almost a quarter of the male work force in the fathers' "generation" to a small fraction (4 percent) in the sons' "generation." At the same time the proportion of upper nonmanual workers doubled, from 15 percent to 31 percent. In effect, technological change generated mobility: recruitment from "below" was necessary to fill the expanding number of slots in the higher reaches of the occupational hierarchy. All analysts agree that this so-called structural mobility largely accounts for the gross rates of upward mobility, not any greater democratic opening up of the system (that is, social fluidity). But to repeat my previous point, the actual flow from specified origins to destinations determines how diverse the origins are of those who become "members" of particular classes and, relatedly, how opportunities are socially distributed. And the flows, detailed in Table 4.1, clearly indicate that members of the classes indicated by the categories in mobility tables have highly diverse origins. Classes are not socially closed groups.

THE (W)RIGHT ANALYSIS?

All the preceding analysis in this chapter, class theorists may claim, is irrelevant, or at least problematic, for establishing whether classes exist as intergenerationally reproduced social groups. They may object that readily available occupational categorizations, however aggregated, aren't classes. At a conceptual level, as I have already suggested, that claim may be reasonable, though these categorizations generally seem adequate to operationally represent the most commonly designated class fissures. Even so, it's worth evaluating Wright's prominent class analysis on its own terms with his own data—especially so because he pointedly argues that class has been misconceptionalized and mismeasured in standard sociological research.

Table 4.2 shows intergenerational "inflows" and "outflows" for males based on a seven-class version of Wright's schema.[3] The upshot is that this categorization in explicit class terms doesn't reveal classes as socially cohesive groups.

Consider first the diagonal in the inflow table. It is striking but unsurprising that most farmers were raised in farming families. That two-thirds of

TABLE 4.2

Inflow and Outflow Mobility: Son's Current Class by Father's Class—Wright's Schema

FATHER'S CLASS	SON'S CURRENT CLASS							
	Employer	Petty Bourgeois	Farmer	Expert Manager	Manager	Expert	Worker	Total
A. Inflow								
Employer	18%	28%	3%	15%	11%	11%	10%	100% (91)
Petty Bourgeois	2	0	15	6	4	4	4	100% (32)
Farmer	23	27	67	7	9	5	8	100% (86)
Expert Manager	3	6	0	18	11	22	9	100% (79)
Manager	24	8	0	16	17	15	22	100% (140)
Expert	7	2	0	3	3	10	2	100% (24)
Worker	23	29	14	36	45	33	45	100% (289)
Total	100% (77)	100% (24)	100% (21)	100% (119)	100% (107)	100% (55)	100% (339)	
B. Outflow								
Employer	15%	7	1	19	13	6	37	100% (91)
Petty Bourgeois	4%	0	10	21	13	7	44	100% (32)
Farmer	21%	8	16	9	12	3	32	100% (86)
Expert Manager	3%	2	0	27	15	15	37	100% (79)
Manager	14%	1	0	14	13	6	53	100% (140)
Expert	21%	2	0	14	11	22	30	100% (24)
Worker	6%	2	1	15	17	6	52	100% (289)

SOURCE: Constructed from Western (1994): app. A.

farmers come from a farm represents substantial social reproduction, but the implications for class theory are slight. The agricultural population has often been ignored or relegated to an afterthought in most class schemas, no doubt reflecting the fact that so few people make their living off the land. (Goldthorpe is the most notable exception, and while they are not class theorists, Blau and Duncan [1967] and Featherman and Hauser [1978] studied farmers as a separate group.) In the contemporary division of labor, who tills the soil has few social ramifications.

Among the other classes in this schema, only the workers have modest levels of self-recruitment (45 percent). But the fact remains that Wright's expansively defined proletariat (including, it may be recalled, blue-collar and routine white-collar workers) is composed primarily of men with *non*proletarian backgrounds. With this diversity, Wright's proletariat can't collectively say, "We've been in this same boat all of our lives."

The classes with productive assets—either ownership, skills, or organizational position—are marked by even more social diversity. Not even a fifth of the employers, petty bourgeois, expert managers, managers, or nonmanagerial experts had class origins that matched their class destinations. And, indeed, in each of these classes, more "members" had working-class origins than were born into their class—usually by a wide margin. All the "exploiting" classes, then, can have very little sense of common background.

The corresponding outflow table underscores the prevalence of intergenerational class mobility. Overall, 70 percent are mobile. (The figure would surely be higher if Wright's twelve-class schema were used to create the matrix.) It is difficult to say how this gross rate is divided between upward and downward mobility because the different bases of exploitation in Wright's schema are not hierarchically ranked. Still, it is worth emphasizing that the exploiting classes don't routinely, or even commonly, pass on their particular asset advantage(s) to their offspring. For example, note the fates of those raised in employer families, presumably the beneficiaries of the most fundamental asset in a capitalist society: a much higher proportion ended up as workers (37 percent) than as employers (15 percent). Similarly, the sons of expert managers—those favored by both skill and organizational assets—were more likely to become workers (37 percent) than become expert managers themselves (27 percent).

Nor is movement out of the working class an unusual accomplishment.

Almost half (48 percent) of working-class sons become some kind of "exploiter" in their own work life. Of course, that means that the other half remains exploited throughout their life (assuming that both the fathers and sons were immobile within the class system throughout their careers). Is this degree of mobility out of the working class high? Such a question, as I've noted before, can't be answered on a priori theoretical grounds, but class origins hardly appear to be destiny. In light of this reality, working-class kids with ambitions to improve their lives were not indulging in unattainable fantasies.

Even so, the outflow analysis in Table 4.2 shows that in some instances class origins are related to destinations. For example, sons of expert managers and of experts—men with skill assets—had higher chances of having a job like their fathers than sons from any other class. Now, what should we make of such proportional differences? Keep in mind that all of the following statements are supported by the data:

1. The *relative odds* of becoming an expert manager favor the sons of this class—e.g. 1.8 greater (27 percent versus 15 percent) than the chances of workers' sons.

2. Even with this relative edge, only a minority (27 percent) of expert managers' sons hold jobs like their father.

3. The *absolute differences* across origin classes in rates of becoming an expert manager are limited—an 8 percent difference between the sons of expert managers and sons of employers, a 12 percent difference between the former and the sons of workers.

Class theorists are likely to seize on the first point; it clearly shows that life chances are not equally distributed—a point that emerges no matter how class is measured. But it's hard to be impressed with these mobility patterns as signs of class reproduction: the overwhelming majority of expert managers' sons don't follow into like positions; indeed, a larger proportion of them "fall" into the working class (as defined by Wright) than retain their class advantage.

Relative Permeability

Some of these class boundaries are more permeable than others. In an extremely sophisticated analysis of these data, Western (1994) attempts to fit a number of loglinear models that represent disproportionate immobility within particular classes, accounting for marginal effects. The technical details of this analysis can't be readily related here. I will simply highlight some key findings. Two of Western's conclusions directly indicate that class location in Wright's terms doesn't structure mobility chances: "Contrary to Marxist expectations, offspring from working-class origins do not routinely have especially bad mobility chances" (127). "Organizational control [i.e., the asset that advantages managers] has negligible effects on intergenerational mobility"(126). But, suggesting class-rooted immobility, he also finds that ownership affects men's mobility, "first limiting movement between self-employment and wage labor, and then further restricting mobility between the capitalist and working classes" (127); and that "skill is clearly the basis for immobility. . . . Sons and daughters [net of other factors] of experts are more than twice as likely as the offspring of nonexperts to become experts themselves, rather than nonexperts" (119).

These latter two conclusions appear to offer some partial support of Wright's class schema, but we should pause before accepting this analysis as indicating class structuration in terms of intergenerational mobility patterns. The "fit" of his loglinear model mean that some variation in observed frequencies can be attributed to marginal and additional mobility effects based on loglinear interaction parameters (at conventional levels of statistical significance). However, that a particular model "fits" doesn't really tell us about the *absolute* level of class effects on mobility chances. As I argued before, to understand class structuration, it is most revealing to simply look at the patterns of gross mobility.

In this light, the simple outflow percentages in Table 4.2 hardly point to prominent structuration. The expertise and ownership "effects" that emerge in Western's models reflect the fact that becoming an employer or an expert manager is uncommon for those raised in *all* classes, but just somewhat less uncommon among those raised in each of these classes.[4] The absolute extent to which families advantaged by ownership or expertise pass on their advantages to their offspring is quite small. By no means is there evidence of class closure based on family possession of ownership or skill assets.

Wright and Female Class Mobility

In assessing Wright's schema, I have concentrated on male mobility patterns to facilitate comparison with the analysis based on the OCG II data, but because Western's analysis indicates some gender differences in class mobility, separate attention to women is warranted.

TABLE 4.3

Inflow and Outflow Mobility: Daughter's Current Class by Family Head's Class

FAMILY HEAD'S CLASS	DAUGHTER'S CURRENT CLASS							
	Employer	Petty Bourgeois	Farmer	Expert Manager	Manager	Expert	Worker	Total
A. Inflow								
Employer	22%	13%	0%	23%	11%	19%	11%	
Petty Bourgeois	6	0	0	3	5	6	4	
Farmer	24	35	82	8	12	13	16	
Expert Manager	10	13	0	12	10	11	8	
Manager	18	14	0	16	15	20	16	
Expert	2	6	0	1	2	5	3	
Worker	16	18	18	37	47	26	41	
Total	100% (57)	100% (24)	100% (4)	100% (57)	100% (81)	100% (71)	100% (33)	
B. Outflow								
Employer	15%	4	0	15	10	15	42	100% (87)
Petty Bourgeois	14%	0	0	7	14	15	51	100% (26)
Farmer	14%	8	3	5	9	9	52	100% (101)
Expert Manager	10%	5	0	12	13	13	46	100% (59)
Manager	10%	3	0	9	12	14	52	100% (103)
Expert	7%	8	0	3	7	19	55	100% (18)
Worker	4%	2	0	9	16	8	60	100% (229)

SOURCE: Constructed from Western (1994): app. A.

To a modest extent, the class locations of male and female workers differ. (The assumption here is that an individual's own paid work determines his or her class location—an assumption that is examined in Chapter 8.) Most notably, women are more likely to be workers than men (53 percent versus 46 percent) and less likely to be expert managers (9 percent versus 16 percent). But mobility patterns within the "female class system" remarkably parallel mobility within the "male class system."

Table 4.3 clearly makes this point. (It should be noted that "class origins" for women is based on their "family head's" position, a procedure that generally means a woman's class origin was determined by her father's work.) Rather than reciting a similar slew of statistical detail, I will merely highlight the most salient patterns.

Except for the few farmers, all classes are composed of women with diverse class backgrounds. A majority of the female workers (59%) came from higher class backgrounds, and only a fairly small minority of the women in each of the exploiting classes were raised in the class that they eventually reached themselves. Workers' daughters represented the *largest* group among experts, managers, and expert managers, accounting for a much larger proportion of each of these classes than women born into each of them.

Like men, women are highly mobile within this class system. Overall, about three of ten inherited their class position. This low aggregate rate reflects the fact that intergenerational persistence within each of the exploiting classes was even lower and that movement out of the working class was fairly common (40 percent). Indeed, by a large margin, a working-class life was the most common fate for women from all social classes.

It is possible to dissect these tables further and note some gender-based differences in intergenerational class mobility, but what is critical here is to recognize the implications of the broadly similar patterns. For both women and men, none of Wright's classes is a socially closed group; social diversity is their defining mark. And for both women and men, class origins are far from class destiny. Irrespective of sex, the favorable odds of those born to class privilege only mean that they have relatively good but still modest life chances. In terms of Wright's neo-Marxist schema, for both women and men, class inheritance among the privileged is much less common than class mobility.

INTRAGENERATIONAL MOBILITY

Until fairly recent years the great bulk of so-called mobility research has essentially been analysis of *inter*generational mobility. Its relevance to class analysis should be abundantly clear by this point: class, so the claim goes, is a persistent, life-defining force transmitted through families over time. That claim turns out to be vastly exaggerated. Oddly enough, much less has been made of the implications of intragenerational mobility for class theory, even though its relevance is at least equally great.

This lesser attention is perplexing and unfortunate because individual work-life histories so directly speak to the claim that class is a persistent force. In obvious ways, the stratification system is very different if most individuals "bounce around" the occupational hierarchy or if most have largely similar experiences throughout their work lives. Karl Mayer and Glenn Carroll (1987: 15) effectively encapsulate the matter: "Fluctuations across classes in the course of a career should undermine class loyalty as well as loosen any potential homogeneity in the material conditions or orientations of a class. . . . If class boundaries can be easily transcended during a work life, then the salience of assumed class distinctions might well be questioned."

In part, this modest concern for what happens in an individual's own work history may reflect a long-standing lack of good data, only recently and partially rectified. My subsequent analysis is plainly limited by the inadequacies of previous research for assessing class structuration. Some of the research on *job* mobility is extremely sophisticated and revealing about career histories, and yet in concentrating on internal labor markets and other within-organization or across-industry patterns, it generally doesn't bring class-related issues into sharp focus. These limitations must be acknowledged, but some good evidence indicates that not only are job changes commonplace, but that "class mobility" within work lives is frequent throughout most of the occupational hierarchy. The interpretative issue before us is how to judge the degree of structuration in light of this mobility.

First to Current Job

The typical way to measure intragenerational mobility has been to compare the occupational category of individuals' (usually males') first job to their current job. As simple and intuitively appealing as this procedure may seem, it is beset with well-recognized problems. First of all, what is a person's "first" job? Many people have a series of short-term, fill-in jobs before settling into a "real" job, one they are serious about. Which job is the first one? Or, at least, which should be designated as first for the purpose of analyzing the class stability of an individual? Or think about the full-time worker going to the community college at night; she gets a degree in six years and then gets promoted a half-year later, partially because of her degree. Is her "first" job the full-time position while in school, which is the same as her posteducation job, or is it the better position that came somewhat later? Obviously, with no difficulty, you can multiply anecdotes from your own set of acquaintances to suggest the ambiguity of the concept "first job." It is especially ambiguous in the American context because the school-to-work transition is so unstructured and the early employment years are so volatile, especially for the lesser educated.

Secondly, not all jobs within a particular occupational/class category, especially for less experienced workers, have the same career potential. Some are much more systematically linked to promotional ladders than others. For example, some sales reps may be in dead-end positions and be fully aware of that fact, while others are being groomed, as a matter of company policy, for managerial responsibility and are equally aware of that too. The first group's immobility seems clear. Is the second group mobile in terms of class (middle to upper middle class), or does this career pattern represent class stability? Whatever the answer on conceptual grounds, it is difficult to imagine having sufficient detail on a wide range of jobs to judge their career-long "class potential."

Together, these concerns about measuring "first job" suggest that a matrix of first job by current job may not accurately capture the extent of class stability within careers. Undoubtedly some part of the apparent class mobility reflects measurement error. And yet this matrix is worth considering because it counters the highly exaggerated sense of career stability that is at least implicitly suggested in much class theory. Moreover, data about job changes within established careers (considered in the next section) also suggest that class is far from a fixed deal, a permanent feature in everyone's lives.

Again, the place to start is the matrix reported in Featherman and Hauser (1978). To keep matters parallel, I'll discuss the data using the same five-category classification as in Table 4.1.

Not only do men often end up in different classes from their father, but even in their own careers they commonly cross class boundaries—mostly to a higher class, but not exclusively so. Indeed, a slight majority (51 percent) of these men changed from one occupational stratum to another. Starting at the top did substantially increase the odds of finishing there (80 percent persistence among the upper nonmanual category). However, a working-class start did not inevitably mean a working-class finish: about a quarter of both the upper-manual and lower-manual starters made it into the white-collar/ middle class in the course of their careers. Moreover, large numbers of lower nonmanual/lower middle class starters ended up in every strata: about as many of the lower nonmanual starters "fell" into the working class (36 percent) as "rose" into the upper middle class (38 percent).

An obvious upshot of all this career mobility is that each occupational stratum has become filled with men having diverse career paths. Even with the general prevalence of upper over downward mobility, 38 percent of the lower manual workers started in another stratum; and even with the advantages of starting at the top, 45 percent of the men who eventually attained upper white-collar jobs started out in a lower stratum, usually blue-collar or farming positions. This openness at the "top" is especially remarkable. That almost half of the men who reached the top stratum started out below attests to both the growth in the managerial-professional category and its related social diversity.

Drawing in men with varied occupational backgrounds, the proprietor/ "capitalist class" reflects the general pattern. Only about a quarter of those who started with their own business persisted as owners, and more of the eventual owners started out in blue-collar rather than white-collar jobs. Ownership, in light of these data, is not a persistent, fundamental divide. The American dream of owning a business is not one that is generally maintained, nor is it one that is foreclosed to even lower-status employees. Of course business ownership has diverse rewards, but it should be apparent that owners of the means of production also took diverse pathways to their positions.

Class Clusters?

Is there "clustering" in the occupational hierarchy that shapes patterns of intragenerational career mobility? The issue here is the extent to which workers stay within specific broad occupational categories (classes) throughout their career, thus furthering structuration. Again, the issue is technically complex and not fully resolved, and because related analyses rely on first job–current job matrices, the previously discussed measurement problems also plague the matter. Snipp (1985) finds a basic blue-collar/white-collar divide underlying other divisions that yield a five-class model. In this analysis both the professions and the manual crafts appear as relatively distinct occupational worlds, and the other divisions are less pronounced. Stier and Grusky's (1990) analysis largely confirms Featherman and Hauser's (1978) argument that occupational persistence is distinctly pronounced among a professional elite and farmers. However, with all the career movement across the intermediate ranks, these analyses find little evidence of class clustering along the commonly specified fault lines—skilled versus unskilled manual workers, blue-collar versus white-collar workers, lower nonmanual workers versus upper nonmanual workers. In sum, class structuration in terms of intragenerational mobility seems largely confined to the professions and the upper (blue-collar) working class.

Within-Career Changes

To restate a point, patterns of first to current job transitions may be misleading because some of the apparent mobility may reflect some "normal" progression in an orderly career. It makes sense, then, to see what happens to people who have in some sense established themselves: do these workers change classes? But this is not an easy question to answer. Clearly you'd expect to see more class mobility the longer the time period, and the younger the workers. There is no obvious right way to define the transition period or the subset of workers to be included. Rather than trying to make a case for a particular approach, I'll simply report two relevant studies that use very different time periods.

First, consider what happens from one year to the next when people change jobs. I report here the findings of a Department of Labor Study (1980) of the 1978 occupations of the 1977 job changers. (These job changers represented 12 percent of the labor force.) Data are reported in terms of nine occupational categories, farm workers and four categories each of blue- and white-collar work.

The key finding is that *a substantial majority* (61 percent) *moved to a different type of job*. Many of these job changes represent changes in class location in light of commonly accepted class designations. Many of the

TABLE 4.4
1969 and 1980 Occupational Categories—White Males

1969 OCCUPATION	1980 OCCUPATION							
	Prof.	*Manager*	*Self-Emp.*	*Cler. & Sales*	*Craft*	*Oper.*	*Serv. & Lab.*	*Farm*
Prof.	64.2%	23.3	1.3	3.8	3.8	0	1.3	2.5
Manager	10.3%	62.9	2.6	10.3	6.0	2.6	1.7	3.5
Self-Emp.	0%	25.9	37.0	11.1	14.8	7.4	3.7	0
Cler. & Sales	12.0%	17.4	1.1	46.7	12.0	6.5	3.3	1.1
Craft	3.4%	9.1	2.8	5.1	64.8	10.2	2.8	1.7
Oper.	0%	7.1	0.8	1.6	26.0	52.0	11.8	0.8
Serv. & Lab	12.8%	7.7	2.6	0	20.5	18.0	33.3	5.1
Farm	3.3%	3.3	3.3	0	13.3	13.3	3.3	60.0

SOURCE: Adapted from Green and Wilson (1992: 119).

changes were between upper (managerial) and lower-middle-class (clerical, sales, etc.) positions as well as between upper (skilled) and lower (unskilled) working-class positions. Yet at the same time many of these job changers crossed the boundary long considered the most fundamental, that between blue-collar and white-collar work. And this boundary crossing occurred in both directions. More than a fifth (22 percent) of the job leavers with white-collar occupations "dropped" to the blue-collar working class, and more than a quarter of the blue-collar leavers "rose" to a white-collar middle-class position. The shop floor and office often provide some distinctive experiences, but with such frequent boundary crossings it's difficult to portray blue-collar and white-collar work as separate worlds. Among the nine occupational categories, only professional-technical workers (50 percent) and clerical workers (52 percent) were notably likely to take a similar job.

Indicating career mobility over a longer time span, Table 4.4 reports a cross-tabulation of 1969 by 1980 occupational job category for a sample of white men (Panel Study of Income Dynamics, or PSID), aged 29–60, who received some labor income in each year of the twelve-year interval. Again, the key finding: *a majority (57 percent) changed occupational categories.* This figure can't be directly compared to the mobility figure for the 1977–78 transition because of the difference in occupational categorizations, but both findings roughly indicate that job changes frequently involve changes in job type.

The diagonals make evident where class structuration is most pronounced:

1. Once at the top (managerial and professional positions), men tend to stay at the top. If a manager or a professional switches, it is to the other one of these categories, though about a quarter of the managers do not preserve their upper middle class status.

2. Almost two-thirds of the craftsmen stay put, and slightly more move up than down.

3. Most farmers (60 percent) stay farmers, and most movement off the land is to the shop floor.

Also evident, however, is the frequent class mobility:

1. A considerable majority of 1969 owners work for somebody else twelve years later.

2. A slight majority of the clerks and salesmen—the most disputed group in class theory—end up in a different type of job, somewhat more often in a higher white-collar position (31 percent) but also commonly in a blue-collar position (23 percent).

3. Almost as many operators change job categories as stay put, and a large majority of service workers and laborers move up.

In short, the upper stratum within the middle class and the upper stratum within the blue-collar working class provide relatively permanent occupational locations, though permanence is hardly guaranteed. By contrast, occupational mobility is commonplace, if not the general tendency, within the lower strata of each class. The difference in mobility patterns, then, is not so much a broad class difference as it is between segments within classes. The professional elite and craftsmen have the highest occupational retention. This pattern likely reflects the relatively strict control of entry through formal certification in these occupations. From the point of view of the individual worker, this certification often represents a substantial investment encouraging occupational stability.

The PSID data offer another perspective suggesting the considerable occupational fluidity in careers. Not only did many workers change occupations in the course of these dozen years, but *several* changes were common.

More specifically, half had two or more changes, 30 percent had three or more. To repeat: these are changes in broad occupational category, not job changes within a category.

How to interpret the magnitude of this occupational mobility—or, conversely, the magnitude of the occupational persistence in careers? The half-empty/half-full teacup answer comes to mind, but it doesn't take us very far. And obviously the magnitude of the mobility/persistence depends on the classification. I've reported findings based on classifications with a relatively high number of categories, thus making mobility appear more likely. Obviously classifications with fewer categories (e.g., blue-collar vs. white-collar) would suggest lesser mobility. Even so, it is evident that many of the transitions in the cited data reflect changes in class location or at least changes of major strata within broadly defined classes.

Occupational changes are so commonplace, I argue, that it is hard to depict *class careers* as the routinely expectable outcome. Within-class careers are common, but so, too, are across-class careers. The latter reality is so prevalent that many people don't feel destined to stay where they started or even where they are after some years in the labor market. Survey results from Wright's comparative Project on Class Structure and Class Consciousness support that conclusion (Clement and Myles 1994:89, table 4.16). To the question, "Do people in positions like yours eventually get significant promotions? That is, a change in job title that brings a significant increase in pay or responsibilities?" employed men replied:

> more than half: 38 percent
> some: 19 percent
> few: 25 percent
> none: 17 percent

Employed women had similar responses. And, remarkably, working-class men and women perceived almost the same opportunity for mobility as others.

This is not to deny the relatively high occupational permanence within certain segments of the labor force. Throughout much of the occupational hierarchy, however, a majority of workers end up as "members" of different classes in their own work lives—a pattern that should undercut class structuration in other dimensions of life.

A DIGRESSION ON INCOME FLUCTUATIONS

A digression on income is in order here. As I explained in Chapter 3, class is not defined by income in any meaningful sense: people have more or less of it, with related degrees of material comfort, but there are no decisive "breaks" in the income distribution that correspond to distinctive social groups. Although analysts can create income class categories like "upper" or "middle," these are convenient statistical creations, not social realities. Yet the volatility of family incomes over time is at least indirectly relevant to assessing class structuration.

Class theory would seem to imply that persistence in class position (i.e., retaining the same sort of job) leads to relatively constant levels of material comfort. Concretely, this means once a factory worker always a factory worker and hence always a modest income, or once a manager always a manager and hence always relatively good pay. Although living standards have certainly received greater attention in Weberian-inspired theory than its Marxian counterparts, the common claim is that class persistently shapes crucial domains of life. To risk stating the obvious, income determines whether a person can sustain or change a particular way of life. Thus, class-related dispositions and practices are reinforced by roughly stable incomes, while mobility up and down the income hierarchy weakens structuration.

Greg Duncan's (1984) analysis of the Panel Study of Income Dynamics—the first good longitudinal data about families' economic conditions—shatters any sense that people generally have stable economic lives. The distributions reported in Table 4.5 clearly indicate that mobility, even substantial mobility, in the income hierarchy is routine. (This table is read as follows: "Of all individuals in 1971, 20 percent lived in families whose incomes placed them in the lowest income quintile, but just 11.1 percent of all individuals placed in the lowest quintile in both 1971 and 1978. The other 8.9 percent had moved upward to the fourth (4.4 percent), third (1.9 percent), second (1.4 percent), or highest (1.2 percent) quintiles" (Duncan 1984: 13).

Consider, first, the fates of the economically distressed, those in the lowest income quintile in 1971. Somewhat more than half ($^{11.1}/_{20}$) were still at this level in 1978, but almost a quarter ($^{4.5}/_{20}$) were in the top three quintiles just seven years after the initial measurement. That is, a substantial minor-

TABLE 4.5
Estimated Fractions of the U.S. Population in Various Combinations
of 1971 and 1978 Family Income

FAMILY INCOME QUINTILE IN 1971	FAMILY INCOME QUINTILE IN 1978					
	Lowest	*Fourth*	*Third*	*Second*	*Highest*	*All*
Lowest	11.1%	4.4%	1.9%	1.4%	1.2%	20.0%
Fourth	4.3	6.9	4.3	2.7	1.8	20.0
Third	2.7	4.7	6.1	3.7	2.8	20.0
Second	1.2	3.0	5.1	6.3	4.4	20.0
Highest	0.7	0.9	2.8	5.9	9.7	20.0
All	20.0%	19.9%	20.2%	20.0%	19.9%	100.0%

SOURCE: Duncan 1984: 13.

ity of the economically distressed population had significantly better lives in a short period of time.

Moreover, having "made it" at one point did not mean that the good life routinely continued. More than half ($^{10.3}/_{20}$) of the top quintile in 1971 fell from this level by 1978, and more than a fifth had moved to the lower three quintiles. I share Duncan's sense of the magnitude of this mobility: "Income position can hardly be considered very permanent if the chance of staying on top for those who begin there is only one in two" (14). Indeed, across the entire range of income levels, mobility was a common occurrence. Overall, 60 percent moved to a different income quintile, and almost a quarter moved at least two quintiles. And, remember, these changes took place within seven years—such a short interval that they can't be attributed to "normal" life-cycle patterns.[5]

This considerable movement up and down the income hierarchy took place in a time when the division of the economic pie remained relatively stable. That is, each quintile's share of total income remained fairly constant (top fifth about 41 percent, lowest fifth about 5 percent), but individual families often changed "income classes." Only with the availability of longitudinal data did this pattern become apparent, but its implications for class theory have not been adequately appreciated. Hout, Brooks, and Manza (1993), for example, cite the stability of the macrodistribution of income as evidence of the continuing reality of class. Yet, as I argued in the introductory chapter, inequality can exist without class structuration in the sense of distinctive socioeconomic groups. "Income classes"—statistical categories—do persist by definition, but over time their "members" are ever changing. It is the individual-level mobility that bears on structuration. Because people frequently move up and down the economic ladder, they often have little opportunity or incentive to develop a sense of collective fate with those who happen to have similar paychecks at a particular time. In short, like occupational mobility, fluctuations in family income undercut class cohesiveness.

CONCLUSION

The simple intergenerational mobility table damns a central tenet of class theory. No matter what class categorization is used in constructing the table, classes are not intergenerationally reproduced social groups. In the contemporary United States, all classes are socially heterogenous: at least half of the working class were not born to the class, and large majorities of the various middle and upper middle classes had different origins from their eventual station. This diversity reflects the widespread mobility, generally upward, in American society. Overwhelmingly, across generations, most Americans are movers, not stayers in the occupational hierarchy. And often the mobility from family origins to personal destination—contrary to many claims—is considerable. Yes, the odds of becoming advantaged do favor those advantaged by family circumstances. Yet maintaining privilege is never routine for the offspring of higher classes, and advancing from the lower classes to positions of privilege is never uncommon. Indeed, class inheritance has been the *atypical* experience of some privileged groups (notably, owners), and upward mobility has been the *typical* experience of relatively disadvantaged groups.

    In terms of intergenerational mobility patterns, class structuration has been undermined by the large-scale shift away from farming and blue-collar occupations and the corresponding increase in white-collar/middle-class occupations. All analysts agree that this transformation, not some democratic "opening up" of the system, largely accounts for the prevalence of intergenerational mobility. In effect, America had to have lots of mobility to meet new demands in the labor market. That macroeconomic force didn't sever the connection between origins and distinctions, but it generated so many openings in the middle-class world that presumed class boundaries proved to be much more permeable than exclusionary. To be sure, analysts can identify some "class effects" on mobility chances independent of this structural factor, but the bottom line is crucial here: *whatever the cause* of all the intergenerational mobility, the *result* is that the American class system is not marked by intergenerational social closure.

Although the related analyses have limitations, all the apparent mobility within careers also undercuts claims of class structuration. Quite commonly, throughout the occupational hierarchy, many job changes represent changes in class location. These changes in class location are evident in comparisons of first job to current job and in the mobility patterns among job changers within the ranks of the established workforce. To be sure, occupational persistence is relatively high within segments of the labor force—high-level professions and skilled craftsmen, in particular—but even there, mobility, in and out, is still notable. Now, perhaps the prevalence of within-class careers will increase because of the ever stronger allocating role of educational credentials, but before indulging speculations about the future, we should remain mindful that class theory is based on the claim that class is now and has always been a routinely persistent feature of life. Analyses of the recent past lend little support for that claim.

The upshot of inter- and intragenerational mobility studies is that the stock characters described or at least implied in class theory are not so common. The son of a blue-collar worker who himself has only a series of blue-collar jobs is often portrayed as the prototypical "working class" guy. So, too, the son of a manager who himself has had a series of managerial positions is frequently represented as the prototypical "upper middle class" guy. These people do exist in substantial numbers. However, even larger numbers don't fit such a pattern: class location commonly changes in the course of a lifetime. Mobility is perhaps the greatest solvent of class structuration.

CHAPTER FIVE

Class Sentiment

How do people identify their own class positions? One ready answer is provided by responses to the General Social Survey. In a fairly standard way, respondents were asked, "If you were asked to use one of four names, which would you say you belong in: the lower class, the working class, the middle class, or the upper class?" In 1990, it broke down this way: 3.1 percent upper, 47.0 percent middle, 45.7 percent working, and 4.2 percent lower class.

In subjective terms, these responses suggest the reality of class divisions. At least Americans are not inclined to *see* themselves as part of some all-encompassing middle class. There's no sign of rampant embourgeoisement or a working class in its death throes. And, indeed, there seems to be a rough correspondence between this subjective class system and the objective class system demarcated in most theoretical maps. In all the class maps outlined in Chapter 3 the class system is primarily constituted by the two large, almost equal-sized groups, the middle and working classes, although their relative size is affected by the placement of routine white-collar workers. The "upper" classes in all class schemas, though constituted in somewhat different ways, are also correspondingly small in size.

Yet the apparent correspondence between how theorists see the world and how (other) people appear to see the world doesn't tell us much about the reality of classes. For one matter, we can question whether responses to such a survey item accurately capture people's sense of their class. Thus in later pages of this chapter I'll necessarily consider some of the methodological problems associated with measuring class consciousness. More significantly, however, the aggregate distribution of self-labeled class position doesn't indicate whether the members of particular *objectively* defined classes are class conscious—or even express similar sentiments on matters like class self-placement that purport to tap this broad concept. That is the key issue to resolve here.

Once again, Marx framed the issue. For Marx, classes are objective, inherent in the relations of production; however, they become agents of change only as they become aware of their collective interests and act on them. Thus in the famous passage in *The Poverty of Philosophy*, the rise of capitalist industrial organization creates a class "as against, but not yet for itself. In the struggle . . . this mass becomes united, and constitutes a class for itself." Marx is not fully consistent in all his many pages in saying whether a class must be conscious of itself as class to be a true class. However, he unambiguously argued class consciousness is a crucial mechanism activating the revolutionary dynamic. Thus the socially significant class, in his view, is the class that exists "for-itself." Marx never really doubted that class consciousness would emerge, and indeed gave relatively scant attention to the concrete social processes that would generate it. But what Marx treated as largely unproblematic can't be sensibly ignored in light of history. After all, the revolution hasn't occurred where Marx thought it would—in the most advanced capitalist societies—nor are there any prospects of one in those societies.

Even if revolutionary consciousness is conspicuously absent among the anointed agents of change, the issue remains of the *extent* to which objectively defined classes are bound by common, distinctive sentiments that may be called "class consciousness." I write with circumspection here because the meaning of "class consciousness" is far from a settled matter. In both conceptual and measurement terms, this is a contested matter. Even so, C. W. Mills (1951: 325) has usefully summarized the most commonly invoked dimensions:

> Class consciousness has always been understood as a political consciousness of one's own rational class interests and their opposition to the interests of other classes. . . . Thus, for class consciousness, there must be (1) a rational awareness and identification with one's own class interest; (2) an awareness of and rejection of other class interests as illegitimate; and (3) an awareness of and a readiness to use collective political means to the collective political end of realizing one's interests.

Mills sets a high hurdle. Obviously no class can be said to have class consciousness in this strong, three-dimensional sense. However, this conceptual perspective valuably suggests that there are relatively distinct *levels* of consciousness, each higher level dependent on the existence of the lower levels. As Chapter 6 makes abundantly clear, there's no point in discussing the third level here. The only real dispute is over the first level—and to stretch matters, the second.

THE RIGHT NAME

I started this chapter with the results from a standard-issue "class self-identification" question because that's how sociologists have typically approached the issue of measuring class consciousness. The common assumption is that members of an objectively defined class are at least minimally class conscious if they name the "right" class. Getting the name right, it is presumed, may not be an *absolutely* necessary condition for the emergence of full-blown class consciousness, but it seems to be a likely starting point. In practice, this approach has entailed a special concern to see whether working-class people use the label "working class" to describe their own situation.

Of course the most obvious objection is that a "success" in responding to the question doesn't mean very much. People can say they "belong" to a class (or, more accurately, select a label from a predetermined list) without "identifying" with any particular set of "interests." It is, in this light, the most minimal of indicators—a limitation that all users of this measure acknowledge to some degree. One certainly can imagine lots of "right" answers without any implication of impending class political mobilization or even common ideological orientations.

But this is only one side of the objections to the measure: a "failure" to answer correctly may also not mean much about class consciousness. A failure may merely signify the respondent's unwillingness or inability to use the imposed, abstract language of the survey researcher in an artificial setting. You can detect "consciousness" only in the context of real life, so the critique goes.

Neither criticism can be dismissed out of hand, but such class-identification measures are still worth considering if for no other reason than that class theory's proponents and critics have so frequently employed them. There is an obvious case for evaluating class theory on the grounds that it has been contested. Also, let's recognize that these measures have been so frequently used because they are likely to tell us something, however ambiguous or limited their meaning may be. That "something" involves a perception of difference and, perhaps, hierarchy. If similarly situated people apply the same label to themselves, that may represent a preliminary step in forming a sense of communal bond. After all, a class "for-itself" must be able to define in some way who are the "us" and the "them." Moreover, given that the word "class" is commonly used in everyday language, it is difficult to see that class-identification questions are so overly abstract or overwhelmingly awkward that responses are devoid of meaning. As it turns out, few leave them blank. I'll reserve comments about the "artificial world" of the survey questionnaire until later. In any case, as I will also show, other measures of class consciousness are no more supportive of class theory.

How closely is objective class location linked to subjective class identification? In general, the answer is that the linkage is weak. But the degree of weakness reflects how the question is asked.

Ever since Centers's (1949) seminal work on class consciousness, researchers have been acutely aware that questionnaire construction affects results. He found that the inclusion of the category "working class" in a class-identification question increased the number of "working class" respondents! (He was responding to a *Fortune* magazine survey that gave respondents three choices—upper, middle, and lower class. About 80 percent opted for the middle category.) But, by the same token, other researchers have amply documented that relatively few Americans describe themselves as "working class" unless they are presented with this choice in a forced-choice format.

Table 5.1 indicates how using an open-ended versus forced-choice format leads to very different pictures of the subjective class system. On the one hand, very few Americans spontaneously claim to be working class—no matter what their occupational circumstances. That term doesn't readily cross Americans' lips. Its absence may suggest that the salience of working-class identification is low. We might well wonder why the working class needs a prompt if class identification has important meaning to that group.

TABLE 5.1

Class Self-Identification by Large Occupational Groups: Responses
to Open-Ended Question and Close-Ended Follow-up

	Executives/ Professionals	*Lower White Collar*	*Blue Collar*
Middle class identification	86%	76%	62%
open question	74	64	50
closed follow-up	12	12	12
Working class identification	9	17	31
open question	3	4	8
closed follow-up	6	13	23
N	(416)	(380)	(471)

SOURCE: Adapted from Schlozman and Verba (1979): 116, fig. 5-2.

We may be inclined to say, then, that we have a middle-class society or, in effect, one that is largely classless. On the other hand, a large minority is at
least willing to select a "working class" response, suggesting some resonance
of this term in their lives. Perhaps the open-ended question is just too vague;
the prompts of a forced-choice format may elicit the necessary focus from
respondents.

Which is the better approach to measuring class identification? This is
an issue that we don't have to settle here. I will concentrate instead on the
results of forced-choice surveys, which is the more common approach, because they allow class theory a greater chance to make its case. The forced-
choice approach at least gives the analyst some variance to explain; the
open-ended approach suggests there's almost no issue to investigate.

Many studies make clear that the connection between class location
and class identification is weak. In one of the more supportive analyses,
for example, Wallace and Jepperson (1986) report a modest correlation
(gamma = .22), which essentially means the higher the class, the lower the
probability of working-class identification. However, correlational language
should not obscure a critical point: a majority of the working class (defined roughly in Wright's terms) made the "wrong" choice. So did a major-

ity (62 percent) of the blue-collar workers in Schlozman and Verba's (1979) study (see Table 5.1). Thus the core of the working class in most objective mappings sees itself as middle class.

In attempting to support his schema, Wright (1985) also reports that only 30 percent of the proletariat selected a working class identification. That, in itself, would appear to be an extraordinarily self-damning finding. Even more damning is the fact that the following five classes had about the same level of working class identification: semicredentialed workers, uncredentialed supervisors, uncredentialed managers, petty bourgeoisie, and small employers. In short, Wright's working class, defined by its total lack of exploitive resources, is generally disinclined to call themselves working class, and no more likely than putatively middle-class groups and even smaller capitalists.[1]

Squinting closely at Wright's findings, it is possible to see some small tendency for the credentialed classes to espouse relatively low levels of working-class identification. However, as Arthur Stinchcombe (1989) aptly notes, this pattern likely indicates some effect of *education* in shaping class identification, because the possession of credentials is built into his definition of class. But as I similarly argued in Chapter 2, such effects—despite Wright's assertion—don't necessarily reflect the effects of an exploitive resource. In any case, the cleavages defined by exploitation in terms of ownership or authority appear inconsequential.

Parenthetically, I can note here that Wright convincingly demonstrates that his own class schema fares better in linking objective and subjective indicators of class than Poulantzas's competing neo-Marxist schema. As should be evident, this is not a great recommendation for either.

In multivariate models alternative measures of class divisions don't suggest that class position affects class identification. Robinson and Kelley (1979) attempted to operationalize Marx's and Dahrendorf's (1959) class models by considering, in categorical terms, control over the means of production and authority in the workplace. Controlling for the continuous stratification variables in the Blau and Duncan model, neither of these class factors alone or in interaction accounts for more than a very minor amount of the variance in men's class self-placement. Among women, these fundamental class factors have no impact on class self-placement. In a follow-up study, Davis and Robinson (1988) find that in the 1980s ownership (and spouse's ownership) has *no* net effect on the class self-placement of men or women.

All this is not to argue that class identification is without social correlates. In a non-Marxist class analysis, for example, Jackman and Jackman (1983) make a strong case that subjective class identification is related to some other subjective orientations (e.g., feelings of "closeness" to other groups). Their analysis does not establish, however, that subjective identification is anchored in objectively defined *class* positions. Their "basic model" of class identification includes three *continuous* measures of status (education, socioeconomic standing, and family income); it explains 28 percent of the variance in class self-placement. By the standards of "attitude-explanations" research, this is pretty high. However, adding categorical "class" variables to their models (including self-employment, job authority, and the manual/nonmanual distinction) adds little or no explanatory weight. That is, richer, more educated people in relatively high-status positions are more apt to say "I'm middle class," but there aren't distinctive class effects on the use of this label.

What the Jackmans' analysis establishes in detail that cannot be related here is that Americans do, or at least can, use the language of class as part of their perceptual maps to understand the multidimensional inequalities in American society. Yet cultural factors like lifestyle and beliefs figure more prominently in their senses of class membership than socioeconomic factors—and much more so than specifically categorical class factors. Although the Jackmans argue that subjective social classes are "social communities," the relevant point here is that these "communities" are composed of individuals with quite different objective class positions. Americans use class language but not in the way class theorists think they ought to.

OTHER INDICATORS

Of course no one should be satisfied with a single indicator of class consciousness, no matter how widespread its use. Class self-identification questions are fraught with too many limitations to make a decisive case; however, the case against class theory does not rest on this evidence alone.

Consider, first, responses to this: "In our society there are groups which tend to be towards the top and groups which tend to be towards the bottom. Where would you put yourself in this scale?" question (Kelley and Evans 1995).

Top   1
             2
             3
             4
             5
             6
             7
             8
             9
Bottom   10

In response to this graphic and relatively unabstract question about hierarchy, Americans overwhelmingly place themselves in the middle. Specifically, 64 percent designate categories 4–6; 85 percent place themselves in categories 3–7. There's no explicit class language here, but the clear implication is that relatively few Americans see themselves as distinctly above or below most others.

Even more notably, as Kelley and Evans (1995) make clear, midlevel self-images predominate among all levels of the objective stratification hierarchy. They further show that continuous stratification variables (especially family income and education) explain a modest amount of variance in this dependent variable, but explicit measures of class division—ownership, supervisory responsibility, and manual status—have very little impact. Of course such class-based resources *are* linked to real advantages in life, but they are not linked to *perceptions* of hierarchical rank.

Nor are they linked to perceptions of class conflict. In the same survey respondents were asked:

> In all countries there are differences or even conflicts between social groups. In your opinion, in the United States how much conflict is there between . . . (a) Poor people and rich people? (b) The working class and the middle class? *Responses*: very strong conflicts, strong conflicts, not very strong conflicts, no conflicts.

Even if Americans tend to view themselves as somewhere in the middle, they appear quite ready to acknowledge "class conflict." Combining scores on these two items into a scale, Kelley and Evans find that a very large minority (43 percent) perceive at least "strong conflict." This is decidedly not a picture of a consensual, harmonious society. However, after assessing the impact of continuous stratification measures and categorical class variables (as in their analysis of self-image), they make the telling point for analyzing structuration: "perceptions of class conflict are largely independent of the objective reality of class" (170).

In short, they report a puzzling pattern: (1) most people put themselves in the middle, yet (2) substantial numbers see significant class conflict, but (3) actual class position is largely unrelated to perceptions of class conflict. Kelley and Evans offer an intriguing explanation that centers on the role of reference groups in shaping perceptions, but *why* objective class isn't linked to class consciousness need not be debated here. To assess the reality of classes, the crucial point is that the linkage is so tenuous.

The indictment can be extended using Wright's (1985) own analysis. In *Classes* he developed a measure of "class interest consciousness" generated by a factor analysis of six items related to the desirable balance of power between labor and management. For example, respondents were asked to agree or disagree with the statement, "Employers should be prohibited by law from hiring strike-breakers during a strike." Unlike the previously considered indicators, this measure purports to tap the *content* of a class interest. In that sense Wright's measure allows inferences about "higher" levels of consciousness that go beyond just a sense of location in the hierarchy or the general ramifications of this hierarchy.

Yet Wright can't turn to his own results as a validation of his class schema. He reports that class location (measured by a slightly collapsed version of his schema) accounts for 6 percent of the variance for men—and none for women! And in a related analysis, Clem Brooks (1994) shows that an alternative measure of the working class—namely, only blue-collar workers—fares no better in distinguishing levels of class consciousness. Of course no statistical criterion can establish whether 6 percent is substantively significant, but all that unexplained variance does suggest that the link between class location and attitudes about workplace organization is very slack.

In any case, as crucial as views about the desirable balance of power between workers and management would appear to be, Brooks also shows that they have limited ramifications. There's virtually no relationship between class consciousness, in these terms, and political commitments. Not only do classes lack the "proper" perception of their workplace-rooted interests, then, but even if they did, it wouldn't be a significant factor in the larger political arena.

Let me cite one more study in support of this indictment. This evidence is particularly relevant to note because Tim Heaton (1987: 614) so clearly reminds us of the issue at stake:

> If disadvantaged and lower status subgroups are aware of their lower status, perceive little opportunity for upward mobility, think society is unfair and favor more egalitarian policies while the opposite occurs among advantaged subgroups, then class formation is solidified. . . . On the other hand, small or inconsistent effects would indicate that class formation is incomplete.

Heaton turns to the General Social Survey to measure four dimensions of class consciousness:

1. class identification (standard way)
2. strength of class boundaries
   a. "In the United States traditional divisions between owners and workers still remain. A person's social standing depends upon whether he/she belongs to the upper or lower class."
   b. "In the U.S. there are still great differences between social levels, and what one can achieve in life depends mainly upon one's background."
3. fairness
   a. "Differences in social standing between people are acceptable because they basically reflect what people made out of the opportunities they had."
   b. "All in all, I think social differences in this country are justified."
4. attitudes about egalitarian policy (questions about governmental provision of jobs, governmental guarantees that various needs are met, and income determination by needs, not just work)

Heaton's LISREL (Linear Structural Relations) models include the standard continuous stratification variables as well as categorical class measures (capitalist, petty bourgeoisie, and manager).

His table primarily represents a great barrage of "unstarred" or small coefficents. Education, by far the best predictor among a weak lot, is related to all four dimensions of class consciousness. However, the class variables are totally unrelated to subjective class and sense of fairness; the capitalists are very slightly inclined to perceive class boundaries, but no other class division makes a difference. As class theory would predict, the ownership class is relatively opposed to egalitarian policies, but the relevant coefficients are notably modest—less than those for race, age, education, and income.

No other conclusion from this study seems plausible: "The lack of a close relationship between objective status and each dimension of subjective consciousness would seem to inhibit the formation of class consciousness" (619). Indeed, this conclusion is all the more believable because the study reaffirms what many other sophisticated studies, using different measures and samples, have also established.

CONSCIOUSNESS IN ACTION

There is little connection between class location and class consciousness; that's the inescapable conclusion of standard issue, survey-based research, even that purporting to be sympathetic to the Marxist tradition. Yes, some class theorists rejoin, that's what *that* research shows, but it is a misguided enterprise. Its measures are inadequate, and even more fatally, its conceptualization of class consciousness misses what is important. Previously I acknowledged my own misgivings about this research, but this critique goes much beyond misgivings. It says class consciousness can be meaningfully comprehended only in the course of specific actions, and is especially vivid in "explosions of consciousness" that emerge as classes struggle with each other. For example, in a widely admired book, *Cultures of Solidarity*, Rick Fantasia writes: "Because I want to begin to free the notion of class consciousness from the purely ideational, attitudinal bonds by which it has been shackled, I will largely dispense with the term 'class consciousness' so that we may be able to consider a wider range of cultural practices *generated in social struggle*" (1988: 17, my emphasis). That is, the uncontextualized responses to abstract survey questions do not capture the dynamic, collective side of class consciousness—and, presumably, the socially transformative potential of class struggle (deemed a good thing by Fantasia and other like-minded critics).

There is no denying the seriousness of this critique, nor its ideological appeal in some quarters. It provides some continuing hopes for the "revolution" or at least some egalitarian reform. After all, those who look for expressions of class consciousness in shop-floor disputes, picket lines, and organizing efforts can surely find them, and their local impact can be notable.

But in the final analysis, this critique does little to save the fundamental claims of class theory.

The part of the critique that damns survey research for failing to appreciate nuances, ambivalences, poles of variation, and the like is true enough, although it is hardly new, nor does it seem distinctly applicable to measuring class consciousness. Virtually any complex concept is difficult to measure in a survey. Subtlety is not the virtue of these instruments. The standard and compelling defense is that these measures can provide a rough approximation of what a representative group of people think about a matter. The compensating virtue of having standardized measures across precisely defined groups shouldn't be dismissed out of hand. Of course these measures can over- or underestimate "true" attitudes; however, since the critique implies that these measures "miss" class consciousness, the point to press here is that if class consciousness is significant, something much more dramatic should be evident in the responses. The face validity of the measures seems considerable.

Much more fundamental is the criticism saying that consciousness can't be studied as matter of attitudes that are analytically and practically separate from action. Here the critics like Fantasia have a useful point to make. As they note, the implicit hypothesis of the survey-based approach is that people have attitudes—presumably stable, coherent, and consistent ideas— that reflect their class position and that in some sense *cause* class-related behavior. This may well be an overly intellectualized view of motivation and behavior. People don't generally form abstract ideas about the world and then act in particular ways because they hold these ideas. How people interpret the world is inevitably shaped by the varying contingencies of their lives, and in turn, their consciousness reflects the ongoing interaction between thought and action. We should grant this point, but at the same time recognize its limited implications for the issue of structuration.

To be sure, abstract ideas don't lead in predictable ways to particular ways of acting. Coherent ideologies are not the *necessary* grounds for action. Yet it is still revealing to know whether people in particular class locations perceive some commonality with others in a similar location, or whether they hold similar views on class-related matters. After all, language *can* matter. If class members can speak the words of commonality, this is at least one sign of group distinctiveness that may foster class action. The fact that there is so little routine connection between objective class location and expressions of class sentiment suggests that this basis for class action is weak.

Indeed, research that takes the consciousness-in-action approach suggests, at most, that certain types of workers in unusual circumstances can express class consciousness. Thus, in intriguing detail, Fantasia tells the stories of wildcat strikes at a New Jersey steel-casting factory, union organizing efforts of women hospital workers in Vermont, and union-busting efforts and their resistance at an Iowa corn-processing plant. The workers in these case studies actively press for collective benefits, and in the struggle they appear to form emotional bonds—what could be called "class consciousness." Yet, of course, most workers rarely, if ever, strike or organize. Fantasia's subjects reveal that "consciousness" can be activated in these atypical circumstances that seem grounded in local grievance with little conscious link to larger social divisions. These responses do not establish that any larger group is class conscious on a routine or consistent basis, the critical matter for assessing this dimension of structuration. If classes constitute significant social divisions, they should have more than episodic impact on few lives. They should have recurrent, pervasive effect.

David Halle's (1984) subtle study of male blue-collar workers in a New Jersey chemical plant is a revealing contrast to Fantasia's findings about workers "on the barricades." The drama of intense worker-boss (labor-capital) conflict is largely absent from their lives. These workers tend to their jobs with reasonable efficiency and little psychic investment; in calculated ways, they comply with managerial authority and subtly subvert it. Based on their at-work experiences, they develop a sense of themselves as "working men"—different from bosses, those who give them orders. Although their expression of the "working man" does not neatly translate into the terms of class theory, they do seem to have a notable, though hardly intense, job-related sense of common fate that transcends their particular workplace. Here are signs of class consciousness that may elude the intrusions of the usual questionnaire.

But the workplace, as Halle makes clear, is not the whole of their lives or even the most important part. In their community lives—as they consume, tend to their homes, and pursue leisure activities with friends and families—they readily see themselves as "middle class." They enjoy their relative affluence with little sense of being below most others. In large measure, their job-related collective identity as "working men" does not extend beyond the factory gates. Moreover, in their political lives their primary identity is being an "American." This identity revolves around traditional meanings of patriotism. As a broadly unifying identify, it at least implicitly denies the significance of class divisions. Taken together, the multiple identities of being a working man, a member of the middle class, and an American mean that class consciousness is muted and significantly delimited.

Of course, no one can say that these workers "speak for" the (male) working class, though their jobs as blue-collar workers in a large factory appear as almost prototypically working class. Even so, the crucial point here is that Halle looks to analyze consciousness in action, grounded in concrete circumstances, and finds a class that has only a very circumscribed sense of *class* consciousness. Halle tells a fuller story than survey researchers, even if its precise reach is unknown. But the finding of limited structuration in terms of class consciousness is largely the same, and I'm unaware of any recent ethnographic study that contradicts this general conclusion.

Like many of the critics of survey-based measures, I'm somewhat skeptical about whether the concept "class consciousness" has been adequately captured in sociological research. Yet at the same time the fact that no research shows more than a weak connection between objective class location and expressions of class sentiment must be accorded its due. I've detailed the absence of such a connection at such length only because the commonsense presumption of a connection is so strong and the implications for class theory are so negative. Quite clearly, we lack evidence of class structuration in this dimension. It is not surprising, then, that class plays a minor role in our political life—the argument elaborated in the following chapter.

CHAPTER SIX

The Politics of Class

The issue raised so directly in Sombart's classic volume *Why Is There No Socialism in the United States?* has long preoccupied American political sociology. No one doubts the premise: however bloody America's labor history and however successful reformist legislation has been in some periods of our history, the American working class has not organized itself as a force for socialism. Historians disagree about how quiescent or resistant the working class has actually been, but the socialist project was never its achievement, nor even its aim in any broad, sustained way. Explanations for this "failure" abound. The implacable hostility of capitalists (and the state); the ideology if not the reality of social mobility; the divisions of ethnicity, race, and region; widespread affluence; and the timely "concessions" of the state in moments of crisis: all of these and more have been offered to answer Sombart's question. Here is not the place to sort through this voluminous and contentious scholarship, but it is worth underscoring that all of it attempts to explain a nonoccurrence. It is presumed that the working class *should* be socialistic. Anything else is deviant.

Indeed, this expectation reflects in particular form the general connection between class theory and political action. For common to all class theories is the statement or at least the implication that class creates "interests"—that is, a systematic stake in maintaining or changing the status quo. Class theory is inherently political in this sense.

To be sure, class theorists differ on what it means to have an "interest." Marxists view it primarily as an objective matter, inherent in the nature of the class system: the exploited proletariat can advance itself (and humanity) only by a revolutionary overthrow of capitalist rule—hence, its objective collective interest. Marxists necessarily concede that this class may not recognize its objective interests and may even deny them; however, in the historical dialectic it is expected that the working class will come to subjectively embrace its interest—in effect becoming, in Marx's phrase, a class *for* itself, not just a class in itself.

By contrast, for the Weberians, "class interests" more literally and narrowly reflect what specific classes actually express an interest in, what they seek as a group. These subjective interests are not rooted in a metatheoretical characterization of capitalism as a social order or in any particular normative philosophy. Rather, Weberians simply expect that classes—with varying degrees of collective intensity—will seek to advance their position, materially and culturally, in competition with other groups. In this view, neither the content of these subjective interests nor the outcome of the ensuing class struggle can be specified a priori. What emerges is historically contingent.

Despite these profound differences in the grounding and meaning of interests, all class theories make the same general prediction: the lower class(es) should be distinctly oppositional and the higher class(es) distinctly supportive of the prevailing political order. Why? Class theorists are vague on the causal mechanism, perhaps because the commonsense observation so obviously presents itself: people tend to want more of the socially defined good things in life like material comfort and esteem, and to rationally pursue strategies to get them. These strategies may include collective action. This rational underpinning of class struggle does not deny the potentially critical role of "irrational," emotional group solidarity in sustaining this collective action. Indeed, a sense of emotional solidarity may be one of the benefits people seek. In any event, political interests and commitments emerge out of the group distribution of social goods. Again, this is the ineluctably political dimension of class theory.

As noted in Chapter 2, however, it is problematic to include class-rooted political action as *constituent* of class structuration. This is because much of the debate in class theory is directly concerned with the relationship between class and political action. That is, many Marxist and non-Marxist theorists ask under what circumstances, and with what consequences, do classes assume political consciousness and take action. In this view classes always have political potential, but this potential is not always realized, nor is the reality of classes called into question because of political quiescence. Quite differently, though, some neo-Marxian scholars incorporate the formation

of a politically coherent or even mobilized collectivity into their class definition. So, in the logic of E. B. Thompson, the celebrated British historian, factory workers became a class—the working class—when they struggled together against their employers for better conditions.

To reiterate my comments in Chapter 2, for the purpose of assessing the
reality of classes, there is no need to take a stand on this definitional dispute.
Structuration is a multidimensional variable: classes are real to the extent
structuration is apparent in key dimensions of social life. By this logic, if proposed class cleavages correspond to the fissures of the political arena, the political mobilization can be seen as one more factor that shows the significance of class in people's lives *and* reinforces class solidarity. Put differently,
if class theory is right, you march to the voting booth, legislative halls, or
barricades with those like yourself, and the march itself builds class bonds
and a sense of collective fate.

THE PARTY SYSTEM

A main lesson of Lipset's *Political Man* (1959) was that with the development of contemporary capitalist society, class conflict had generally moved
to the political arena, transformed to an electoral contest among competing
political parties. The result was the democratic class struggle. Based on a
calculation of interests, at least in the short term, the "natural" alignment
became this: the working (and lower) class was attracted to the programs
and ideologies of the left, and the upper and middle classes to the right—
especially as these terms distinguish orientations to the welfare state. Whether
the reformist impulses of democratic socialists represent the "true" long-
term interests of the working class has been hotly debated throughout the
century, primarily by radical theorists. But more than any organization, the
reformist parties of the left have been the mechanism for working-class political mobilization.

The American experience clearly indicates, however, that the seemingly
"natural" proclivity is by no means inevitable. In Europe political party systems have been organized in significant measure along class lines (though the
current extent of class voting is not pronounced, as discussed in Chapter 11).
At the institutional level, there has been no comparable American development of the "class war" in the political arena. It is impossible to character-
ize the Democratic Party as the party of the working class in anything like

the way that the British Labor Party or the Swedish Social Democratic Party fits the label. Its class appeals have generally been muted, almost an electoral necessity with such a socially diverse electorate and a winner-takes-all system.

Labor unions have been a significant interest group within the very inclusive Democratic Party coalition. But that's all it is, just an interest group, not the dominant, central force running the party's operations. At times such as the New Deal they were perhaps the leading block within this coalition, even exercising close to veto power on some issues. Yet, even in their heyday, union leaders never directly assumed leadership positions within the party, and intraparty compromise, even on matters of intense union concern, was generally the rule. Unions have generally made politics a very secondary concern, preferring to push for a larger share of the pie through collective bargaining (Gompers's vision of more, more, more) rather than pressing for more general gains through state policy. Now, representing a small and declining share of the work force, they have marginal clout. Union endorsements can even imperil candidates' chances because unions are now often perceived as a narrow and selfish "special interest." Their politics-goes-second strategy may have once been a matter of some choice; now it is a necessity.

For their part, business leaders and organizations have had disproportionate impact on the affairs of both major parties, without encountering sustained class-based opposition to their conservative preferences. Their decisive influence in the electoral process and their preponderant representation in key executive branch positions in Democratic and Republican administrations alike is well documented (see, e.g., Domhoff 1983 and Dye 1990). This long-standing influence has surely undermined the emergence of distinctive class-rooted ideological differences between the parties. Even though Democrats and Republicans have embraced elements of the welfare state with varying degrees of enthusiasm, the parties have not presented themselves as coherent ideological alternatives. The result is that class divisions have not structured the political party system.

This constricted range of political debate may well reflect the dominance of capitalist ideology and control structures. As so-called structural Marxists as well as some "mainstream" theorists like Charles Lindblom argue, the political system has a built-in bias to favor capitalist interests without capitalists needing to take any specific action on their own behalf. All governments must be attentive to business interests or face the disastrous consequences of an investment strike. If the economy fails, suffering is widespread and governments fall; business confidence is therefore inevitably a prime concern of the state. Lindblom aptly writes, "Businessmen consequently do not need to strain or conspire to win privileges already thrust on them by anxious legislators and administrators" (1978: A19). Government policy, then, has distributional consequences and generally buttresses the capitalist underpinnings of our economic order.

But it is one matter to say that the political system favors *capitalism* and quite another to say that the political system reflects the mobilization of *classes*, much less that it reinforces their solidarity. As I argued before, the reality of classes is not inherent in capitalism. However tilted the bias of the system toward preserving what Robert Heilbroner (1985) has called the "regime of capitalism," the point remains that class divisions per se have not structured the political party system. And just as the party system does not give institutional form to class conflict, class position does not significantly shape individual political behavior and attitudes.

VOTING

The most obvious matter to consider is whether classes have distinctive voting patterns. Typically this issue has been addressed by constructing class voting indices, measures of the extent the working class votes for "its" party, the Democrats, and the middle class votes for "its" party, the Republicans. As the preceding discussion suggests, this identification of the Democratic Party as a party of the left is surely open to question, but it does seem fair to view it as less conservative than its electoral rival and somewhat more open to initiatives that favor the disadvantaged. (Of course the lack of parties with class appeal may be in part the cause of low class voting, not just its effect.) One may also question the methodological adequacy of commonly used measures of class voting, like the Alford Index, but substitute measures don't lead to substantively different conclusions. Indeed, the general point can be stated unequivocally and briefly: in presidential elections class divisions in voting patterns are very modest.

TABLE 6.1

Percentage of Democratic Voters by Respondent's Class (Goldthorpe Categories)
and Among Intergenerationally "Class Stable" Respondents

	SERVICE		ROUTINE NONMANUAL		PETTY BOURGEOIS		MANUAL WORKERS		FARMERS		AGRICULTURAL WORKERS		TOTAL
	All	Two Generation[1]	All	Two Generation	All	Two Generation	All	Two Generation	All	Two Generation	All	Two Generation	
Democratic Vote	33%	31	38%	21	35%	39	46%	49	35%	34	39%	63	40%
Inflow Mobility[2]		38		10		15		53		84		14	

NOTES: [1]Two Generation refers to respondents whose father's class was the same as their own. [2]The percent of each class that is composed of "Two Generation" class members.

SOURCE: Adapted from De Graaf et al. (1995): table 2; data: seventeen GSS files 1972–90.

Halle and Romo (1991) show that the blue-collar working class didn't even consistently cast a majority of its votes for Democratic candidates in the 1980s; and controlling for a set of sociodemographic variables, blue-collar workers were about as likely to vote for Bush in 1988 as lower and upper white-collar workers. Using the GSS (General Social Survey), I found that my Omnibus Measure of Class (see pp. 51–52, Chapter 3) explained 1 percent of the variance in the 1988 presidential vote. The difference in the Bush vote between the highest and lowest categories was 15 points.

To get still one more perspective on the matter, consider the voting distribution by class (a modified version of Goldthorpe's schema) in Table 6.1. No class, not even manual workers, went to the "left." And the range in votes for the Democrats was limited: 33 percent among the service class and 46 percent among the manual workers.

Moreover, class voting was low even among those who were "stable members" of a particular class by virtue of family origins *and* personal destination (see the figures for "two-generation" class members in Table 6.1). Most notably, the voting difference between the two-generation service class and the two-generation working class was only slightly larger than the difference between all members of these classes. Mobility effects are apparent for only two classes: the immobile routine nonmanual workers were less Democratic than routine nonmanual workers from other origins, and the (few) immobile agricultural workers were more Democratic than their counterparts from other origins. More generally, however, within each class, the mobile and the immobile voted in similar ways.

This general pattern suggests that the high level of class mobility in the United States doesn't account for low class polarization in voting. Consistent with many other theorists, I had surmised that class mobility undercuts other forms of structuration, including the political dimension. By this logic, class differences in voting should be more pronounced among the two-generation class members (longer, more consistent class socialization) than those who were class-mobile across generations. And, relatedly, because of their early political socialization, the downwardly mobile should "pull" their destination class to the right, and the upwardly mobile should "pull" their destination class to the left—the aggregate effect being the dilution of class differences. Reasonable speculation perhaps, but for the most part, this is not the way things are. Lots of social mobility means socially diverse classes, but the low level of class polarization in voting cannot be explained by the "compositional effect" of incorporating people with different family experiences into the same class (DeGraaf, Nieuwbeerta, and Heath 1995: 1022).

A NEW DISSENT

The view that class doesn't notably shape voting behavior is the increasingly orthodox position, but it hasn't gone unchallenged. The sophisticated critics Hout, Brooks, and Manza (1995) rightly contend that much of the research relies on crude measures of class and dichotomous measures of voting behavior (Democratic or Republican, among those who actually vote). Rather than a blue-collar/white-collar divide, they prefer a six-class model: professionals, managers, owners-proprietors, nonmanagerial white-collar workers, skilled workers, semiskilled and unskilled workers. This is intended to be Goldthorpian in spirit. And rather than simply consider the main two-party split, they look at third party votes and nonvoting as significant political behaviors. They are concerned to trace the trajectory of what they call "total class voting," which "includes all sources of statistical association between class and voting behavior, including not voting at all" (ibid.: 809). They contrast this concept with "traditional class voting"—"that proportion of the statistical association between class and voting behavior that arises from the affinity of blue-collar classes for left-leaning parties and the affinity of white-collar classes for right-leaning parties" (ibid.). This latter concept is tightly linked to the Alford Index.

So, based on this approach, do findings effectively challenge the orthodoxy? Their index of total class voting—"the standard deviation of class differences in vote choice in a given election"—fluctuates quite widely across elections from 1948 to 1992 without any clear trend. This finding is the basis for their claim of *no decline* in class voting. Their analysis also reveals some *realignments* in class voting, even as the "traditional" class alignment has broken down. Most notable is the movement, post 1968, of both nonmanagerial white-collar workers and professionals to the Democratic Party. At the same time the commitment of skilled workers to the Democrats has varied significantly from election to election. With the stronger support for the Republican candidates among owners and managers, the net effect is no diminution in class voting, but the pattern of class voting has altered.

TABLE 6.2

Percentage Distribution of Partisan Choice by Class, Recent Elections

	Professionals	*Managers*	*Owners and Proprietors*	*Non-managerial White-Collar Workers*	*Skilled Workers*	*Semi- and Unskilled Workers*	*Total*
Democratic Vote							
1988	44%	28%	28%	53%	28%	58%	42%
1992	61	49	36	63	60	67	58

	Alford Index		*Class Voting Index for Choice (Partisan Kappa)*	
	1988	7	1988	53
	1992	9	1992	43

SOURCE: Adapted from Hout, Brooks, and Manza (1995): table 2; data: American National Election Studies.

The problem here is interpreting the magnitude of class vote. Their sophisticated index (called *kappa*) doesn't have any obvious intuitive meaning about the size of class effects, even if it is useful to track trends. Granted, in some lights, class voting may not have declined, but that's not the same as saying it was ever much to begin with. To see what their index summarizes, consider their results for the two most recent elections in their analysis (see Table 6.2). In 1988 the partisan kappa score was 53; in 1992, 43. The most obvious point is that classes are hardly persistent in their electoral support. At the extremes of volatility, skilled workers went from a large Republican majority (72 percent) to a substantial Democratic majority (60 percent), as did professionals (56 percent Republican to 61 percent Democratic). If there's class voting in particular elections, there's little evidence of enduring class politics.

Now, the class differences in partisanship in each election are surely important in deciding electoral outcomes, and particular contrasts between the most partisan classes are notable, especially between "capitalists" and "workers." In both of these elections the difference between these classes (about one-third of the labor force) was about 30 percent—not a small matter. But what are we to make of the fact that in 1992 *no* other class differed from the overall Democratic total (58 percent) by even ten points? Looking at the overall pattern, I'm inclined to agree with the critics' own assessment: "Although the United States has had *low* but significant class voting throughout the postwar period, class politics has *never* grown from it" (806, my emphases).

In short, in recent decades the voting booth has not registered class conflict to any significant degree. Of course one could say that recent decades reflect an aberration, that class voting can reemerge if voters are mobilized to pursue class-resonant political agendas. Perhaps. Yet it should be recognized that any "decline" is from modest levels and has extended through many changes in administrations and through many ups and downs in the business cycle. Moreover, the very suggestion that class voting *could* be mobilized indicates that it is not the routinely expectable outcome. In voters' minds the pocketbook is only one concern that competes with others. We should expect some fluctuation in the saliency of economic issues, including those involving distributional concerns, but the historical record suggests that these fluctuations will be short-lived, hovering around a low baseline level.

POLITICAL ATTITUDES

The ballot box and the public-opinion survey register similar findings: very small political effects of class. The existing opinion research rather convincingly indicates that class position per se does not fundamentally shape individual political attitudes. To give some particulars to this critique, I will consider the findings of five methodologically sophisticated studies that incorporate a wide range of attitudinal matters. All of these studies, I should note, test class theory in multivariate analyses, incorporating continuous stratification measures and categorical measures of class. As I argued in Chapter 2, these analyses thereby speak more to the causal force of class than to the sheer presence of class divisions, the structuration that might be evident in bivariate analyses. Even so, the fact that the *combined* effects of the categorical and continuous measures of stratification tend to be small poses a severe challenge to even the most expansive understandings of class.

Government Interventions

Using data from a 1983 survey of Indiana residents, Knoke, Raffalovich, and Erskine (1987) explored attitudes toward government interventions in the marketplace on matters including provision of job guarantees, the desirability of economic planning, government assistance to minorities, and payment for medical care. Dealing with redistributive issues, each of these concerns would seem to have inherent "class implications." Their structural equation models included occupational prestige, education, income, race, and age, as well as a six-value class measure approximating an early version of Wright's class categorization. For the most part, the class variables had no discernible impact, and the few statistically significant coefficients for class were small, less than the coefficients for the continuous stratification measures. In their understated words this analysis "challenges theorists who argue that stratification plays a central role in shaping political attitudes" (155).

Economic Ideology

Form and Hanson (1985) conducted a similar study, but rather than examining only specific policy preferences, they considered attitudes related to a more general sense of economic ideology. Their 1979 survey of Illinois residents included thirty-four variables that addressed such concerns at the fairness of personal earnings and that of various groups, the equity of various forms of income redistribution, political self-identification, and optimism/pessimism about economic conditions. Included as independent variables in their survey were measures of income, education, race, sex, age, and a four-value measure of class—employers/self-employed, managers (employees with supervisory responsibility), professionals, and workers (employees without supervisory responsibility). Their findings reveal a barrage of nonsignificant coefficients, and the instances of statistically significant "class effects" point to almost trivial substantive significance. Explained variance in their "class model," which included their class measure *and* continuous measures of the other "stratal" variables, exceeded 10 percent in only four of the thirty-four dependent variables.

Evaluating Political Actors

Wallace and Jepperson's (1986) study of the impact of class structure on popular evaluations of political actors—a key component of political culture in their view—is still another story of the missing or minor effect. Analyzing responses to a mid-seventies nationally representative sample, they regress attitudes toward "five significant political actors" (unions, the Democratic Party, civil servants, small business, and big business) on class and other stratification, organizational, and demographic variables. Class was measured in terms of a seven-value classification that largely follows Wright's (1985) schema.

Class has *no* effects whatsoever on attitudes about the Democratic Party or big business—arguably the two most politically salient groups considered. The lower classes tend to have relatively favorably attitudes toward civil servants and relatively negative attitudes toward small business, but these are matters of slight degree. In each case, the R^2 for *all* the variables in the model is .07.

Social Issues

Furthermore, class location is barely linked to views on so-called social issues—noneconomic matters like minority rights, civil liberties, personal freedom, law and order, and gender equality. Analyzing twenty-one standard GSS items in light of a four-class model (owners, managers, semi-autonomous workers, and workers—a schema derived from Wright), Zipp (1986) finds some modest bivariate differences on these matters (the semi-autonomous workers generally being the most liberal). However, controlling for education and a few other sociodemographic variables, social class has *no* statistically significant effect on fifteen of the twenty-one items, and the statistically significant effects were minor. Zipp reports similar results using a crude alternative definition of class, manual versus nonmanual workers.

Other Class Measures

These findings of limited political effects are not limited to the three specifications of class structure already considered. Robinson and Kelley (1979), as noted in Chapter 5 regarding class sentiment, operationalized Marx's and Dahrendorf's class models by considering, in categorical terms, control over the means of production and authority in the workplace. Over and above the explanatory power of the continuous stratification variables in the Blau and Duncan model, these class measures have no or virtually no effect on confidence in labor, political-party identification, ideological self-description, or presidential vote.

This is not to make R^2 (and its statistical cognates) the Holy Grail of socio-logical research, but the search for substantial "class effects" across the wide range of political behaviors and attitudes considered here has turned up little. Although there are *some* class effects, they are so infrequent and modest that class can't be considered a fundamental source of political division.

To these analyses of the general impact of class location, it is now useful to add some specific consideration of the political impact of ownership. The property divide has a central place in much class theory, but its political ramifications have received, oddly enough, little attention. If the division between owners and the employed represents a fundamental fault line in the class structure, then it should be a division with political consequence.

OWNERSHIP

We have many capitalists in our midst if ownership per se defines the capitalist class (see Chapter 8). These "capitalists," it is commonly believed, have a direct incentive to promote government policies and a social environment that favors their investment. As a result, they become socially active conservatives—that is, citizens with a broad commitment to the status quo.

That all seems sensible, but however sensible, class theory can't turn to empirical analyses for support. Studies of the sociopolitical ramifications of ownership are remarkably few. Perhaps the translation of imputed "interest" to political orientation is considered so automatic that empirical documentation is unnecessary. Capitalists are rarely alleged to have false consciousness, after all. Yet what research is available poses a challenge to the parts of class theory that depict business ownership as a fundamental sociopolitical cleavage.

First, I will recall some analyses discussed in the previous chapter on class sentiment. Davis and Robinson (1988) found that ownership had no effect whatsoever on class self-placement. And Wright reported that larger owners were only modestly inclined to take a conservative position on his measure of "class interest consciousness," while smaller owners were barely distinguishable from many lower classes of wage laborers.

Some of my own previous research, "Having a Stake in the System" (Kingston and Fries 1994), is pertinent to the question of the specifically political dimension. Using the GSS we tested these hypotheses: business ownership and home ownership are independently associated with (1) participation in community affairs, (2) participation in political activities, (3) conservative political orientations, and (4) affirmations of individualistic ideology and the essential beneficence of the political-economic system. These hypotheses all follow from the general idea that owners have an "objective" interest in being conservative activists.

Obviously the measurement of ownership involves conceptual decisions with possible substantive implications. However, with the GSS it is only possible to know whether a respondent is "self-employed" in her or his primary occupation. This definition still includes a diverse group—owners of large and small businesses, blue- and white-collar workers, the financially successful and the less successful. There's no best way to represent this variability. We simply divided the owners into two groups: the self-employed with a blue-collar/service occupation (52 percent) and the self-employed with a white-collar occupation.[1] In our regression models we controlled for the "normal suspects": continuous measures of socioeconomic standing and standard demographic variables. We also separately considered men and women because the sociopolitical participation of each sex is differently influenced by various factors (see, e.g., Abowitz 1990) and because men and women own different types of businesses (Silvestri 1991).

We sought to have a broad-gauged view of political views and activities and therefore examined the following in our regression models:

Political views: party identification (0 = strong Democratic, 6 = strong Republican); 1984 Presidential vote (1 = Mondale, 2 = Reagan)

Political participation: voted in 1984 (1 = yes, 2 = no); attempted to sway others' vote (1 = often, 4 = never); worked on campaigns (1 = most elections, 4 = never); interest in political affairs (very = 1, not = 4)

Social participation: worked to solve community problems (1 = yes; 2 = no); formed group to solve community problem (1 = yes, 2 = no); number of memberships in voluntary organizations; attend religious service (0 = never, 8 = several times a week)

Political-social ideology: ideological self-identification (1 = extremely liberal, 7 = extremely conservative); government should reduce income inequality (1 = strongly feel so, 7 = strongly against); government should do everything possible to improve conditions of all poor people (1 = strongly agree, 5 = strongly agree people should take care of themselves); government involvement in country's problems (1 = strongly agree do more, 5 = strongly agree too much)

Evaluation of system: how people get ahead (1 = hard work most impor- tant, 3 = luck most important); confidence in institutions (banks, major com- panies, Federal government, and Congress) (1 = complete confidence, 7 = no confidence at all); responsiveness of local government (1 = lots of attention, 4 = none at all); personal influence on local government (1 = a lot, 4 = none at all)

In our article the results section was brief because the analysis indicated that business and home ownership, net of the control variables, had either small or, more commonly, no relationship to political involvements and at- titudes. "NS's" dominate the table. Here I'll be even more succinct; the lim- ited exceptions to the general pattern are evident in Table 6.3.

In general, owners turned to the Republican presidential candidate (a 12–15 percent Reagan advantage compared to nonowners). Yet only male white-collar owners distinctly identified with the Republican Party, and even this inclination is modest.

Nor are owners distinctly "good citizens," active in political or com- munity life. They do not go to voting booths in unusual numbers, and they aren't overrepresented in voluntary organizations. If they have financial in- centive to be involved, there's no indication that they act on it.

Nor are owners, in general, distinctly inclined to have a favorable view of our political and economic institutions. If these institutions work to the disproportionate advantage of capitalists, the presumed beneficiaries don't reciprocate with any special confidence in how they function. *Nor* do own- ers espouse any distinctive sense of political efficacy.

Nor do owners have any special allegiance to a conservative identifica- tion. At the same time, though, owners, particularly those in white-collar occupations, are relatively skeptical of government activism, especially on behalf of the less advantaged. That is, they modestly favored the "conserva- tive" position even as they were not particularly inclined to call themselves "conservative."

Even allowing for the impact of ownership on some matters, the overall pattern of results points rather unambiguously to a general conclusion: in it- self, having a stake in the system by owning a business does not significantly foster sociopolitical involvement or a conservative political orientation. If, as is sometimes argued, to be an owner is to be a capitalist, then the capitalist class is not a distinctive political force.

TABLE 6.3

Effects of Ownership Dummy Variables on Indicators of Sociopolitical Attitudes and Behaviors, Net of Control Variables, with Separate Equations for Men (M) and Women (W)

Ownership Variables	PARTY IDENTIFICATION		PRESIDENTIAL VOTE 1984		VOTED IN 1984		POLITICAL INTEREST		TRIED TO SWAY VOTE	
	M (1)	W (2)	M (3)	W (4)	M (5)	W (6)	M (7)	W (8)	M (9)	W (10)
White-Collar Owner	0.73 (.11)	NS	0.23 (.15)	NS	NS	NS	NS	NS	NS	NS
Blue-Collar Owner	NS	NS	0.20 (.12)	0.24 (.12)	NS	NS	NS	−0.29 (−.08)	NS	NS
Homeowner	NS	NS	NS	NS	−0.14 (−.14)	−0.16 (−.17)	NS	NS	NS	NS
R^2, total model	.08	.08	.13	.13	.18	.23	.11	.14	.06	.05
N	598	553	348	363	559	511	605	560	602	558

Ownership Variables	GOVERNMENT INVOLVEMENT		GOVERNMENT HELP POOR		GOVERNMENT EQUALIZE INCOME		EFFORT REWARDED		CONFIDENCE IN FINANCIAL INST.	
	M (23)	W (24)	M (25)	W (26)	M (27)	W (28)	M (29)	W (30)	M (31)	W (32)
White-Collar Owner	0.37 (.10)	0.35 (.09)	0.32 (.08)	NS	0.70 (.10)	NS	NS	−0.31 (−.09)	NS	NS
Blue-Collar Owner	NS	NS	NS	0.59 (.13)	NS	0.80 (.10)	NS	−0.29 (−.10)	NS	NS
Homeowner	0.35 (.14)	0.28 (.11)	0.22 (.09)	NS	0.66 (.16)	NS	NS	NS	NS	−0.18 (−.14)
R^2, total model	.11	.12	.07	.06	.11	.08	.02	.04	.04	.03
N	579	532	590	546	602	558	602	556	599	558

NOTE: Cell entries are unstandardized regression coefficients, with standardized coefficients given in parentheses. Control variables were age, race, family income, occupational prestige, education, marital status, and length of community residence. Measurements are indicated in the text. All noted coefficients were significant at $p < .05$. NS = not significant. Kingston and Fries 1994.

WORKED ON CAMPAIGN		STARTED LOCAL GROUP		WORKED ON LOCAL PROBLEM		NUMBER OF MEMBERSHIPS		ATTENDED CHURCH		IDEOLOGICAL IDENTIFICATION	
M	W	M	W	M	W	M	W	M	W	M	W
(11)	*(12)*	*(13)*	*(14)*	*(15)*	*(16)*	*(17)*	*(18)*	*(19)*	*(20)*	*(21)*	*(22)*
NS	NS	NS	NS	NS	NS	NS	NS	NS	NS	0.51 (.12)	NS
NS	NS	NS	NS	NS	NS	NS	NS	NS	NS	NS	NS
NS	NS	NS	NS	NS	−0.10 (−.10)	NS	NS	NS	NS	0.52 (.18)	NS
.07	.09	.06	.06	.11	.16	.15	.18	.05	.09	.04	.02
604	559	604	550	606	560	605	556	604	558	580	533

CONFIDENCE IN BUSINESS		CONFIDENCE IN FEDERAL GOVERNMENT		CONFIDENCE IN CONGRESS		LOCAL GOVERNMENT RESPONSIVE		INFLUENCE ON LOCAL GOVERNMENT	
M	W	M	W	M	W	M	W	M	W
(33)	*(34)*	*(35)*	*(36)*	*(37)*	*(38)*	*(39)*	*(40)*	*(41)*	*(42)*
NS	NS	NS	NS	0.37 (.18)	NS	NS	NS	NS	−0.36 (−.09)
NS	NS	NS	NS	NS	NS	NS	NS	NS	−0.39 (−.10)
NS	NS	−0.22 (−.15)	NS	NS	NS	−0.25 (−.14)	NS	NS	NS
.05	.03	.03	.02	.04	.02	.04	.04	.06	.13
587	548	594	553	592	551	596	552	599	549

CONCLUSION

Of course individual survey items and model specifications may be questioned. The point here is not to defend the validity of individual findings, but rather to emphasize the overwhelming *pattern* of results. The conclusion that class has minimal effects on political orientation is based on measures of voting, party identification, ideological self-description, attitudes about numerous specific policies, and general evaluations of the political-economic order. If class position fundamentally structures political behavior and culture, something more should have turned up. All kinds of reasons may be adduced for why the theoretically expected connection hasn't been made, but the fact of the matter remains that classes are not structured as distinct political groups.

CHAPTER SEVEN

Class Culture

Even if the idea of class cultures has long been standard fare, the analysis of culture has moved to the cutting edge of class theory. It's now impossible to deal with the cultural component of class analysis without delving into new vocabularies and new conceptualizations of culture, class, and their connection to each other. Amidst all the conceptual joustings, however, some common themes are apparent: culture is significant, complex, and insufficiently appreciated in class analysis. I agree, but I'll argue in this chapter that less is being said about class than is often imagined, and that the case for distinct class cultures is notably weak.

Before attending to any of the intricacies of these at-the-edge discussions, I'd like to highlight one very conventional study, James Davis's "Achievement Variables and Class Cultures: Family, Schooling, Job, and Forty-nine Dependent Variables in the Cumulative G.S.S." (1982). This analysis confronts the key issue of the present chapter: do classes significantly differ in their cultural outlooks and practices? Its approach suggests the value of attending to concrete matters, and it usefully deflates some of the bombast related to the let's-bring-in-culture argument. I also highlight this work as a matter of personal indulgence, because it was so influential in spurring me to develop the larger thesis of this book.

A PERSONAL EXCURSUS

Before first reading Davis's analysis about a decade ago, I certainly had qualms about the existence of discrete classes. To my eye, for example, mobility tables seemed to show lots of movement, despite the contrary spins that many of my colleagues favored. Yet my "Intro" students still heard about classes. They heard somewhat modified versions of what I had heard in my own undergraduate and graduate days. Not to be flip, but what else would be expected from a "progressive" educated in the seventies?

Davis's article, in its simple, direct way, shook my complacency on the matter because it refuted what I "knew" to be true. I couldn't dismiss or ignore the findings. Perhaps more significantly, it activated a more general reassessment of what I had read about classes—a reassessment that respected, above all, the weight of social scientific empirical evidence. Reading Davis's analysis, then, wasn't akin to Saul's experience on the road to Damascus— a sudden, complete conversion. Yet more than any other analysis, it crystallized my emerging doubts and pointed the way to a wider investigation.

CASTING THE NET

Davis writes without theoretical pretension. What's the meaning of culture? Why should class be related to specific cultural beliefs or practices? How best to measure class? He doesn't even try to answer such questions. Rather, he's resolutely empirical, almost promiscuously selecting forty-nine items from the General Social Survey that previous research had at least suggested should be related to "achievement variables" like occupation. As will be evident, his results are devastating to this Common Wisdom.

As data-driven and theory-light as Davis's exercise may be, it valuably indicates the very wide range of cultural matters that are unrelated or weakly related to class. Davis categorized these forty-nine items in five groups that I list and illustrate: (1) *morale*: satisfaction with various dimensions of life; (2) *attachment*: memberships in community organizations, religious sentiments, socializing patterns; (3) *politics*: party identification, spending policies; (4) *values and tastes*: sought-after job characteristics, TV watching, newspaper reading; and, (5) *social issues*: sexual relations, crime policy, the role of women.

Following Census Bureau classifications, he coded occupations into five categories: (1) professional, technical and kindred, managers, and administrators; (2) clerical and sales; (3) craftsmen and kindred; (4) operatives, laborers, service workers; and (5) farmers. Obviously this classification does not fully correspond to any of the theoretical depictions of the class structure, especially in its lack of attention to ownership and authority relations.

However, even if there are some misclassifications of class position, it should be sufficiently sensitive to detect important class divisions that may exist.

Davis found that occupation has a net substantive effect on only eighteen of forty-nine items. (Besides occupation, his models include only education and father's occupation, not a full set of control variables.) Moreover, these effects are narrowly clustered and small. Here are some of the details leading Davis to conclude that his findings "cast considerable doubt on the 'class culture' notion that occupational strata have vast and diffuse effects on the texture of our lives" (580–81):

> Only one of eleven "social issues," attitude toward the death penalty, is related to occupation.
> The widest "class spread" on any of the eight items relating to values and tastes is for newspaper reading: the difference between professional/managers and operatives in daily reading rates is 15 percent.
> The effects are concentrated on items that tap cynicism (trust of others, optimism about the future, attitudes toward public officials) and items related to jobs and economic security; they are totally absent for other social orientations like free speech, race relations, gender roles, drugs, sexual behavior, divorce, marital and general happiness, and socializing patterns.
> Of the minority of items that did show differences by occupational strata, no particular "class break" (blue collar vs. white collar, upper white-collar vs. lower strata, or skilled vs. unskilled manual workers) is generally most pronounced.

Davis also investigated another pertinent question: are class *origins* related to cultural outlooks and practices? A common presumption in class theory is that people acquire lasting, important cultural outlooks in childhood and that their cultural lessons vary across classes. So class theory would predict some notable connection between class origins and later cultural orientations. Yet, to the contrary, Davis's findings indicate that people readily escape any cultural impress of their family's class. Within the non-farm population, father's occupation had *no* net effect on *any* of the forty-nine items. That is a serious challenge to class theory.

Now, as I argued in Chapter 2, the case for or against class theory should primarily rest on the showing of bivariate differences—but Davis's analysis is multivariate (in a very reduced form). The obvious question, then, is whether his "controls" for education and father's occupation obscure such differences. In brief, the answer is that notable class differences are few.

I largely replicated Davis's study using the 1994 and 1996 GSS and my five-category Omnibus Measure of Class. Compared to Davis's "class" schema, this categorization, by incorporating a group that many would recognize as an upper middle class or what Goldthorpe calls the "service" class, would seem to increase the probability of finding any class structuration. On a few matters relating to what Davis called "morale" there are very modest differences (gammas less than .1)—for example, job satisfaction and general happiness. But the absolute differences don't point to distinct class cultures. To a somewhat greater degree, class is related to judgments about other people's "character"—for example, their trustworthiness (see Table 2.1) and helpfulness. Elite professional managers are particularly inclined to see the good in others; lower blue-collar workers are inclined to see the darker side. As Table 2.1 indicates, only a slight majority of the elite (57 percent) think you can trust people most of the time, as do fairly sizable minorities of all other classes. Yet that also means a fairly notable tendency to distrust others among all nonmanagerial classes. The significance of such class-related differences on these few items can be debated.

However, the general pattern is that class is very weakly associated with the sorts of "culture" items that Davis considers. Rather than relate a slew of details here, I'll refer to specific matters as they become relevant in later sections of this chapter and the next. Considered together, they support Davis's conclusion about the lack of evidence for class cultures infusing "the texture of our lives."

As I said, the analysis of class cultures is hardly a novel enterprise. What Davis's analysis does is attack a staple line of argument in class theory. For the long-standing common presumption in both the Marxist and Weberian traditions is that members of a particular class have relatively distinctive beliefs, customs, values, and morals that accumulate over time and become shared. The emergent class cultures, so the argument goes, significantly reflect differences in economic experiences *and* reinforce them. Yet Davis's analysis is decidedly "old-fashioned," unattuned to recent controversies about the role of culture in the stratification system.

Although Davis doesn't invoke a formal causal argument, his statistical models suggest the conventional sense of the relationship between class and culture: economic circumstances (occupation is the independent variable) determine or at least largely shape cultural dispositions (the dependent variables). That is, economics are primary and culture is derivative—or as some prefer, epiphenomenal. The Marxian legacy of structure-superstructure weighs heavily here.

The new wave of theorizing about the relationship between class and culture challenges this formulation on several fronts. To summarize baldly, the new theorizing suggests that the conventional view of the class-culture relationship is insufficiently dialectical, unduly static, and inattentive to the autonomy of the cultural realm and its significance in affecting the distribution of privilege. That means culture affects class and vice versa, that the connections between class and culture can change, that culture is not always derivative of class, and that culture can independently affect who gets what.

If we want to understand the complex relationships between various forms of social inequality and culture, these premises are a good place to start. As Davis's analysis and many other studies considered in the following pages suggest, the conventional view of distinct class cultures doesn't take us far. The critics rightly make the case that the world is much more complex than that. Yet, it should be recognized, this insistence on complexity—in particular, the separate identities of gender, ethnicity, and religion; the separation of lifestyle from economic position; and the role of agency in selecting from the cultural "tool kit"—does not save class theory. Rather, it reveals the important limitations of class theory, despite some professed intentions to the contrary.

This point, I recognize, is controversial. Perhaps it can be best appreciated in light of Pierre Bourdieu's extraordinarily influential work that reconceptualizes the relationship between class and culture. As I will elaborate, Bourdieu's work offers promising ways to think about inequality but doesn't point the way to finding class structuration in cultural terms. The discussion here focuses on that part of Bourdieu's work that is relevant to the central question of this book: are there classes?

BOURDIEU ON CLASS: A PRIMER

What Bourdieu really, really means about class and culture is hard to say. His style is elliptical, as seemingly prized in French intellectual circles: a mixture of highly abstract formulations (couched in idiosyncratic vocabulary), detailed empirical analysis (not always tightly connected to the theoretical argument), and some lyrical expression. As Lamont and Lareau (1988) convincingly show, even his central concept of "cultural capital"—now practically a buzzword in sociological circles—admits of many, not fully consistent meanings, all resisting good measurement. Some of his very general arguments about the diverse, socially constructed bases of "classes" are clear enough, and there is some appeal to reading that class boundaries are like "a flame whose edges are in constant movement, oscillating around a line or surface" (1987a: 13). Even though readers of his many pages can readily find many "Bourdieus," it is possible, without too much ambiguity, to summarize his main ideas that are relevant to the issue of class structuration.

First, the essential point to recognize is that the main thrust of Bourdieu's work is *not* about class—despite his own frequent use of the word, and despite the common claim that he adds a cultural component to class analysis. Indeed, in some respects, his argument in *Distinction* and other writings is an attack on class theory in its conventional meaning. Above all, Bourdieu wants to elaborate the processes by which social groups of various sorts come to be distinguished by their conditions of existence and their related dispositions. (Yes, there is a close parallel to what Weber meant by "status groups"—social groups that *may* be based in common economic circumstances, but frequently are not.) Bourdieu refers to these groups as "classes," but he emphatically argues that significant social divisions are often rooted in "other principles, ethnic, racial or national, and more concretely still, with principles by the ordinary experience of occupational, communal and local divisions and rivalries" (1987a: 7).

Of course Bourdieu can use the word "class" as he sees fit. Yet, to the extent that culturally based divisions shape the distribution of social resources and are not derivative of economically based divisions, Bourdieu challenges a central tenet of class theory. In this light his argument does not refine the theoretical claim that class is *the* central axis of differentiation; rather, at minimum, it is a call for attention to multiple axes of differentiation.

Bourdieu focuses on the ways various social groups employ their particular endowments of "capital"—economic, cultural, and social—to advance their positions within "social space." By "capital" Bourdieu means the varied resources that have "market value" in the struggle for privilege. Economic capital refers to conventional material resources like wealth; social capital to social networks that provide institutional access; and cultural capital primarily to the knowledge, tastes, and personal style that can be used to establish socially recognized distinction. The cosmopolitan elite, for instance, presumably knows how to "appreciate" modern art, thus forming bonds of taste within their own groups and barriers to the less privileged and sophisticated.

Manners as well as money, then, can be used to create privilege, and these manners are largely the product of family upbringing and educational experiences. Cultural capital is like money: its value can appreciate (a group's consumption tastes become widely valued), or depreciate (certain tastes can become too common), and it can be used to obtain other resources (like access to economic positions). Because of varying endowments of these forms of capital (what Bourdieu calls its "composition"), social groups develop and are shaped by a distinct "habitus," a basic lifestyle, "understood as a system of dispositions shared by all individuals who are products of the same conditionings" (1987b: 762).

In analyzing these "conditionings," Bourdieu stresses both the interdependence of these "capital" markets and their significant independence. He thus expects economically based groups—specifically, broad occupational aggregates—to develop some cultural commonality. He even uses occupational categories to develop his empirical analysis of the French class structure, though he treats these categories as "good and economical" indicators of location in "social space" rather than as "real classes" per se. His central message is that important cultural divisions tend to roughly correspond to divisions in the economic order, but that the boundaries of "real classes" are ever changing (the moving flame), created by various mixtures of economic and cultural conditions.

Bourdieu argues compellingly about the possible boundary-creating significance of both cultural and economic capital, as well as the reinforcing *and* independent ways in which they can operate. Yet it should be recognized that his analysis is much more a brief for a particular theoretical approach to analyzing inequality than an empirical claim about the contours of the class system. Based on some rather crude analyses of how occupational groups in France differ in their cultural practices, Bourdieu makes some sweeping generalizations about "middle class" and "working class" culture. (His quantitative empirical analyses are very conventional in technique and logic, even if sometimes ambiguously presented.) However, his more subtle and important theoretical argument suggests that there are many socially consequential groups. These groups have different bases of commonality, vary in internal cohesion, and change in distinctiveness and hierarchical position. It is therefore necessary to narrow Bourdieu's theoretical approach if it is to inform the issue of *class* structuration.

As noted, Bourdieu takes a very expansive view of class, but the reality of classes shouldn't depend on definitional inflation. The conventional way of framing the issue still poses a significant question in its own right: do classes—defined as economically based groups—have distinct cultures, collective ways of thinking and acting? That's the meaning of "class culture" for most class theorists. In answering this question, however, we should be alert to how consumption tastes, interpersonal style, and the like that figure so prominently in Bourdieu's analysis of culture may affect class structuration.

To the Bourdieuians and others who say this approach is still too "economistic," my rejoinder is that class theory *is* economistic and that its economistic failings should be made apparent. And to the Bourdieuians who say this question implies a static approach, missing his concern for process and change, my rejoinder is that we need to know whether Bourdieuian processes (and others) have created relatively permanent structures that can be called classes. Indeed, as I argued in Chapter 2, the question of whether a structure exists seems logically prior to the question of how it came to be— and, in any case, the former can be addressed without resolving the latter.

In short, Bourdieu's infusion of cultural concerns into class analysis doesn't redirect the search for structuration so much as it prompts a renewed appreciation of the complex bases of contemporary stratification—a theme developed in the concluding chapter. However, my immediate concern is to show that cultural practices in families and communities do not significantly and pervasively differ across classes—counter to what Bourdieu often claims, and counter to the conventional beliefs in class theory.

FAMILY LIFE

Long before Bourdieuian language became commonplace, discussion of class "cultures" most pointedly, and perhaps most significantly, revolved around alleged differences in family life. Not much has changed in this respect, and understandably so. For it is *in* the intimacy of families that class should be most saliently expressed—and hence produced and reproduced as a social force. So when Bourdieu writes of the creation of habitus, he emphasizes its underpinnings in patterns of family life. And in the more prosaic language of our introductory texts, the family is usually portrayed as the key agent of socialization. That is, within families, people define themselves, acquire their sense of social possibilities and limitations, and pick up the repertoire—Swidler's "tool kit"—of orientations and strategies that guide their approach to social life.

Class theory commonly extends this general insight: different class experiences produce (or at least are associated with) different types of family lives; and, in turn, these family experiences reinforce, if not reproduce, the class system. This argument is significant, most obviously because what happens in the "haven" of the family is so crucial to the overall quality of a person's life. But it is also significant because of its bearing on the overall level of class structuration. To the extent that classes learn distinctive "lessons" and enact different practices in their family lives, they may develop more intense feelings of "us" and "them" and different capacities to deal with the "heartless" outside world. All of these ramifications, moreover, may reinforce the transmission of class position across generations.

Generalizations about the particular characteristics of *the* working-class family or *the* middle are long-standing staples of sociological analysis and popular discussion. Of course all analysts allow for exceptions—and then the overriding class-rooted commonalities are stressed for such defining matters as intimacy between spouses, parental values and child-rearing style, and involvement with kin. In brief, the commonly cited contrasts are these:

1. Middle-class marriages are relatively compassionate, warm, and equalitarian; working-class marriages involve more sex-segregated activity, greater emotional aloofness, and a more dominant role for husbands.

2. Middle-class parents are presumed to value self-direction and imagination in their children, while working-class parents are presumed to value compliance and acceptance of authority. Relatedly, the middle-class parental style stresses reasoning, and the working-class parental style stresses punishment, often physical.

3. Middle-class families have relatively extensive, nonfamily social networks; especially among the upper middle class, cosmopolitanism is common. Working class families, by contrast, are primarily enmeshed in networks of kin and neighbors; they are locals.

With varying emphases, all of these claims have been so frequently reiterated that they have an almost unassailable status as received wisdom. Yet support for these claims rests on a thin evidentiary base and, indeed, some good research substantially undercuts arguments for class-based differences.

Marriages

Consider first the common notion that working-class and middle-class people have different kinds of marriages. Qualitative studies, now somewhat dated, like Komarovsky's *Blue Collar Marriage* (1964) or Rubin's *Worlds of Pain* (1976) are the prime basis for this claim. These studies are richly textured, evocative and probing in detail. Undoubtedly, the working-class respondents in Rubin's study felt "pain," but at the same time you must wonder if working-class wives *generally* feel the same sorts of pain, or if their pain is *distinct* from the experiences of wives in other classes. These concerns are particularly nagging because quantitative survey-based research presents a quite different picture.

First, to establish a rough baseline, recognize that reports of marital happiness are unrelated to class. Up and down the class hierarchy, Americans most typically report being "very happy" in their marriages. (This finding and the immediately following are based on the 1994 and 1996 GSS and my Omnibus Measure of Class—see pp. 51–52, Chapter 3.)

Moreover, to a remarkable degree, attitudes about the normative ideals of marriage and family life are similar across classes. Are concerns for personal freedom more important than the commitments of marriage? No difference by class. Ideal number of kids? Generally two and, to a lesser extent, three in all classes. Do kids interfere with parents' freedom? Across the board, almost no difference by class, though to a very slight degree the managerial-professional elite disagrees more than all others. Is financial security the main advantage of marriage? The same pattern. Should the man be mainly responsible for economic provision and the woman for hearth and kin? No difference by class. Do people prefer that men and women in a relationship do most things in their social life together or do separate things that interest them? Quite decidedly, people in all classes opt for togetherness, though the rate is slightly lower among the elite group. Do they prefer a relationship where the man and woman are emotionally independent or dependent? There's a fairly even split in all classes.

Considered together, these survey items suggest the absence of class-based differences in the normative ideals about family life—and, indeed, the considerable general consensus on many matters. Of course one might argue that people feel socially obliged to espouse these ideals, that the reality of their lives departs from these ideals. Possibly so. But even the idea that so many people in different classes may feel this "obligation" undercuts the force of any distinct class cultures.

Analyzing more subtle aspects of marriage, Anne Locksley (1982) presents another challenge to the class-culture argument as it applies to relations between spouses. She drew on long-established, standard procedures for measuring how spouses felt about each other and how they actually interacted with each other. Her fourteen survey items represent well-validated indicators of what people commonly mean by "good" and "bad" marriages. She measured class with a modified version of Wright's early class categorizations (managers, semiautonomous workers, and workers) and then considered whether class was related to marital quality, and also whether it was independently so. Notably, her models included education as an independent variable.

She found that class (net sex) was associated with five of the fourteen items: marital happiness, ever having had a problem with marriage, frequency of irritation with spouse, frequency of work interference with marriage, and spending leisure time with spouse. However, controlling for education as well, class had an independent effect on only one of the fourteen items—frequency that work interferes with marriage. By comparison, education had an independent effect on twelve of the items, sometimes a substantial effect.

Here it is pertinent to reiterate my earlier argument that education is not class, nor is it even a surrogate measure of class. What Locksley's analysis tells us is that something about education, other than its impact on careers, affects marital quality. And, conversely, even if education affects career attainments, occupation—the defining underpinning of class—isn't per se related to marital quality. Reflecting on the frequently posited notion of a working-class culture, Locksley writes, "What is taken for working class culture, insofar as it comprises attitudes and values regarding the marital relationship, may actually be 'high school culture'" (1982: 438). Like other findings alluded to throughout these pages, Locksley's analysis suggests the need to figure out why education has such crucial impact on people's lives.

Life at Home

So that's how people talk about their marriages to researchers. What about what they actually do—arguably, a more vital concern? To answer that question, I looked at time diaries of married couples from the 1981 Study of Time Use (STU) (Juster and Stafford 1985).[1] How people spend their time is a simple but most telling indicator of their commitments.

Drawing on the detailed diary reports, I calculated the actual number of minutes that couples committed on a Sunday to the following activities:

  1. *The time spouses spent together in any kind of activity.* This addresses the issue of whether middle-class families are distinctly "companionable" while working class families are distinctly inclined to gender-segregated lives.
  2. *The time each spouse spends at home.* Are there class-based differences in home-based "privatized" life?
  3. *The time each spouse spent doing housework and the husband's share of it.* Working-class husbands, it is often alleged, are particularly reluctant to take on domestic chores (other than repairs), while their middle-class counterparts are somewhat more open to sharing them. Really?
  4. *Time spent in leisure.* Do the exigencies of life create different class-related opportunities to pursue leisure activities?

I looked at diaries for Sunday because it is the most domestic day, when choices are generally least constrained by employment opportunities. I used a slightly modified version of the five-category Omnibus Measure of Class.

These time diaries generally undermine notions of distinct class cultures in the domestic life of married couples:

  There is no tendency for "companionable" middle-class marriages and "go-their-own-way" working class marriages.
  There are no class differences in home-based "privatized" life.
  There are no differences in the housework of husbands and wives across classes; accordingly, no class is distinctly egalitarian or traditional in the household division of labor.
  To an extent, the rich managerial-professional elite is the leisure class (a difference partly reduced if TV time is added to the leisure total), and the lower working class is the least inclined to recreational activities (though not because of greater housework).

I should add here that Erik Wright (1997) has strongly confirmed my findings about the division of household labor. Rather than using time diaries, he relied on respondents' reports of the percentage of each of five primary household tasks that they did and their spouse did. These were combined into a weighted scale. Significantly, he also created a measure of *family* class by cross-tabulating the husband's job class by the wife's job class. Our measurement strategies differ but our results do not—a fact that adds to the credibility of the conclusion.

More specifically, here's what Wright found: According to the wives' reports, at the bivariate level, family class location explains *2 percent* of the variance in husbands' contribution to housework (and only families with a self-employed worker significantly differ from the omitted category, "pure middle-class households"). Also according to wives' reports, *none* of the co-efficients for family class location is significant once the wife's education is controlled for in the statistical model. As Wright acknowledges, the results unambiguously indicate that women bear a largely disproportionate burden, irrespective of their class location.

In short, in terms of actual time commitments, the broad contours of domestic life for married couples are remarkably similar across the classes. Admittedly, though, this analysis has some obvious limitations. For one important matter, these diaries don't tell us about the *meaning* that couples may attribute to particular activities, like their time together. You can readily imagine, for instance, that some couples are more intimate and egalitarian than others, even though they spend the same amount of time together— and conceivably that there are class-related differences in this intimacy. Or, similarly, there may be class-related differences in the enjoyment of away-from-home activity. But even so, actual commitments of time represent significant, concrete statements about what people prefer to do in their marriages and significant constraints on what marriages are like. To argue that there are class differences in marital relations, then, you'd have to emphasize the significance of relatively subtle differences in the meaning of activities. Moreover, survey data on couples' feeling about their marriage suggest that any differences must be just that—subtle, not the basis for "class types" of marriages.

Raising Children

A central claim of the class-culture argument is that classes raise their children differently. In brief, this comes down to saying that the distinctive job experiences of the classes teach them different lessons about how to deal with the world and, further, that parents pass these lessons on to their children. Thus, working-class kids learn to become working-class adults, the same goes on for the middle class, and the class system is reproduced.

The empirical case for this argument most prominently rests on Melvin Kohn's (1969) now classic work, *Class and Conformity*. Based on innovative surveys, Kohn contended that working-class parents are more inclined than middle-class parents to value their children having characteristics like good manners and obedience. Such characteristics are presumed necessary to deal with the later demands of working-class jobs that often require unquestioning deference to authority. And the flip side is that middle-class parents more highly value independence of mind, creativity, and self-control than working-class parents do. These are the sorts of traits that are presumably valued in managerial and professional positions. Now, of course, Kohn can't (and doesn't) claim that these parental values are successfully transmitted to kids (many parents would surely be skeptical about their own success). But the force of the class-culture argument rests on the presumption that this transmission is successful and that these values are related to children's later fate in the occupational world.

Given the prominence of Kohn's work, it deserves some careful consideration. His intellectual contributions truly are significant, but it is essential to see what he did and did not accomplish. His findings tend to moderately support class theory, though less than commonly supposed.

Although the significance of parental values for children's later economic attainment is not clear, Kohn initially established that various dimensions of *stratification* are at least moderately related to some parental values and behaviors. (Even so, the modest or even weak nature of many reported relationships should not be overlooked.) What is not clearly established, however, is a strong relation between *class* and these matters. Even though Kohn's influential study has been often cited as support for the class-differences argument, his notable contribution here was somewhat different—a point that Kohn and Schooler (1983) later explicitly acknowledged. In *Class and Conformity* he showed that a multidimensional measure of socioeconomic status (the Hollingshead scale) was moderately related to parental values about the qualities children should have. Only in later work did he directly (and briefly) consider the explanatory power of class as a variable.

In this later work Kohn and Schooler examined the relationship between class (a rough approximation of Wright's schema) and parental valuation of self-direction for their children—a presumed important "middle class" orientation. The zero-order correlation is fairly notable (eta = .47); the blue-collar proletariat are the outliers, distinctly low in their regard for self-direction. (This correlation between class and valuation of self-direction is largely attributable to the association between class and what Kohn calls "occupational self-direction"—a continuous measure that taps the amount of initiative, thought, and independent judgment involved in a job.) Thus, to an unusual degree, we see evidence of class structuration, with the blue-collar/white-collar divide being especially pronounced.

At the same time, Kohn and Schooler's multivariate analysis suggests that class per se doesn't have much impact. For as we know, education is related to both class and parental values; but education is *not* included in the statistical models that purport to show the causal effect of class. Some of Kohn and Schooler's other analyses strongly suggest that this omission is critical. Here are the relevant details. The correlation between a continuous SES measure and valuation of self-direction for children is substantial (.66), but this correlation reflects the effect of education that is incorporated in the SES index. That is, net of occupational position, education is strongly associated with this parental value; however, net of education, occupational position—*substantially associated with their class measure, .72*—is *not* related to it. We can sensibly expect, then, that apparent "class effects" would be greatly reduced with the inclusion of education in the model. And, again, I must insist that education is not class.

My point here is not to belabor the details of model specification, much less to establish the true causal effects of class. At minimum, however, this discussion should indicate that Kohn's work points to some class differences in parental values, but that it doesn't establish that class position creates these differences.

Kohn's work is not the only word on the matter, despite the surprising paucity of research that looks directly at the connection between class and child-parent relationships. How do kids themselves perceive their parents' child-raising efforts? That's what Steven Messner and Marvin Krohn (1990) investigated, using the well-studied though somewhat dated Richmond Youth Project Study—a large survey of teens in California.

From thirty-four survey items they devised three scales of family "compliance structures": *normative*—essentially whether parents explain their parenting decisions; *coercive*—whether parents scold, have unfair rules, or use restrictions to punish; and *utilitarian*—whether parents promise things in exchange for good behavior. Following a self-described "neo-Marxist reconceptualization," they identified three classes among the employed and considered the self-employed as a separate class. If the family-class-cultures argument is correct, lower classes should favor coercion more than others, classes in the middle should be relatively inclined to utilitarian persuasion, and the higher-level classes should most frequently rely on normative appeals. The theoretical presumption is that there is a correspondence between the compliance structures parents face in the workplace and compliance structures that they impose in the home.

Class theory fares badly. By the accounts of these teens, there's either very weak or no connection between parents' class and how parents attempt to direct their teen's behavior. This conclusion holds for both boys and girls. And like other researchers, Messner and Krohn find that class is unrelated to delinquent behavior (Hirschi's index of self-reported delinquency) for boys and very weakly related for girls. In short, class distinguishes neither distinctive parenting styles or distinctive involvement of kids in minor criminal behavior.

As a final point about child-rearing practices, it is worth noting findings about the alleged tendency of working-class parents to spank their children— presumably, in some views, a significant practice that fosters working-class authoritarianism, greater child abuse, and a general subculture of violence. The first point to make is that the research cited to support this claim generally uses problematic measures of class. Secondly, as Erlanger's (1974) review of this research shows, the correlation between various stratification measures (with varying claims to measuring class) and spanking, as well as attitudes toward corporal punishment, is low, "probably . . . not strong enough to be of great theoretical or practical significance" (81).

CLASS AND THE ARTS

> The distinction between "high" and "low" culture seems less and
> less meaningful.
>
> —Susan Sontag

> We have in recent decades begun to move gradually but decisively
> away from the rigid, class-bound definitions of culture forged at the
> close of the nineteenth century.
> —Lawrence Levine, *Highbrow/Low Brow*

An important part of the Bourdieuian argument about class formation rests on the premise that classes consume different sorts of arts or at least consume a particular art in a distinctive way. As Paul DiMaggio and Michael Useem (1978) contend, "to the extent that classes and class fractions do possess characteristic cultural consumption patterns, their possession becomes a convenient instrument for class identification." Moreover, consuming arts in the "right" way—essentially meaning expressing the cultural tastes of social elites—can be a form of cultural capital, useful for solidifying privilege or fostering social ascent.

Here's a concrete way, deliberately exaggerated, to depict this abstract argument:

The Brahmin, at the intermission of the symphony's performance, discusses the Mahler piece with some of his peers at other investment banks. The banker and his wife (who serves on the board for the orchestra) had attended such performances with their families while growing up, as had most of his business associates. After knowledgeably discussing the merits of the new director, the banker arranges a squash game with one of the other businessmen, who had also learned the game at prep school. Later in the week, they started work on a joint venture which proved profitable for both. On the drive home that night, after scanning the radio dial with some displeasure, his wife remarked, "It's good to know some people still have taste."

A young executive at the Brahmin's firm attends the same performance, hoping that she looks suitable in her surroundings and, more particularly, that her superior at the bank will notice her. No one in her family had gone to such concerts, but she and her husband had studied classical music in college and had come to like it, especially when they sat with others in the sophisticated surroundings of the symphony hall. Later that week, the Brahmin surprisingly turned to her in the elevator and asked if she, too, didn't think the Mahler was rushed. She joined his team on the joint venture; she changed sports from racquetball to squash.

Obviously my unsubtle intention is to present a parable of cultural capital in action—the consumption of elite art / high culture to maintain and create social privilege. At issue, however, is whether this kind of consumption actually has pervasive, significant resonance in the stratification system. This miniparable does reflect social processes that do occur. And you could surely adduce similar scenarios for people at all levels of the social hierarchy. In many ways, blatant and subtle, all kinds of social groups use cultural cues to build solidarity and exclude others, but there is good reason to doubt whether such processes are systematically linked to class-based expressions of culture.

The Performing Arts

For the most part, the cultural-capital argument as it bears on class structuration turns on the role of *elite* cultural consumption—hence my allusions to the Mahler. Now, surveys of attendance at classical music concerts—commonly deemed "high" or "elite" culture—do show that the audience is primarily composed of affluent managers and professionals (though teachers fill many seats too). Accordingly, the occupational elite is disproportionately represented at these gatherings of elite culture. But this crucial matter is also true: only a small minority of *any* class goes regularly to these concerts. Mahler—who? or who cares? In effect, that's what large majorities of *all* classes say. Given this fact, an appreciation or even a feigned interest in classical music is hardly necessary for acceptance into elite class circles; much less can it be seen as an active force promoting upper-class solidarity. Probably the most that can be said is that some small segments of the economic and academic elite have a distinctive taste for classical music, but any economic ramifications of this shared taste is far from clear.

What I've said about classical music applies with equal force to other "elite" art forms—classical and modern dance, "serious" drama, opera, and "serious" literature. Audiences at the ballet and the local repertory company are disproportionately drawn from elite circles, and these art forms could not exist without the philanthropy of wealthy people, many of whom appear quite conscious that their generosity buys standing within some "cultured" segments of the economic elite. Some of these benefactors of "high" culture even view their financial support as an obligation of their economic privilege (Ostrower 1995). Yet only a small proportion of any group that could be defined as the upper class actively consumes these "elite" art forms. Neither this class nor the upper middle class stands apart as a cultural group sharing a sense of "refined" artistic taste.

Musical Taste

Nor does any lower class mark itself by a distinctive attachment to a particular musical style. Richard Peterson's research (1992) and the research he's done with Albert Simkus (1994), based on the national 1982 Survey of Public Participation in the Arts, clearly documents this point. If classical music and opera are considered the defining essence of elite musical taste, then country-western is commonly considered the most prominent expression of (regionally flavored) working- or lower-middle-class musical taste. Yet when asked to name their favorite musical style, only some 20–30 percent among blue-collar and routine white-collar workers chose country—just slightly more often than "higher managers." Indeed, among managers "lower status" country beat out "higher status" classical by more than two to one.

Additionally, however, Peterson and Simkus show that a "taste hierarchy" of some thirteen different musical genres is related to the occupational hierarchy, but they specify, "the taste hierarchy represents not so much a slim column of taste genres one on top of the other as a pyramid with one elite taste [i.e., classical music] at the top and more alternative forms at about the same level as one moves down the pyramid to its base" (1994: 168). In other words, segments of the economic elite like classical more than anyone else, but in all classes significant numbers like jazz, folk, big band, rock, musicals, country, gospel, and so on. The most distinguishing feature of the tastes of the more privileged classes is that their tastes are wider than the tastes of lower classes. Perhaps the relatively privileged know Mahler, but they are also likely to know Sondheim, Springsteen, Monk, and Brooks. These are the people Peterson and Simkus call "omnivores," consumers of many different forms of cultural expression. In contrast, lower status people are more apt to be "univores," limited in their range of taste.

This perspective redirects conventional understandings of the connection between class and artistic taste as a cultural marker. What the uni-/omnivore distinction suggests is that higher-status people tend to have more *elaborated* cultural codes, not distinctive ones. And perhaps this cultural versatility is a useful resource for the omnivores, facilitating personal exchanges in a variety of settings. By the same token, the limited cultural repertoires of the univores may hinder their success in dealing with people unlike themselves. But it is a relatively subtle matter to consider variations in the elaboration of cultural codes. It's difficult to imagine that upper-status omnivores feel some strong common bond because they can say, "People like us like everything." And by the same token, it's unlikely that all the lower-status univores, with a wide range of tastes among themselves, see restricted tastes as a unifying force or some common barrier to social ascent. Surely no research has established these points.

Reading

Being "up" on the currents of contemporary literature ("Didn't you just love Kingsolver's way with . . .") or knowledgeable about the classics ("As Ovid reminds us . . .") may have some currency in some social circles (besides the academic), but you'd be hard pressed to argue that distinct class cultures are defined by literary taste. The reason is simply stated: reading books has a minor place in American cultural life.

Surveys show that a considerable proportion of the populace claim to have read a book within the last year, with predictable gradients by occupational status and education. Yet Americans have a thin commitment to reading. To specify: overall, some 40 percent reported reading at least one novel in the year, but a quarter of these readers couldn't name the novel, and another 30 percent named only works of light, popular fiction. About a tenth of American adults claimed to have read anything with some pretension to literary distinction.

This small number of "serious" readers is particularly pertinent to the class-culture argument. As I already mentioned, participating in elite/highbrow culture potentially provides the most cultural capital: this activity marks the "refined" person who stands above the masses. Yet few can use this currency. Even if researchers can't specify the number of highbrow consumers of literature within particular classes, we can surely infer from the aggregate figures that they are uncommon if not rare at *all* levels of the class hierarchy. This is so even if the reading sophisticates are disproportionately concentrated within the ranks of the (female) upper and upper middle class. Indeed, in a culture that widely favors straightforward expression, those who drop the learned literary allusion may run the risk of being labeled pretentious, even in many elite circles.

On the other hand, reading Clancy or Steele, King or Krantz can provide no cachet. They are too commonplace, read by the sales clerk, sales manager, and executive's wife. Precisely because they are so popular, they can't be the basis of class-based cultural distinctions.

Hanging Pictures

David Halle's *Inside Culture* (1993) takes us inside people's houses to examine the meaning of art in their lives: what do they hang on their own walls, and how do they think about these pictures? This unusual and fascinating analysis is very instructive about the connection between class and art. He visited homes in four communities, two characterized as middle or upper middle class—the Upper East Side of Manhattan, and Manhasset, a suburb on Long Island; and two as "working and lower-middle class"— Greenpoint, Brooklyn, and Medford, Long Island. These cases would seem likely to highlight any class-based differences that may occur.

Predictably enough, the Catholics in Greenpoint had more religious scenes on their walls than the East Siders, and people in the affluent communities spent more on their art than their less affluent counterparts; but hands down, the winning choice for subject matter across the class hierarchy was the (depopulated) landscape. To be sure, abstract art—often taken as the sign of sophisticated taste, in part because its "appreciation" requires abstract verbal support—was more prevalent on the East Side than elsewhere. Yet Halle cautions that the ability to "decode" some cultural meaning in this art is far from profound: "the urge to decorate plain white walls, a central factor underlying the liking for abstract art, is widespread" (197). And even if it's true that some segment of the affluent has somewhat distinctive taste (or consumption pattern), the socioeconomic payoff of having this art is not apparent. Nor does it seem to represent some insuperable cultural barrier. Halle sensibly asks, "How hard is it to take down the reproduction of the *Last Supper* in the dining room and replace it with a reproduction of a Picasso, Matisse, or Mondrian?" (197).

I've considered a number of studies in various cultural realms related to "tastes" that presumably underlie forms of cultural capital. The general point should be clear, but I'll have Paul DiMaggio (1994: 459), one of the leading analysts of cultural capital, summarize the matter: "Although taste is *differentiated* by social status, there is no sign of discrete taste classes with sharply *segmented* preferences . . . [and] although all research reports positive associations between measures of socioeconomic status and taste, the proportion of variance of these measures is low."

SEARCHING FOR BOUNDARIES

Michelle Lamont's work, *Money, Morals, and Manners* (1992) brings a new level of sophistication to analyzing the connection between class and culture. Rather than simply looking at who does what (e.g., goes to art museums) or who holds particular values (e.g., desires intimacy with a spouse), she seeks to explore the symbolic boundaries that upper-middle-class males actually *use* to separate themselves socially from others and, reciprocally, to define their own sense of group identity. In her words, "My efforts were aimed at obtaining an adequate picture of the labels participants use for describing people whom they place above and below themselves" (18). In lengthy interviews she probed these men's senses of what makes others worthy or unworthy, appealing or not, in effect letting the respondents themselves define how they make social distinctions. Obviously her focus on this one group restricts the analyses, but it is undeniably rich in detail and incorporates a broad sense of the kinds of distinctions that may be used in establishing social boundaries.

The potential payoff of this approach is significant: *if* the symbolic boundaries of the upper middle class are distinctive, and *if* the symbolic boundaries of other classes are distinctive as well, then culture can be seen as an important force promoting structuration. However, Lamont's much heralded book does not make this case. What we first need to do is to recognize what her American respondents said about their boundary-setting distinctions in three realms—moral, socioeconomic, and cultural.

On the moral front, Lamont tells us, upper-middle-class men say that they dislike "the phonies, the social climbers, and the low-morals types" (60). And being a "low-morals" type means violating the ethical code of the Judeo-Christian tradition. At the workplace the most prized colleagues are friendly, hard-working team players who also maintain an ambitious, self-directed side. The remarkable thing about these orientations is that they appear so unremarkable.

After all, it seems so American to reject "phonies"; they aren't the objects of scorn just for Holden Caulfield and upper-middle-class men in New York and Indianapolis. In a culture that *generally* seems to value a straightforward, genuine approach in social interactions, the phony is the commonplace symbol of what not to be. Similarly, the social climber runs up against

the widespread egalitarian ethos. By the same token, these men would be social deviants if they *didn't* endorse the strong cultural prescriptions to be
friendly and work hard.

Lamont also tells us that the men of this advantaged class admire economic success, especially if coupled with moral probity. Money is the mark
of achievement, but neither privileged origins nor particular occupations
have much effect in defining social boundaries. The language of class is notably absent in Lamont's accounts, and their admiration for economic success seems widely shared. Indeed, Lamont reminds us, these findings won't
surprise the readers of Tocqueville's *Democracy in America* or Lipset's *The
First New Nation*.

Further, of the three types of symbolic boundaries, these upper-middle-
class men care least about specifically cultural concerns in making social
distinctions. In rating the weight each respondent gave to moral, cultural,
and socioeconomic boundaries, Lamont attempted to identify "the principle of organization implicit and explicit in all their answers" to questions about "choice of friends, child-rearing values, and feelings of inferior-
ity and superiority," and other related matters. She then coded into broad
categories the frequencies of statements that supported various principles
underlying social distinctions. Here are the results of this impressive, in-
depth exercise:

For cultural concerns, the statements of upper-middle-class men in the
for-profit sector generally suggested only "indifference" or "occasional" significance. Their average scores for moral concerns were somewhat higher,
between "occasional" and "somewhat frequent." Their concerns for distinctions based on socioeconomic matters were most pronounced, averaging
between "somewhat" and "very frequent."

Those upper-middle-class men designated as "social and cultural specialists" gave equal weight to cultural and moral concerns (between "occasional" and "somewhat frequent" on her scale) and slightly greater weight
to socioeconomic concerns.

As affirmed in Lamont's study, the upper-middle-class commitment to
traditional American virtues and the success ethnic hardly appears distinctive; these men seem to espouse the general American ethos. On the cultural
front, however, we must be less confident in judging their distinctiveness,
largely because relevant studies are sparse. (Perhaps other classes have even

lesser regard for culture-based distinctions.) Even so, as Lamont incisively argues in her conclusion, the accounts of these men directly contradict Bourdieu's argument that cultural distinctions play a significant role in social reproduction. Is it likely that "manners" have such impact if men profess so little concern for them?

In *Money, Morals, and Manners* Lamont discursively contrasts upper-middle-class orientations and the orientations of other classes (as do I here), but this comparison is necessarily limited and unsystematic for the good reason that related research does not scrutinize other classes in similar terms. Do working-class males define worthy people in a different way from their upper-middle-class counterparts? That she really can't answer, as her call for research on other classes indicates. To remedy this deficiency, Lamont, Schmalzbauer, Waller, and Weber (1994) turn to the Culture Module of the 1993 GSS to assess the determinants of moral and cultural boundaries in the general U.S. population.

You might imagine that Lamont, the in-depth interviewer, might take some exception to measuring "culture" by close-ended survey items: too unsubtle, too unnuanced. Not so. She readily accepts the measures as appropriate to test her argument about class-based symbolic boundaries. She quotes Peter Marsden and Joseph Swingle, writing in *Poetics* (not a bastion of positivistic survey research), that these items specifically measure "tastes, preferences and activities that serve as symbolic indicators of membership in and boundaries between social groups." So if Lamont accepts the GSS items, we can decide whether she makes the case for class cultures on her own terms.

Lamont focuses here on moral and cultural boundaries. Moral boundaries refer to the personal qualities that are important to people in establishing who is worthy of their esteem; and cultural boundaries to the manners and tastes that govern how people live. These admittedly complex matters are captured in the following terms—*moral boundaries*: items related to (1) whether the respondent believes he/she should take care of himself/herself first, (2) the importance of marriage and children, (3) attitudes toward premarital sex and homosexuality, and (4) the personal importance of faith in God; *cultural boundaries*: items related to (1) the importance of having cultured, creative friends and (2) importance of being cultured in one's life.

She measures class as a dichotomy: the upper middle class (high and low managers, high and low culture workers, artists, high and low technical workers, and high sales workers) and the working class (clerical, skilled and unskilled manual, and service occupations). Obviously this specification does not capture the full complexity of any developed class schema, but it seems roughly suitable to assess whether the upper middle class—those most apt to engage in cultural boundary work, according to Lamont—is truly distinctive.

Employing multivariate regression, Lamont and colleagues show the relative influence of class, other stratal measures (education, income, race, and gender), and "lifestyle enclaves" (marital status, "high culture" tastes like watching PBS, and religious activity). It's not much of a contest between the stratification variables and the lifestyle variables—the latter win in a landslide. Measures of being involved in the high-culture lifestyle are the best predictors of the cultural boundaries; measures of being included in the traditional family and religious lifestyle enclaves explain the most variance in the moral boundaries. *Class is almost totally irrelevant in constituting these boundaries.* The upper middle class does not significantly differ from the working class on any of the cultural boundary items, and does so for only one of six moral boundary items. Net of the other variables in the model, the upper middle class is slightly less apt to "put themselves first"—an indication of some greater self-professed altruism. The other stratification variables have sporadic, small impact, though they do not establish the reality of *class*-based boundaries.

Moreover, the class-cultures argument cannot be saved by invoking indirect class effects—that is, being religious or a family traditionalist is part of an upper-middle-class way of life that, in turn, induces particular moral or cultural orientations. To be sure, the class and other stratification measures are modestly related to the lifestyle measures. Yet models that incorporate the stratification variables and exclude the latter still show that class has no effect whatsoever.

Lamont and colleagues resist their own clear findings, oddly concluding, "Theories on symbolic boundaries must be de-centered from a wholly class-centered approach to be able to account for this reality [that people belong to cross-cutting status groups]" (23). Their "centering" language seems designed to say class is still significant, but perhaps less so than expected.

Given their findings, why should class remain the reference point? A more reasonable conclusion is that their analysis revealed no evidence whatsoever of class-based moral and cultural boundaries. That is a powerful indictment of attempts to infuse cultural concerns into class analysis.

METAPHYSICS, MORALS, AND CLASS

Culture, in the sociological gaze, has many meanings and levels, ranging from such mundane activities as child-rearing practices to senses of beauty to epistemological and fundamental moral commitments. This latter, "deep" level relating to Truth and Goodness has received little empirical attention, perhaps because such matters seem either too sublime or ineffable to be captured by the profane tools of social science. (Kant considered the sphere of morality to be one of the three abstract value spheres that constitute culture, and Parsons made it a central component of his action schema, but, it's fair to say, neither theorist inspired much empirical research.) Arguably, however, such foundational commitments constitute the most fundamental aspect of culture—notwithstanding the great difficulties in operationalizing relevant concepts. To the extent that such commitments shape or guide more specific thoughts and actions, they are important to consider in assessing claims of class cultures.

My colleague James Davison Hunter has recently ventured into the problematic territory of charting individuals' moral-cultural compasses. Using cluster analysis, he and Carl Bowman (1996) sought to identify subgroups of the population that differ in their core commitments on three crucial dimensions:

> "*license vs. restraint*," measured by acceptance of such adages as "live for today," "look out for number one," and "good fences make good neighbors";
>
> "*relativism vs. absolutism*," measured by reactions to statements like "All views of what is good are equally valid" and "We would all be better off if we could live by the same basic moral guidelines";
>
> "*traditional vs. progressive morality*," measured by reactions to divorce, premarital and homosexual sex, pornography, cigarettes, alcohol, marijuana, interracial marriage, and swearing.

Then, in terms of these core commitments, they identified six distinct patterns of moral commitments, briefly noted here:

1. *Traditionalists.* This is the most conservative group in regard to self-sacrifice, foundationalism, and traditional morality.

2. *Neotraditionalists.* This is the second most conservative group, moderate versions of the first group.

3. *Conventionalists.* These represent a moderate to conservative cluster, seemingly so "more out of habit and accepted practice than out of conviction."

4. *Pragmatists.* Traditional in personal morality, they also reject relativism but are the most hedonistic of all clusters.

5. *Communitarians.* This group tends to be somewhat skeptical about traditional moral principles and somewhat relativistic in views of truth, but have a strong willingness to subordinate immediate gain and personal satisfaction to future gain or the common good.

6. *Permissivists.* These are the most relativistic, dismissive of traditional morality and hedonistic—"moral improvisers."

Americans appear remarkably divided in their moral orientations, but these differences are also remarkably unrelated to class cleavages (see Table 7.1). What's clear here is that classes don't collectively espouse a distinctive moral-cultural view; in no class does even a narrow majority fall into a particular cluster. The permissivists are the most common overall (about a third) and the most common within *each* of the classes. Generally, within-class moral differences mirror the differences within the society at large. Hunter and Bowman's "social elite"—a quasi- "new class" designation (see Chapter 10) of high-income, graduate-educated people—is the partial exception. This elite eschews conventionalist and traditionalist orientations, but given their attraction to all other orientations, they hardly constitute some anticonventional avant-garde.

At the same time, for very fundamental matters, class doesn't structure religious orientations. Overall, Americans are a religious people, and religious observance is fairly common throughout the class hierarchy. Responses to the General Social Survey analyzed in terms of my Omnibus Measure of Class (pp. 51–52, Chapter 3) indicate that frequency of church attendance is unrelated to class and frequency of prayers is only very minimally so. Belief in the existence of God is widespread and only weakly related to class. Opium or inspiration, religion isn't a unifying component of distinct class cultures.

The only conclusion to be drawn is that class divisions are not reinforced as moral-cultural divisions. And the important implication is that

TABLE 7.1
Patterns of Moral Commitment by Class

Moral Commitment Cluster[1]	Poor Workers	Low- and Mid-Income Workers	Managers/ Entrepreneurs	Professionals	Social Elite	Total
Conventionalist	19.9%	13.2%	18.5%	9.2%	0%	13.6%
Traditionalist	7.3	8.5	13.3	10	2.3	9.2
Permissivist	33.1	33.9	27.7	34.9	39.5	33.3
Pragmatist	11.9	13	12.7	10.9	16.3	12.5
Communitarian	13.2	16.2	16.8	18.3	16.3	16.3
Neotraditional	14.6	15.2	11	16.6	25.6	15.1
Total	100%	100%	100%	100%	100%	100%
N	(151)	(507)	(173)	(229)	(43)	(1103)

NOTE: [1]See text for definitions.

SOURCE: 1996 Survey of American Political Culture, Post-Modernity Project, University of Virginia. Special Analysis, Carl Bowman (Hunter and Bowman 1996).

all the moral-cultural conflicts that so animate our political realm cut across class divisions. Culture has a political life of its own that is neither derivative of class or epiphenomenal.

ALL THE SAME?

Overall, then, there are few signs of distinctive class-rooted cultural dispositions. This conclusion holds for a wide range of realms of life often deemed "cultural": patterns of family life, consumption of the arts, and moral commitments. Hence, Bourdieuians face a quandary: how can distinct cultural dispositions reproduce the class system if there aren't class-rooted distinctions to activate?

Let me stress, however, that this does not mean that all Americans are culturally alike or even that cultural dispositions are unrelated to economic status. Of course, cultural homogenization is apparent in important respects. A few people turn on *Masterpiece Theater*, disproportionately the well educated; but almost all of them, along with everyone else, also watch *Seinfeld* or its equivalents. Jane Austen may enjoy a flurry of exposure in movie theaters and video stores, but the movies based on this "serious" novelist's work are necessarily popular in the literal sense of the word—just like all the action flicks, sci-fi adventures, and romances that dominate the lists of "top grossers." And by the same token, Americans (especially males) widely and enthusiastically participate in what Robert Lipsyte has called Sports World. This is the collective obsession with "big time" sports—in effect, morality plays with stars of iconic status. Cutting across classes, its appeal is reflected in spectating rituals and ever greater commercial promotion.

At the same time, American culture is also a niche culture. We're far from alike. The inhabitants of Sports World can focus their energies on particular sports; virtually any religious conviction can and does find expression in some organization; the music store (or cyberspace outlet) can cater to a huge variety of tastes; and parents can raise children with a variety of "styles" and in a variety of circumstances. Yet these niches are generally not aligned in class terms.

As lifestyles and cultural commitments proliferate, they are linked to many social identities—diverse, cross-cutting, and often impermanent. The successful Tribeca gallery owner, say, may share with her fellow urban cultural entrepreneurs some appreciation of avant-garde theater, good French wine, sexual expressiveness, and involvement in organizations promoting civil liberties. The Brahmin investment banker's wife, who previously appeared in the parable of cultural capital, may have similar affluence and partially share some of these enthusiasms, but feels much more culturally comfortable in her traditionalist, blue-blood social circles. And the CEO of a substantial company in Indianapolis may care nothing about any of these matters: he's involved in a breakfast prayer group at his church, Little League coaching, and his weekly golf game. In each case, their cultural commitments may facilitate success within their particular localized sector of the upper-status world, but in cultural terms, their distinctive common ground is slight, surely nothing suggesting an overarching unity within an upper class.

Of course the fact that Americans differ so widely in economic circumstances means that they also differ in their ability to buy their way into various cultural niches. But few of the barriers are absolute; class-based divisions readily blur. Landscape paintings are available at an almost infinite range of prices, as are clothes of particular cuts and fabrics, foods and drinks, recreation clubs, cars and home appliances, and, indeed, almost all imaginable consumer goods. Any status distinctions that people draw must necessarily be finely calibrated. The class signals of cultural consumption patterns are further muted because people create their own narrow niche by making different choices across the many realms of cultural life. Indeed, U.S. marketing experts do not target broad classes in their promotional efforts, but instead identify much narrower "lifestyle enclaves" that are not defined by class. One widely used analysis, for instance, has identified, through cluster analysis techniques, some *forty* different neighborhood types (Weiss 1988). That sort of fine differentiation better characterizes the American condition than the larger categorizations of class theory.

And so it is that dual processes of homogenization and differentiation undermine class structuration in the cultural dimension. Distinct class cultures aren't maintained in these conditions, only a many-sided confluence of partially competing and often changing status groups. This alternative perspective receives greater elaboration in the concluding chapter of this book.

CHAPTER EIGHT

On the Domestic Front: Friends, Residences, and Families

To what extent does class shape the content of off-the-job social networks? That's the organizing question of this brief chapter. It's an important question because the answer indicates whether classes exist as communal groups bound by unifying patterns of social interaction. If the divisions of the workplace are reinforced by divisions in community life, then class becomes more significant for individual identity and possibly collective action. On the other hand, without intimate communal reinforcement, class is less likely to generate distinctive cultures and political dispositions. Besides considering friendship and residence patterns, I focus as well on the feminist challenge to class theory, especially the problematic location of families in the class structure.

FRIENDSHIPS

Here's the imagery consistent with class theory:

> Some blue-collar guys in the assembly plant meet at a local bar after work, have a few beers, and plan a fishing trip together. They decide to invite some other guys from their neighborhood who work in another factory in town.
> A lawyer's wife arranges for some other lawyers in her husband's firm and their wives (two stay-at-home, one realtor, one teacher) to come over for a dinner party. She also includes a fellow member of the Junior League who is married to a physician.
> A young secretary calls three of her high school girlfriends, all with clerical jobs in three different offices, to discuss her difficulties with her boyfriend who is about to join the Marines.

That is, the bonds of work actually forge friendships or people gravitate to others who are similar in class terms.

This imagery of class-patterned friendships is probably accurate for some locales, but Huckfeldt's (1983: 658) bold claim that "the [class] homogeneity of friendship groups is well established in social science research" is hard to sustain. Indeed, there's remarkably little research that specifically addresses the class basis of friendships. But the available research, including Huckfeldt's own, indicates the considerable class *heterogeneity* of friendship networks.

Using data from the 1966 Detroit Area Study, Huckfeldt reports the social class distribution (a tripartite division of professional-managerial, clerical-sales-service, and blue-collar workers) of respondents' three (non-relative) best friends. These white males were somewhat likely to have close friends within their own class, but their choices hardly reflected class-*homogenous* social worlds. Just under half (43 percent) of the upper-middle-class men had at least one very close working-class friend, as did a majority (59 percent) of the lower-middle-class men; a substantial majority of the lower-middle-class men had a close upper-middle-class friend (67 percent) and a working-class friend (59 percent); and working-class men often counted (46 percent) an upper-middle-class man as one of their three closest friends.

With the same data set Laumann (1973) used smallest space analysis to examine friendship patterns. He found that those at the very top, self-employed professionals, and those near the very bottom, laborers in manufacturing, had unusually high tendencies to choose friends from their own occupational group; but overall the relative proximities of the occupational groups to one another was determined by gradations of status rank (especially as indexed by educational attainment) and size of the workplace. These findings, Laumann concludes, undercut claims of differentiated class subcultures because "[g]roup 'boundaries' are simply too permeable— that is, are too often 'breached' by members' choosing outsiders as intimates" (82).

This conclusion also aptly describes the friendship patterns revealed in Wright's recent national survey, which asked respondents to name the three people—friends or relatives, not including immediate family members—to whom they felt "personally closest." Wright and Cho (1992) rigorously analyzed the *relative* permeability of different class boundaries to cross-class friendships. All three boundaries in Wright's class schema—property, expertise, and authority—created at least some obstacle to the formation of

TABLE 8.1
Respondent's Class by Class of Three Best Friends—Wright's Schema

RESPONDENT'S CLASS	FRIEND'S CLASS							
	Emp*	PB	EM	Mgr	Sup	Pro	Semi-Pro	Wrk
Emp	23%	13	19	6	5	1	5	26
PB	22%	20	11	2	4	2	4	35
EM	12%	5	34	2	9	4	10	25
Mgr	16%	6	18	4	14	4	2	37
Sup	5%	7	18	5	16	1	5	44
Pro	6%	2	29	6	2	15	13	27
Semi-Pro	9%	5	23	1	5	5	27	26
Wrk	10%	5	13	3	10	2	5	54

*KEY:

Emp	Employers
PB	Petty Bourgeosie
EM	Expert Managers
Mgr	Managers (excludes supervisors)
Sup	Supervisors
Pro	Professionals
Semi-Pro	Semiprofessionals
Wrk	Workers

SOURCE: E. O. Wright, Comparative Project on Class Structure and Class Consciousness. Adapted from unpublished data.

friendships. The divisions created by property had the largest impact, followed by expertise and then authority. However, this emphasis on relative permeability obscures just how common cross-class friendships actually are. What's crucial in assessing class structuration is the *absolute* amount of cross-class friendships—that is, seeing who is friends with whom.

Table 8.1 reports these data; it cross-tabulates respondents' class by their three best friends' class (including relatives who are not in the immediate family and excluding all friends not in the labor force). The class categories are Wright's own slightly collapsed version of his recent class schema.

The most obvious point is that cross-class friendships are very commonplace: 62 percent of the friendships are off the diagonal. Only among the working class are a majority (54 percent) of friendships within class; in all other classes the rates of within-class friendships are much lower. Moreover, the working class is by no means socially isolated. At least a quarter of the members of all other classes have a very close working-class friend. Indeed, the capitalists, managers, and supervisors report *more* working-class friendships than friendships within their own class—surely more a sign of porous than impermeable boundaries.

To some large but unknown degree, the frequency of cross-class friendships reflects the fact that relatives are the people that we often feel "personally closest" to and that relatives are often differentially located in the class structure. The family picnic or Christmas get-together is frequently a multiclass experience! Yet whatever the source of cross-class friendships, the fact remains that class location does not significantly circumscribe friendships.

Moreover, survey data indicate that members of particular classes don't "hang out" with distinct sorts of intimates—despite speculations to the effect that the working class tends to a home-centered, familial orientation, while the middle class favors interacting with non-kin friends. Respondents to the GSS were asked about their frequency of socializing with relatives, neighbors, and friends. I cross-tabulated responses by my five-category Omnibus Measure of Class (pp. 51–52, Chapter 3). For each group the association was trivial. True, questions about the frequency of interaction don't tap subtle aspects of how people socialize, but in light of these data, the case for a substantial class division in basic interaction preference is hard to sustain.

RESIDENCE

The communal anchors for class are also not generally evident in residence patterns, even though some class-rooted communities exist—and seem to draw much attention in much public commentary. The working-class enclave, often ethnically homogenous, is a staple of ethnographic research; here, in the neighborhood, class cultures are presumably transmitted in day-to-day interactions in yards and homes, as well as in local shops, schools, and recreational facilities. At the other extreme, the gated community—with its tight restrictions on appearance and behavior—has become the reigning symbol of the alleged secession of the elite from the larger community. Yet the obvious issue is how common are such enclaves. Or, in a complementary light, how common is it for members of particular classes to live in relatively class-homogenous locales?

Obviously Americans are spatially sorted by economic means. Zoning laws and development patterns conspire to separate residential areas by housing costs. But an income filter is not necessarily a class filter. As noted before, the overall connection between class and income is pretty modest (.4, according to Hout, Brooks, and Manza 1993). That means that many people of disparate classes can buy into a "good" neighborhood and, conversely, that many others of disparate classes have to settle for a "lesser" neighborhood. At the same time, with the prevalence of the car culture that severs the necessity of living close to the workplace, people can shop around for the best that their money can buy.

As a result, the limited available evidence suggests there is considerable class mixing in where people live. (Social scientists have been much more concerned with documenting racial segregation and to a lesser extent the dispersion of "income classes.") Laumann (1966), for instance, found that the men in Belmont, Massachusetts, only *tended* to live near others with the same type of occupation, certainly not to the degree that would suggest class-based residential enclaves. (In this analysis he used a five-category classification, three levels of white-collar work and two of blue-collar work.) Overall, almost two-thirds of the men had a next-door neighbor with a different occupational status from their own. Only among the lowest occupational category, semi- and unskilled workers, did even half (56 percent) have neighbors from their own status level. The manual-nonmanual divide was hardly impermeable: 39 percent of the skilled workers had a white-collar next-door neighbor, as did 21 percent of the lower blue-collar workers.

Yet analyses of the occupational composition of census tracts suggest a somewhat greater tendency to class-based residence patterns. Simkus (1978) computed the degree of occupational residential segregation in 1970 in ten urban areas with Duncan's index of dissimilarity as applied to eight occupational groups. The "segregation" between occupational groups rose in the predictable directions (income and occupation are obviously linked), but some class clustering was also evident. Among whites, upper white-collar workers (managers, professionals, and salesmen) modestly *tended* to live off in certain tracts as a group, as did blue-collar workers, with clerical and service workers spread between these clusters. However, perhaps a quarter of occupational segregation reflected the effects of race. Blacks, then as now, were very disproportionately concentrated in certain tracts.

Admittedly, the evidence here is limited. What's available, however, largely indicates the sorting effects of income and race, not class. And the forces of suburbanization and the spatial dispersal of economic activity all seem to work against the general prevalence of class-based residential communities.

ALL IN THE FAMILY?

By focusing on women and their economic role within families, feminist scholarship has surely thrown a large monkey wrench into the assumptions of class theory. Feminist scholars have long decried the neglect of women in studies of stratification and social class (Acker 1973)—a neglect that many recent sophisticated analyses of gender stratification have done much to rectify. These analyses tend to advance one of two points. The first is to establish that gender per se constitutes an independent axial principle of stratification that is not reducible to economic/class relations. The second is to "engender" class analyses, noting, for example, the distinctive class locations of women, the reciprocal effects between class and gender relations, and the interactions between gender and class in determining interests.

I endorse the first point. Because it is not directly relevant to my focus on the existence of classes, however, I'll sidestep reviewing this large claim. Arguments that seek to "engender" class analyses are more directly relevant to my critique because they presume the existence of a class system—however inadequately that system may be understood in an ungendered light. In other words, so the argument goes, class analysis may be sexist, but it deserves to be revised, not rejected. I'll argue, to the contrary, you can't save the baby of class theory by changing the water in the tub.

The feminist critique within this revisionist perspective questions the assumption that the family is the proper unit of analysis in class theory and, relatedly, that the male worker in the family is the economic actor determining the class position of the entire family. This critique does attack a central tenet of class theory, for as Annemette Sorensen notes, "All classical theories of social stratification and social class share the fundamental assumption that the family is the unit of stratification. This means that members of the same family are assumed to occupy a single position in the stratification hierarchy" (1994: 27). In response, critics sensibly and forcefully question whether the experiences of contemporary women are given their due attention. After all, a substantial majority of women have jobs, so that they directly experience themselves the (allegedly) class-creating force of paid work, and large numbers of women live without a male breadwinner.

If work experiences and labor market rewards create class, how can these realities be ignored? The common remedy, then, is to make the *individual* the unit of analysis. Thus wives and husbands in the workforce have their own class location, and only unemployed spouses with an employed partner have a derivative class. Less commonly, the proposed remedy is to create some sort of "family measure" of class, jointly accounting for the work experiences of both spouses.

When this issue about the proper unit of analysis has been contested on empirical grounds, it has been essentially played out on the matter of subjective class identification. That is, does the class location of husbands largely determine the class identification of themselves and their wives (the conventional view), or does the class location of wives independently and substantially affect their own class identification, and possibly that of their husbands (the revisionist view)? Sorensen's cross-national review of the many back and forths of this debate suggests that a weak version of the conventional view has generally been supported. Employed wives may be affected to a small degree by their own work experience, but their husbands' experience is *relatively* decisive. However, Marshall and colleagues' (1995) recent, sophisticated analysis indicates that only in the United States and Britain do employed women identify more strongly with their husband's class than their own.

So, is the family or the individual the right unit of analysis? The protagonists can't really decide. Wright counsels that the theoretical merit of these approaches depends on whether class location is significant primarily because it identifies a "set of micro-experiences on the job that shape subjectivity" (1989: 37) (if so, go for the individualistic approach) or primarily because it shapes "material interests" (then, go for the family approach). Yet, I contend, all this debate misses the essential point: *however* conceptualized and measured, class location is weakly related to class identification.

The debate on the unit of analysis has turned on the *relative* explanatory power of the family and individualistic approaches, but too readily neglected is the fact that it is a contest between two very weak opponents. As the review in Chapter 5 indicates, there's meager evidence of structuration in terms of class sentiment, and surely employed females are not the vanguard of advanced class consciousness. Just recall Wright's finding that the class location of women, measured by their own work experience, accounted for absolutely no variance in his index of "class interest consciousness" (for men, there's a modest association). By the same token, although the overall association between class (individually measured with a collapsed version of Goldthorpe) and vote is minor, it is nonexistent among women.

Similarly, all the debate about any differences in the "mobility regimes" of women and men should not obscure the implications of their common high mobility rates for class structuration. Tables 4.2 and 4.3 make abundantly clear that intergenerational class mobility (origins defined by "family head's" class, and destination by one's own work) is commonplace for both sexes. That means that the class origins of the women and men in each class are notably diverse. The exclusion of women may have been rooted in sexist assumptions, but their inclusion doesn't substantially change the story.

If anything, including women's mobility patterns may point to lesser overall structuration than indicated by males-only research. Erikson and Goldthorpe's comparative analysis in *The Constant Flux* (255) indicates that women had *greater* mobility from their class origins than men. Moreover, analyzing the relationship between origin measured by father's class and destination as determined by the "dominance principle" (i.e., family class = the class of the spouse with the better job), they showed that chances of upward mobility were *higher* among all households than indicated by analyses of male-only mobility tables. Sexist research practices, then, may have led to an overstatement of what is in any view a low level of structuration. In short, because mobility is the great solvent of structuration, undoing the sexist practices of mobility research may also mean a further challenge to class theory.

The feminist critique suggests a reason why class structuration is so low: large numbers of married women have gone to work in a substantially gender-segregated labor force. It seems reasonable to expect that the class system is more firmly structured to the extent that family members experience similar conditions on their job, thereby having closely aligned material interests. Conversely, "cross-class" families would seem to undermine the structural roots of the class system.

If classes need a stable home to flourish, the reality is unencouraging: many spouses belong to different classes. Of course the prevalence of cross-class families depends on how class position is designated. Wright (1989) indicates that one-quarter of all households have earners from different classes—a figure based on a six-class categorization, counting all one-earner families (60 percent of the total) as class consistent. Other categorizations point to even higher rates of mixed-class families, especially if they use the manual/nonmanual divide as an indicator of class division. Using the 1988 GSS and the same five-category class schema that I previously employed, I found that the spouses were located in different classes in 65 percent of dual-income couples. Even in light of a tripartite division (blue-collar, lower white-collar, upper white-collar), the prevalence of the mixed-class family is significant: 53 percent. Couples with a blue-collar husband and a lower white-collar wife account for a good proportion of all cross-class families, but it is clear that at least a significant minority of all families have divided class positions in terms of any structural map.

The possible implications are easy to imagine. Even if the spillover of work experiences into nonwork realms of social life is fairly modest, spouses in cross-class families are exposed to different sorts of work mates and work conditions, all of which can shape social networks, cultural outlooks, and political orientations. As spouses attempt to reconcile these different experiences within the day-to-day interactions of their married life, they can only further blur structuration—which, to recall Giddens's meaning, involves the "modes in which 'economic relationships' become translated into 'noneconomic' social structures."

By way of summary here, the issue of the unit of analysis—the family or the individual—is largely moot because neither approach suggests substantial structuration. Indeed, the male biases of the research tradition may have actually overstated the degree of structuration. A possible rejoinder here is that class situation of women is being examined in *"male* categories"—a doomed enterprise. True, analysts outlined the main contours of the class system before women were so prominent in the workplace. As well, "gender skews" in the distributions of women and men across occupations, and in work situations within occupations, are quite pronounced (see, for example, Wright 1997: ch. 12; Clement and Myles 1994; Esping-Andersen 1993). Yet the fact that men and women have different sorts of jobs doesn't establish that there are distinct male and female class structures. The unmet challenge is to demonstrate that the classes identified in some female class structure are distinctive in terms of mobility, culture, and other dimensions of structuration. In the absence of even any preliminary evidence to this effect, it's hard to believe that new female-oriented depictions of the class system would lead to notably different results.

CHAPTER NINE

Lives of the Rich and Poor

In this search for class structuration, those at the top and bottom of the economic hierarchy have received little attention so far. In part that's because they live largely outside the sociological gaze—absent from mobility tables, surveys of the general population, studies of social interaction patterns. Rigorous analyses of the *class* characteristics of economic elites and the poor are truly sparse. Even so, the reality of these classes is frequently portrayed as self-evident. Yet a critical look at what we do know about the rich and poor is in order. What is often taken as self-evidently true about these groups doesn't withstand critical scrutiny, in many respects.

Here I take up in order: (1) the distorted and conflated portrayals of the upper class, the capitalist class, and the rich—again, I'll make the point that inequality doesn't mean class structuration; and (2) at the other extreme, the underclass, a group largely defined by its exclusion from the occupation-based class system. The prevalence of poverty amidst our plenty is not in doubt, but whether a substantial proportion of the poor may be usefully viewed in class terms may be seriously questioned.

AFFLUENCE, OWNERSHIP, AND PEDIGREE

Wealth isn't what it used to be. Bill Gates's estimated worth is more than fifty billion; in today's dollars, John D. Rockefeller peaked at about twelve billion dollars. Some 340 Americans have now amassed enough wealth (in constant terms) to qualify for 1918's top-thirty list—a roster that included fabled names of American commerce and industry like Pierre Samuel du Pont, Andrew Carnegie, William Vanderbilt, and J. P. Morgan. What's more, the numbers of Americans with spectacular incomes has greatly surged. In 1994, just over 68,000 IRS tax returns declared incomes in excess of one million dollars (.059 percent of all returns). In 1979, only some 13,505 filers declared equivalent incomes, about five hundred thousand dollars.[1] However counted, the rich are alive and well, perhaps more so than ever before. In light of these figures, skepticism about the reality of an upper class might seem to be a gross waste of time.

At this point I'm obliged to allude to the famous sociological debate between Fitzgerald and Hemingway. You'll recall that Fitzgerald, the class theorist, opined to Hemingway that the rich are "different from you and me"; to which the latter, the stratification theorist, replied, "Yes, they have more money." That debate crystallizes the issue before us. Of course, there's great inequality with small numbers of people enjoying lives of immense affluence, but that in itself doesn't mean there's class structuration at the top, an upper class. What's crucial to assess, as for other presumed classes, is the extent that this (varyingly defined) "top group" has demographic identity and social cohesion.

I'm inclined to say that, for the most part, Hemingway has the better of the debate. But it's not a debate that's easy to settle. For one matter, what may be generically called the "upper class" has been defined in many different ways. Recall from Chapter 3 that this elite class has been varyingly delimited by substantial ownership (how big?), or some combination of ownership, high managerial/professional position (how high?) and high income/ wealth (how much?). Further compounding the difficulty of making this assessment is the fact that much relevant data are simply unavailable, no matter how the group is defined.

In the following pages I'll make some necessarily limited, data-driven forays into the Fitzgerald-Hemingway debate about the nature of the economic elite. Here I advisedly use the term "economic elite" because it's impossible to systematically assess structuration for any specific theoretically designated "class." Rather, I'll refer to facts about elite groups (e.g., millionaires or executives in some large corporations) that would seem to overlap with various designations of the upper class. I'll also consider the validity of certain common indicators (e.g., prep school attendance) of upper-class membership.

Of course, structuration is most expectable among the economically favored. They have the greatest incentive to close ranks and preserve privilege, and the greatest capacity to do so. And indeed, many chroniclers of this class believe they've had considerable success in this pursuit. Yet the best available evidence, I believe, is substantially at odds with images of an hereditary, castelike grouping bound together by common socialization experiences and distinctive lifestyles.

Ownership

Apply a Marxian definition of the capitalist class—owners of the means of production—and you'll readily find members of that class. All of the mega-rich and virtually all of the mere millionaires (to be discussed below) would qualify. But so, too, would many others. Indeed, in this perspective, it may be said that America has created a mass capitalist class.

Erik Wright (1997) finds that almost 15 percent are self-employed: 1.8 percent of the self-employed have ten or more employees ("capitalists"); 6 percent have two to nine employees ("small employers"); and another 6.8 percent work by themselves or with one employee ("petty bourgeois"). Moreover, almost a quarter of the workforce (a third of men) have been self-employed at some point in their work career. As owners of the means of production, they'd all be capitalists.

But while self-employment makes ownership appear tangible and direct, it hardly defines the universe of owners. Corporate executives are employees (highly paid hired help), but they are also often partial owners of the businesses they run. And while their ownership stakes may account for a small, even trivial proportion of their firm's value, these stakes can have great personal value. In 1995 the CEOs of the one hundred largest companies owned, at the median, $8.4 million worth of stocks in their own company (Hacker 1997).

What's more, the widespread popularity of personal mutual funds and the investment of employee pension funds in equities lends some reality to the notion of "people's capitalism." Recent estimates (constantly being revised upward) indicate that about 40 percent of households have some ownership stake through stock ownership. Of course for most of these nominal "capitalists" the stakes are absolutely small, accounting for a relatively small proportion of their income. Their voice is absolutely irrelevant to the direction of corporate policy, except, possibly, as a collective "exit" choice that depresses a stock's value. Yet, in a strict legal sense, ownership of the corporate economy is widely dispersed.

The issue is how to make sociological sense of these various forms of ownership. Particularly pertinent here are two questions: do the self-employed constitute a class, and what are implications of the so-called managerial revolution for the character of the contemporary upper class? The new legions of stock owners would hardly seem to constitute a class, even if political appeals to their interests may have some resonance. Indeed, the very dispersal of stock ownership maybe one factor, among many, that undercuts other forms of class structuration.

The Self-Employed As a Class

Do employers ("capitalists") beget the same? To answer this question, let me briefly refer to material noted in Chapter 4. Wright's analysis shows that the overwhelming majority of employers' sons did not end up as owners themselves; only 15 percent became employers, another 7 percent became petty bourgeois. Small owners were even less apt to have sons within the ranks of the self-employed: 4 percent became large owners, none had positions like their fathers. This meant that the ranks of both the employers and petty bourgeois were very predominantly composed of men with origins in non-owning families. If ownership defines a capitalist position, then this class lacks demographic identity.

Clearly, the ranks of Wright's employer class incorporate a diverse lot, and few truly large owners are likely to be found in the mobility matrices of his data. (To a limited extent, this deficiency is remedied by considering mobility patterns among the mega-rich and millionaires in subsequent sections.) However, Wright's data effectively make the point that the property divide, as defined by self-employment, is frequently traversed.

Recall, as well, that the sociopolitical ramifications of ownership are generally slight—class sentiment (Chapter 5) and political commitments (Chapter 6). This limited impact is expectable at least in part because the nature of work among the self-employed is so varied (owners of an investment advising firm, a clothing boutique, a home plumbing operation), as is their income. Kalleberg and Griffin (1980) have convincingly shown that ownership independently affects income, over and above standard human capital and occupational variables, but the fact remains that owners have vastly different levels of income—and, hence, greatly varied capacities to purchase particular lifestyles.

Managers As Nonrevolutionaries

The presence of salaried executives at the head of large corporations has raised acute problems for class theory, particularly theories that make property per se the axial division in the class structure. Although Berle and Means's *The Modern Corporation and Private Property* (1932) wasn't the first to broach the matter, this book surely brought it to a head. Berle and Means argued that the actual owners (i.e., many stockholders) don't control the corporation and that the actual controllers of the corporation (salaried managers) don't own it—and that the new controllers seek ends other than profit maximization. If so, a question almost inevitably arises: has the capitalist class dissipated with the dominance of large publicly held corporations in the contemporary economy?

It's now well established, most convincingly by Edward Herman in *Corporate Control, Corporate Power* (1981), that a central premise of the thesis is correct: an overwhelming majority of large corporations are now run by professional management, not by a controlling block of family-organized owners. These professionals are owners themselves, but their control is linked to their organizational position, not the prerogatives of ownership. At the same, however, Herman effectively showed that the managerial revolution has *not* meant a change in business goals. No doubt spurred in part by their own financial stakes, these salaried managers run their companies with no loss of fervor for profits or their own well-being.

In effect, these well-compensated managers act as capitalists are supposed to act, and they surely have the economic means to enjoy very privileged lives. Class theorists might sensibly regard this corporate elite as modern-day capitalists—along with the old-fashioned types, the members of wealthy family dynasties, and the owners of lucrative small businesses. Ownership may have defined elite economic position within nineteenth-century capitalism, but in the contemporary capitalist economy the decisive factor is usually participation in high-level decision making, mostly in publicly held organizations.

Both in terms of power and reward, this participation defines the economic elite. Recognize that a woman who owns a diner with ten employees would be a member of the capitalist class by the ownership definition; the salaried chief financial officer of a Fortune 500 company, with substantial stock ownership and net worth in the millions, would not make it. Sociological reality is turned inside out and upside down if the former is located within a dominant elite class and the latter is relegated to some lower category of well-paid hired help. Indeed, ownership status can often be more a matter of accounting convention and tax considerations than sociological reality. What counts is being in a position to reap the highest rewards; legal proprietorship is neither necessary nor sufficient to reach this position.

Any sensible definition of the upper class, then, would incorporate large owners, very high-level corporate executives, and some ancillary professionals. In a following section, I'll assess, necessarily in a partial way, the class structuration of this corporate elite. But before that, I'll relate some characteristics of two economically favored groups that partially intersect this corporate elite—the mega-rich and millionaires. Obviously these groups are defined by an inherently arbitrary cut off figure of monetary success, not by a theoretical conceptualization of class location. Yet seeing what they're like is revealing about the top of the economic hierarchy.

The Mega-Rich

America is now in an era of the mega-rich, unprecedented in history.[2] *Forbes* recently estimated—estimates are necessary because all relevant data aren't publicly available—that 137 Americans had personal fortunes of at least a billion. Moreover, in recent years the fortunes of the nation's wealthiest have increased spectacularly. To be counted in *Forbes*'s top 400 in 1982 required about $90 million; it took about $415 million in 1996 (a real increase of almost *three* times).

These lists of the mega-rich do include a good number of people living off the successes of their family predecessors or in some sense "running" their family's business. Their intergenerational privilege suggests something in the way of an upper-class existence. And yet even at this extraordinary level of wealth, many fortunes were also amassed quickly in one generation. As difficult as it may be to make an absolutely clear-cut distinction between the self-made and inherited fortune, the openness of the very top of the American monetary hierarchy is dramatically underscored by estimates indicating that half or more of the top-400 fortunes are self-made. This is not to say that all of these self-made fortunes represent stories of rags to riches (John Kluge, the poor immigrant's son); others are like Sumner Redstone, who parlayed his father's chain of drive-in theaters into an entertainment-related empire, and others are like Bill Gates, who enjoyed the benefits of having parents with affluent professional backgrounds.

Still, at the point in the economic hierarchy where you'd expect inheritance to be the very highest, a family background of privilege is not the necessary ticket for entry. Nor, indeed, is an elite education. While college and professional degrees are commonplace among this group, less than a fifth (in 1989) had an Ivy League degree. Ivy Leaguers are vastly overrepresented within the ranks of the mega-rich—some acquiring these credentials by family tradition, others by individual merit alone—but the overwhelming number aren't bonded by some common socialization at an elite academic institution.

In the complementary light, it's relevant to note that arriving at the very top doesn't mean staying there. From year to year substantial numbers drop off the *Forbes* lists. Of the forty-one families at the top in 1982, seventeen didn't make it in 1996. And staying at the top over a longer time is even harder: of 1918's thirty wealthiest Americans, only Rockefeller, Ford, and du Pont had any relatives on the recent top-400 lists. This doesn't suggest riches-to-rags stories; most descendants of "downwardly mobile" families like the Astors, Cabots, and Kennedys are more than comfortable. Yet because some fortunes get divided among many heirs and new fortunes constantly emerge, there is surprising fluidity at the top.

The Millionaires (Net Worth)

Down from the rarefied level of the super fortunes, the millionaires are in many respects common folk—*not* idle coupon clippers, *not* people born with the proverbial silver spoon in their mouth, *not* particularly flashy consumers. That's the message of Thomas Stanley and William Danko's aptly titled study, *The Millionaire Next Door* (1996), which provides the best available evidence about this affluent group—a level of net worth that perhaps 3.5 million households have attained (out of 100 million).

Counter to the born-to-the-manor image that's so common, Stanley and Danko find:

> more than half never received *any* inheritance and fewer than a fifth inherited 10 percent or more of their wealth;
>
> fewer than a quarter received a gift of ten thousand dollars or more from a family member;

almost half never received any college tuition from parents or other relatives.

Overwhelmingly, these millionaires "made it" by dint of their own efforts, not by the careful selection of wealthy parents. Eighty percent are currently working; of this group about two-thirds are self-employed, primarily as entrepreneurs and secondarily as self-employed professionals. The authors describe the millionaires' businesses as "dull-normal": "welding contractors, auctioneers, rich farmers, owners of mobile-home parks, pest controllers, coin and stamp dealers, and paving contractors" (9). Their jobs pay well but not spectacularly: median = $131,000; average = $247,000. Their wealth reflects the high saving rate (on average, 20 percent of yearly income) that their high paying jobs allow.

Furthermore, as a group, this wealthy elite doesn't greatly flaunt the trappings of money. The average value of their home is $320,000, and the great majority of their neighbors are not fellow millionaires. Only a quarter of the men have ever bought a suit that cost more than $600; half haven't ever paid more than $235 for a watch. Their car maker of choice is Ford—the F-150 pickup, America's overall best-seller, is especially popular.

A PEDIGREED ELITE?

Sociological chroniclers of the upper class like E. Digby Baltzell (1958, 1964) and William Domhoff (1967, 1970, 1983) stress that intense class bonds are forged as its members pass, from birth to death, through exclusive institutional settings with their own distinctive styles, rituals, and values. These chroniclers describe a small class-conscious world: listing in the Social Register at birth, life in residential enclaves (with primary and summer locations), school days at a boarding school (chosen from a small set of the "right" ones), debutante balls and other class-exclusive social events (to further class homogamy), attendance at a prestigious university or college (if possible), a career in businesses/firms dominated by others so privileged, and membership in certain downtown men's clubs and country clubs—all in a pattern to be passed down to the next generation. This distinctive life thus reflects long-standing wealth and creates a socially cohesive class, mobilized and capable of defending its interests. In short, the upper class is an aristocracy of wealth and status.

Let there be no mistake about it, this privileged world exists. As Peter Cookson and Caroline Persell compellingly document in *Preparing for Power* (1985), for instance, affluent students are trained in a class-conscious way at elite boarding schools. Families listed in the *Social Register* congregate in a few luxurious summer vacation spots (Higley 1995). Intraclass marriage is high (Ostrander 1984). And those privileged by this background enjoy highly disproportionate success in the corporate world (Useem and Karabel 1990).

How big is this world? That's hard to say. Domhoff (1983) has estimated that it constitutes about .5 percent of the population. This estimate is based upon the numbers of students at certain private schools, listings in the Social Register, and interview studies in Kansas City and Boston. (How he used the latter—Coleman and Rainwater [1978]—is not specified.)

There's good reason to be skeptical, however, that Domhoff's key indicators of upper-class status (used by many others) suggest a population anywhere near this big. First, recognize that the number of families listed in the Social Register—less than thirty-five thousand—represents about .05 percent of all families. Second, as I detail below, the number of students going to "upper class" private schools is very small—depending on degree of eliteness, between .05 and .17 percent of secondary enrollments.

At some points Domhoff also uses membership at a small set of men's clubs, some thirty or so in total—for example, Century (New York), Rittenhouse (Philadelphia), and Union (Cleveland)—as an indicator of upper-class membership. While membership totals aren't listed, the numbers wouldn't seem sufficient to create a class of the size that Domhoff estimates. Moreover, membership in these clubs may frequently be a poor indicator of upper-class origins. Many executives join because of their corporate position; they enjoy the perk and desire access to a place where they can make valuable contacts. Thus, membership may often be the consequence of business success, not an affirmation of upper-class origins.

However inflated Domhoff's estimates of this "class" may be, the larger question is whether an upper class should be primarily defined by *social* affiliations. Analysts who use such indicators are surely right in presuming that the great number of the so-designated "upper class" are wealthy, or at least economically comfortable. The social elite is rich. But the relevant question is this: what proportion of an *economically* defined upper class (e.g., large owners and top executives) has "aristocratic" affiliations? Essential to keep in mind here is that class is fundamentally rooted in economic life; patterns of social affiliation may solidify classes, but they don't define classes.

To address this matter I first interject a fairly lengthy criticism of prep school attendance as an indicator of upper-class position. This indicator has a strong but distorting hold on the imaginations of many class theorists; it deserves scrutiny.[3] I then indicate that relatively few of the economic elite had high-status origins, at least as indicated by commonly used markers of "aristocratic" life.

Preppydom

Is being a "preppy" a valid indicator of upper-class status? And, relatedly, are elite private schools key agents in the reproduction of some presumed upper class? It's useful to have a sense of the numbers involved.

Here I draw on William Domhoff's lists that have appeared in publications such as *The Higher Circles* and *Who Rules America Now?* Domhoff acknowledges that attendance at an elite prep school is not a perfect indicator of upper-class status. But neither he nor many others seem inclined to doubt the great usefulness of the indicator. Along with Baltzell's work, his research is almost ritualistically invoked to suggest that prep school attendance is a defining mark of upper-class life.

In his latest list, Domhoff (1983) indicates 103 upper class schools.[4] By my count, according to *Peterson's Guide to Secondary Schools* (1994–95), these schools enroll about thirty thousand students. This amounts to .17 percent of all high school enrollments. The so-called Elite 16 that Baltzell focused on—including "St. Grottlesex," Andover, Exeter, and a few other schools that have long been identified as the most elite—enrolled less than ten thousand, about .05 percent of high school enrollments. Enrollments at these schools are trivial within American secondary education.

By reasonable reckoning, these schools also appear irrelevant to the educational arrangements that the great majority of the current economic elite makes for their children. To substantiate this point it would be desirable to know what proportion of some upper class (defined by economic position) actually send their children to an "upper class school." That information isn't available, but some rough-and-ready approximations can be instructive.

First, assume that about 2 percent of the population is "upper class."

Wright (1997) estimates that 2–3 percent of the population primarily derives its income from capital assets (a "capitalist class"); other estimates of the upper class as a owner-corporate elite group are in this range (e.g., Rossides 1990). Then assume that this top two percent of families produced 2 percent of all high school students. Now further imagine—against evidence to be cited below—that *all* of the thirty thousand students at the "upper class" schools were raised in a "top 2 percent family." That would mean that only 8.6 percent of the kids in economically elite families went to an upper-class school. By the same calculations, only 2.7 percent of the elite's kids would attend an Elite 16 school.

Obviously these assumptions and resulting calculations can be called into question at several points. Yet this exercise should show that prep schools can't have major impact as institutions of social reproduction at the top end of the hierarchy. The simple reason is that they enroll so few students. To be sure, elite families *disproportionately* send their offspring to these schools (to their kids' benefit in college admissions and later careers), but doing so is far from a *general* strategy even among the elite. And I'll show in the following section that the current elite generally did not have a prep school background themselves.

If the prevalence of preppies in elite circles is exaggerated, so too is the current "upper classness" of these institutions. When Baltzell himself attended St. Paul's, the top boarding schools of New England were truly bastions of blue blood families. The scholarship boy was an oddity, at some schools consigned to distinctive servantlike work duties. Now, though still heavily skewed to the affluent, these schools enroll a much wider mix.

Consider the proportion of students at the Elite 16 schools receiving financial aid. Recently the range was from 40 percent (Andover) to 18 percent (Middlesex) with an average of 27.5 percent. Although tuitions are staggering, it's hard to see a scholarship student as being, by birth, a member of the upper class. Perhaps the socialization experience is so intense that these schools *create* upper-class-oriented kids. (I doubt it commonly happens; just talk with a cross-section of preppies.) Yet the fact remains that going to Groton or Choate per se doesn't reliably signal the intergenerational transmission of great privilege. In effect, then, using preppiness as an indicator of upper-class origins is likely to cause a good number of false positives—and if it's used as a necessary criterion, it's likely to lead to many false negatives.

Still, for all the limitations of this indicator, it's worth detailing that preppies are much less commonly ensconced at the top of the corporate hierarchy than is commonly suggested.

Looking for Aristocrats

All the best evidence indicates the following about the presence of "aristocrats" in the corporate suites: (1) they are hugely overrepresented, especially among the so-called "inner circle" that is involved in dense interbusiness networks, and (2) they are a small minority, even at the most elite levels of the corporate world.

In 1977 Michael Useem and Jerome Karabel (1990) studied almost 3,000 managers and directors of 208 large firms. These firms represented a broad mix of industries and included the very largest companies within each industry type as well as large yet more modest sized firms (e.g., manufacturing firms ranked 451–500 in sales, commercial banks ranked 41–50). All of the managers in the study were vice presidents or higher; a quarter served on at least two corporate boards. By any reckoning, all these managers would qualify as full-fledged members of the corporate elite, and many were at the top of the elite.

By their calculations, one-sixth of these senior managers were born into the upper class. They defined "upper class origins" as those who had attended an elite prep school (fourteen of the sixteen on Baltzell's list) *or* were listed in the Social Register. Now, clearly, those so favored early in life had greatly disproportionate success. (Recall that much less than a percent of the population had these advantages.) And Useem and Karabel further document that the benefits of aristocratic origins were relatively pronounced within the ranks of executives involved in business associations and multiple directorships. Yet, by the same token, the fact that 82 percent did not qualify by these criteria means that the corporate elite did not "bond" as a whole by trading stories about prep school days or by referring to a published listing of "people like us."

In the late 1980s, Thomas Dye (1990) examined the secondary school backgrounds of 4,425 top executives, a complete listing of the presidents, officer directors, and outside directors of the very largest industrial corporations (one hundred), utilities (fifty), banks (fifty), insurance companies (fifty), and investment firms (fifteen). Compared to Useem and Karabel's sample, Dye looks at an even more elite group. He finds that about a tenth of this corporate elite had attended one of thirty-three prestigious prep schools. (He cautions, however, that his sources may underreport this information, perhaps up to a factor of two.) Even allowing for some undercounting, Dye's analysis indicates that a prep school background is far from the common experience among the corporate elite.

Nor are there signs of an ongoing WASP ascendancy in the religious commitments of business leaders. The favored church of Baltzell's (1964) "Protestant establishment" was the Episcopalian, a church whose membership has amounted to a few percent of all church membership. Socially privileged businessmen, raised and committed to this church, did come to dominate some sectors of the economy in the earlier parts of the century, especially in East Coast finance. Now, however, that dominance has dissipated with the rise of Catholics, Jews, "low church members," and the irreligious—a phenomenon graphically detailed in Robert Christopher's (1989) *Crashing the Gates: The De-Wasping of America's Power Elite*.

True, Episcopalians appear to remain *overrepresented* among the corporate elite, but the fact remains that they constitute a small minority. A recent careful analysis of the religious background of what Pyle (1996) called the "power elite" (mostly corporate executives and lawyers) in a recent *Who's Who* indicates that almost 19 percent listed this affiliation among those who listed any affiliation.[5] That proportion is fairly significant, but it's crucial to recognize that two thirds of this elite claimed no affiliation at all. Thus only 6 percent of the total "power elite" claimed to be Episcopalian. Whether the large numbers with no affiliation reflects low religiosity among this elite or just reluctance to make a public statement about religious commitments is impossible to judge. Nonetheless, this "power elite," a group that largely overlaps with the most influential segment of the corporate elite, doesn't commonly signal membership in the "Episcopacy."

The common thread through the preceding discussion is that the offspring of high-status families enjoy unparalleled access to top corporate positions but are a small privileged minority within the corporate elite. Nicholas Lemann gets it right: "There is a tremendous difference between the notion that some upper-class WASPs are very powerful, or the notion that the WASP style is popular, and the notion that a small, cohesive group of WASPs runs the country. It's this last notion that Baltzell correctly assesses as having become ridiculous" (1992: 42). The reference to Baltzell may appear odd. After all, his work is so commonly cited to support arguments for the existence of a cohesive, powerful Protestant establishment. Too often forgotten, however, is that Baltzell wrote about a group that, by his own estimations, had its heyday in pre–World War II days and, to a lesser extent, just after the war. By the time he had published his most substantial work (1958, 1964), the days of this establishment had already substantially passed. When Baltzell "revisited" this establishment in recent years, he (somewhat ruefully) proclaimed its death. "What remains of the Protestant establishment," he writes, "has been watered down beyond recognition" (1991: 76).

Yet if the corporate elite is generally nonaristocratic in origin, this is not to say, of course, that it represents a cross-section of America. Drawing on an early 1970s survey of top executives at very large corporations, Moore and Alba (1982) report that slightly more than a quarter (27 percent) had "capitalist" fathers, while another quarter had "petty bourgeois" fathers and 36 percent had "manager" fathers. (They used Wright and Perrone's 1977 class categories. "Capitalists" had ten or more employees.) Clearly those favored by birth, especially the sons of "capitalists," were overrepresented within the ranks of the corporate elite—and, indeed, to an almost equal extent, within all sectors of the political economy. But most of the "capitalists" here (a group including farmers) are a far cry from socially privileged aristocrats, as are almost all of the petty bourgeois and managers. Moore and Alba find a "broader stream of recruitment" than elite theorists like Domhoff imply, so that there is "considerable over-representation of individuals who do not have upper-class origins" and a "stronger representation of a class group [small owners] within the elite than is true of the upper class" (57).

NEW ELITES?

Necessarily, this analysis of the corporate elite has relied on somewhat dated information (pre the PC revolution in many cases!) and has been biased in focusing on executives at the very largest companies. Obviously these executives have been and still are powerful figures, but much of the recent dynamism in American business has come from smaller ventures, often in high-tech fields. Excluded from these analyses of the elite are all the Silicon Valley millionaires (and their like throughout the country), the entrepreneurs who have "gone public" with their health care, communications, or bioengineering companies, and the burgeoning corps of investment professionals not housed in large firms.

What are their class origins? Systematic data to answer that question aren't available. It seems reasonable to expect, however, that success in established larger corporations is more dependent on upper-class linkages than success in newer forms of small business. In the former, existing elites have had the opportunity to establish gatekeeping and promotional procedures to favor people like themselves—though their success appears very partial. By contrast, because the route to the top is less routinized in the world of emerging businesses, the significance of status distinctions is likely to be even less salient. Although a complete social history of the new small-business-based elite has yet to be written, many accounts suggest that people from non-elite backgrounds—though often possessed of prestigious credentials—are commonly at the forefront of this development (see, e.g., Reed 1988). To the extent that's so, the class structuration of the economic elite becomes ever more tenuous.

THE UNDERCLASS

Many commentators—scholarly and popular alike—have discerned the emergence of an underclass, at the very bottom of the economic hierarchy. Yet political contentions surrounding this claim far exceed its analytical precision. Depending on their political inclinations, analysts have characterized this underclass in widely divergent terms: everything from menacing threats deserving scorn and punitive control to beleaguered victims warranting compassion and ameliorative social policy. The concept has been condemned as a conservative, racist code word as well as an exaggerated liberal conceit designed to justify the welfare state. And whatever the politics involved, the conceptual and operational meaning of the concept is far from settled. Depending on its (politically fraught) definition, this class can appear fairly large or puny—or is considered inherently unmeasurable.

I'm inclined to agree with Joel Devine and James Wright's observation, "When all is said and done, the notion of an 'underclass' is less a concept than a metaphor, and metaphors (unlike concepts) do not admit of precise definition" (1993: 78). Nevertheless, they confront this socially potent metaphor in light of social science evidence, and I will too. For all the ambiguity, there is sufficient consensus on the meaning of "underclass" and sufficient evidence that bears on that conceptualization to question whether the notion of a distinct class helps us understand contemporary poverty.

Of course the poor have always been with us in substantial numbers. In 1992 the official poverty rate stood at 14.5 percent. It had declined steadily from more than a fifth of the population in 1959 to just more than a tenth in 1973, and since then has moved up and down within a range of 11–15 percent. Whether this official rate over or understates the poverty population is a matter of definition and political preference.

This official definition represents a cutoff figure based on calculations of the cost of an "emergency temporary low budget diet" multiplied by three and adjusted for family size and location. Although frequently invoked, this federal standard has been subject to diverse criticisms with different implications for the size of the poverty population. To reduce the number of poor people, add in (sensibly) the value of government transfers and keep the same cutoff figures. To increase this population, argue (sensibly) that the cutoff figures are arbitrarily derived, that people living substantially above this standard still have miserable lives, and that new higher cutoffs would represent a more humane vision.

In any event, using this absolute definition makes clear that many people live very badly in American society. And, moreover, relative to those in typical circumstances, the poor are worse off than they used to be. In 1959 the poverty cutoff was 55 percent of the median family income; in recent years, about 40 percent. This simple calculation dramatically points to the great distance between the poor and the economic mainstream.

Yet, in all depictions of the underclass, there's something more implied than the existence of many impoverished people. To use the language of the previous chapters, the common implication is that there is class structuration in one or more dimensions: (1) the underclass is composed of the chronically impoverished, barely making ends meet without employment or at least any steady legal employment; (2) it is a spatially concentrated group, largely in inner cities, which is cut off from the economic and social mainstream; (3) and it is a socially deviant group whose behaviors and dispositions (e.g., violence, drug use, illegitimacy, despair/anger) violate general norms, locking them in poverty. Underclass theorists vary in their emphasis on these economic, spatial, and cultural dimensions—and how they may be related to each other. But in all cases, the idea (metaphor) of an under*class* implies the existence of a fairly large group more or less permanently beneath or marginal to the occupation-based class system.

Perhaps the most important point to make against this claim is that long-term *persistent* poverty per se doesn't define a sizeable class. Duncan's (1984) analysis of the Panel Study of Income Dynamics—one of the few available longitudinal data sets—found that only 2.6 of the population were poor for at least eight years in the decade 1968–78, and fewer than 1 percent were poor throughout the decade. Now, Duncan's cutoffs for persistent poverty may be somewhat stringent, and more inclusive definitions surely indicate a larger group. For instance, Devine and Wright (based on the Panel Study of Income Dynamics, or PSID) show that between 1969 and 1987 only 1 percent of the population were constantly poor but some 5 percent were poor for at least fifteen years, and almost 12 percent were poor for at least ten years. But their analysis of shorter stretches also shows that for every five-year "window" in these years (e.g., 1974–78, 1975–79), those who had been poor for five straight years constituted, on average, less than a quarter of the poor population, though the proportion of chronically poor increased in the 1980s. So if some *persistent* poverty is the defining bedrock of an underclass, it seems fair to say that this class is quite small and that most of the currently impoverished population is not part of it.

Furthermore, it is essential to recognize that the *jobless* urban poor also represent a fairly small fraction of the poor population. This fact is important because the usual depiction of the underclass excludes the infirm, the elderly, the young—that is, those who are poor through no "fault" of their own; instead, it focuses on the inner-city residents who could potentially work but don't. In effect, some analysts resurrect the old distinction between the "deserving" and "undeserving" poor. Whatever their "deservingness," some simple arithmetic with Census Bureau data—following the lead of Devine and Wright—clearly points to the limited size of the urban jobless poor.

Consider that in 1990 there were 33.6 million poor people, *but* only 16.6 million were poor adults of typical working age, *and* only about 8 million were jobless throughout the year, *and* only about 3.2 million of these lived in central cities. Thus, this group of *poor, urban, jobless adults* represents about a tenth of the entire poor population and a fifth of all poor adults. Obviously these calculations are crude, especially because the "working poor" here includes those who had only sporadic employment. Even so, no amount of reasonable tinkering with the numbers can create a "class" larger than a few percent.

Nor do many of the poor live in blighted urban ghettos. Paul Jargowsky and Mary Jo Bane's (1991) analysis provides a necessary caution against seeing poor blacks living amidst socially concentrated poverty—the usual depiction in the popular press and television specials—as typical of the general poor population. In 1980 about 1 percent of the population lived in census tracts in which at least 40 percent of the population was poor, and less than 9 percent of all poor people did so. Even among impoverished blacks, a large majority (79 percent) did not live in one of these poor ghettos.

Of course the 40 percent cutoff is in some ways arbitrary: are neighborhoods with 38 percent poor really different from those with 42 percent poor? And why not use, say, 30 percent as the cutoff, as William Wilson (1987) argues in *The Truly Disadvantaged*? Jargowsky and Bane, after intensively examining conditions in Memphis and Philadelphia, make a reasonable defense of their 40 percent cutoff. The 40 percent poor neighborhoods correspond more closely to common notions of the "bad" urban ghetto than neighborhoods with half this rate of poverty. Even so, using a 20 percent cutoff, 1990 data indicate that just more than a third (37 percent) of the poor lived in a poor ghetto. In a few cities, largely in the East and Midwest, larger proportions of the poor live in impoverished neighborhoods, but more generally the reality is that poor people are spatially dispersed, not concentrated in places like the South Bronx, Roxbury, or Englewood.

The underclass is still harder to pin down if you try to think of it as a socially deviant group. Of course the idea that the poor are beset by a debilitating culture is hardly novel, even if analysts who suggest as much go out of their way to distance themselves from the now out-of-favor "culture of poverty" thesis, often by arguing for the structural roots of dysfunctional behaviors and attitudes. The argument for an underclass culture essentially rests on observations that black inner-city neighborhoods have very high rates of violent crime, drug use, illegitimacy, unstable families, low academic achievement, and school dropouts. The prototypical symbols of this culture are: (1) the violent black male, a high school dropout, living off the proceeds of illegal activity like drug dealing, cohabiting with a series of women; and (2) the young unmarried black mother, unable or unwilling to hold a job, content to live off welfare support (and incidental money from other sources). To be sure, it is sadly true that such people exist—in hard-to-determine but nontrivial numbers; yet still at issue is whether *many* people even approximate this presumed constellation.

To date, no one has made a rigorous case for a culturally distinct underclass—and, indeed, some evidence casts serious doubt on this claim. For one, survey data indicate that the poor and long-term unemployed are neither unusually fatalistic nor politically alienated—as many depictions of the underclass suggest they might be. Gordon Marshall and colleagues (1996) defined the poor as the lowest 5 percent income group and long-term unemployed as those without a job for at least a year. They compared the responses of these groups to those of the nonpoor and the employed on such standard items as: "People get rewarded for their effort," "Rich people are rich as a result of the economic system allowing them to take unfair advantage," and "Public officials don't care much what people like me think." Despite some slight differences from the rest of the population, the poor and the unemployed appeared remarkably mainstream—as did the very long-term unemployed, poorly educated young people, and single mothers. Even if the meaning of these data aren't beyond question, the results run strongly counter to the implications of underclass theory.

Furthermore, Christopher Jencks's (1991) careful review of aggregate-level trends suggests good reason for considerable caution in accepting the reality of an underclass. True, through the 1980s among blacks there were increasing rates of long-term joblessness and unwed parenthood; but there were also rather stable or slightly declining rates of welfare use, violence, and teenage motherhood, and significant improvement in academic attainment and skills. These contradictory trends are hard to square with the argument that a "new" growing form of poverty is emerging, rooted in some multi-faceted deviant culture.

It seems essential to recognize that those at the very bottom are a "heterogenous grouping," as William Wilson insists in his definition of the truly disadvantaged. Ken Auletta (1982), whose early qualitative work did so much to give currency to the term "underclass," draws attention to four very different subgroups: the *"traumatized"*—"drunks, drifters, homeless shopping-bag ladies and released mental patients"; *violent street criminals*, often linked to the world of drugs; *nonviolent hustlers* who get by through various activities in the underground economy; and *long-term welfare recipients* lacking the job skills, personal demeanor, and ambition to find regular work. This very diversity suggests that almost the only common denominator is poverty, and some of the criminals may have short-term economic success. And to the extent that's so, the analytical value of seeing them as part of a class is problematic.

Christopher Jencks has issued a pertinent warning:

> To understand what is happening to those at the bottom of American society, we need to examine their problems one at a time. . . . Instead of assuming that the problems are closely linked to one another, we need to treat their interrelationships as a matter for empirical investigation. When we do that, *the relationships are seldom as strong as our class stereotypes would have led us to expect.* (1991: 97)

In other words, the signs of class structuration are weak if the underclass is thought to include any more than a modest fraction of the poor. Yes, we have truly disadvantaged families and individuals, but the notion of an underclass obscures the diversity of their circumstances and often seems to exaggerate the magnitude of the problem they represent.

I should note here that Jencks embeds his remarks about the underclass in a more general point about class analysis: "We use class labels precisely because we want to make the world tidier than it is" (ibid.). That message undergirds my central thesis; I'll elaborate on it in the concluding chapter.

CHAPTER TEN

The Postindustrial Effect

Here I consider arguments suggesting that the development of a postindustrial economy has been accompanied by the emergence of new classes that are not evident in conventional class maps. In an economy that promotes professional-expertise and service-sector employment, it is often alleged, new "winners" and "losers" have been created: a "new class" of elite professionals and a low-skilled, service-based working class that faces even bleaker conditions than the traditional manufacturing-based working class.

I first address the politically charged notion of the "new class," a purportedly oppositional elite. As for all class analysis but perhaps unusually so, ideological concerns loom large in the related debates. I then analyze the alleged emergence of a new service-sector-based working class, most frequently symbolized by the lowly paid fast-food worker. Rhetoric about the McProletariat, I'll contend, appears to far exceed evidence for its reality.

A NEW CLASS?

In the 1970s, the idea of a "new class" gained currency, especially in neo-conservative circles, though to a limited degree also on the left. What was allegedly new was the emergence of a professional-managerial elite that was at once politically and economically powerful and hostile to the organization and culture of modern capitalism. It was seen as the product of a knowledge-based economy that prized its skills and provided opportunities for the expression of its ideas. This class of "knowledge workers," so it was further claimed, threatened the dominance of business owners and executives—the "old" class.

This idea of an oppositional elite was generally expressed in essays driven more by ideological passion than conceptual precision and empirical verification. It represented the fears of conservatives (e.g., Irving Kristol) and, to a lesser degree, the hopes of radicals (e.g., Alvin Gouldner). At the time new class theories gained prominence, they did have some plausibility, at least on a superficial reading of political developments.

Opposition to the Vietnam War was dramatically prominent in the academic world, as was a general distrust of governmental authority in the aftermath of Watergate; antinomian tendencies in the arts flaunted traditional conventions; and some public officials promoted an activist welfare state and an activist role for government in regulating business. Observers may disagree about the extent and depth of these developments, but there's no doubt that some segments of the professional, artistic, and intellectual elites advanced an agenda of dissent. However, we should still ask two questions: Did this dissent represent the ideology of some distinctive *class*? And, perhaps even more crucially for new class theory, is there any dissent *now* apparent that continues to breathe life into the concept of the new class?

Answering these questions is bedeviled by the fact that analysts define the new class in quite different terms. Stephen Brint (1984) has helped us see the variety of visions—more or less restrictive. (See Figure 10.1). The Ehrenreichs (1977) offered the most inclusive view: all salaried professionals and managers. This group is essentially the upper middle class in many conventional class schemas. Gouldner's (1979) "new class" included professions in scientific and technical fields and occupations involved in cultural production. And Kristol (1972), most restrictively of all, included only professionals in the arts, media, and the academy as well as those in governmental regulatory and welfare-related activities.

While new-class theorists could point to this or that "dissenter" as an example of an oppositional elite class (people associated with the National Endowment for the Humanities were favorite exemplars), more systematic analyses have posed a severe challenge to their central claims. Most devastatingly of all, Brint (1984) simply compared the views of new-class members, in various configurations, to business owners and executives on a host of survey items relating to (1) antagonism to business, (2) egalitarianism, (3) receptivity to liberal efforts, and (4) personal values (e.g., a concern for self-fulfillment and restrictiveness on moral issues). Brint's important conclusions: "First, none of the new-class aggregations show important differences in response from the business comparison group on the two attitudes

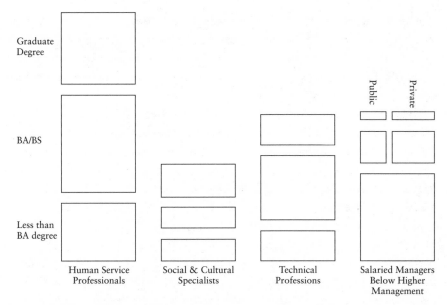

Occupational Segments by Educational Attainments (Professionals and Managers Below Higher Management).

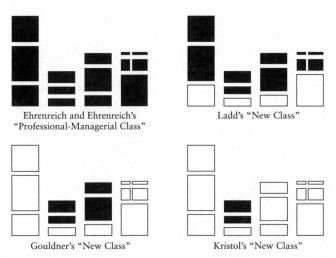

Occupational and Educational Distribution of Four "New-Class" Aggregations.

SOURCE: Brint (1984): figs. 1 and 2.

FIG. 10.1. New Class Aggregations

that most clearly represent potential challenges to business interests—the variables measuring egalitarianism and anti-business sentiment" (37). Like their "old class" counterparts, new-class members were quite conservative, generally much more so than the "working class," which Brint equates with blue-collar workers.

On the matters of reform (vote for McGovern?) and personal values (homosexual sex okay?), Kristol's cultural-intellectual elite did tend to take the liberal position more often than business people, but their views were hardly radical or unified. For example, only a bare majority voted for McGovern and not even a majority favored increased funds for social programs. Brint's second conclusion addresses these findings: "Second, the only aggregation to show a consistent, strong pattern of liberalism on the remaining issues—Kristol's aggregation of arts and social science related occupations—is clearly not a class" (ibid.). Brint (and I) define a class as a large group of people who share broadly similar resources in the labor market or a common relationship to the means of production (e.g., ownership). Against this standard, Kristol's aggregation of a few specialists in the intellectual-cultural realm falls far short.

What economic resource or relationship to the means of production do these specialists (few in number) have in common *and* that other managers and professionals lack? The answer can't be involvement in the production or manipulation of symbols or knowledge because so many other occupational groups do the same. Indeed, in Kristol's formulation, the central underpinning of the new class seems to be some alleged common oppositional mind-set. That is, it is defined politically, not economically. As Robert Westbrook has observed, "Membership in the New Class, then, is not a matter of social class but of ideology" (1996: 69). But in any case, neither the breadth nor depth of oppositional sentiments runs deep in these occupational segments.

Brint's later work *In an Age of Experts* makes clear how misleading the concept of the new class is for understanding the structural position and political role of professionals. He reminds us of what should be readily evident:

> Professionals vary widely in the pay they command; not all credentials are created equal or are even remotely comparable.
> Professionals are distributed across the for-profit, governmental, and voluntary sectors; they fill positions of different ranks within organizations in each

sector; and they are further split by the division between the self-employed and the salaried.

Professionals ply their skills in the interests of different social purposes and in different spheres, including business services, applied and basic science, culture and communications, civic regulation, and human services.

Given this structural diversity, it's understandable that differences on many political matters *within* the ranks of professionals at least match differences *between* professionals and the "old class." At the same time, their tendency to be relatively liberal on social matters (e.g., tolerance of "alternative" lifestyles and support of civil liberties) seems to reflect the orientations of the well educated, not some specific class-based sentiment.

I've focused here on the politics of the alleged new class because its theoretical proponents have almost exclusively defined its structuration in political terms. New-class theorists tend to be relatively silent about patterns of social mobility into the new class, its members' class consciousness, and other dimensions of class structuration. Yet it is worth recalling some findings from previous chapters that bear on these matters:

1. Hunter's "social elite"—managers-professionals with some graduate education earning at least fifty thousand dollars—approximate some of the more expansive definitions of the new class. This elite is not bound by a common moral code: 40 percent were deemed "permissives"; 16 percent were "pragmatists" and an equal number were "communitarians"; and 26 percent were "neo-traditionals." And lest this elite be thought of as a distinctly permissive sort, recognize too that overall more people (33 percent) were categorized as "permissives" than any other moral cluster (see Chapter 7).

2. Wright's "expert managers" (4 percent), "expert supervisors" (4 percent), and "expert non-managers" (3 percent) are all "new class" members in some light. Hardly oppositional, each of these groups takes a slightly *pro*capitalist stance on Wright's working-class-consciousness scale. And their views virtually match the sentiments of owners, large and small (see Chapter 5).

3. Professionals and (nonowner) managers have diverse social origins. For example, only 29 percent of the manager-professionals in the OCG II study were raised in such a family. And less than a fifth of all male "expert managers" in Wright's schema had fathers of a similar class (see Chapter 4).

In short, the "new class" has always been a "muddled concept," as Daniel Bell has famously observed, but it is also a concept that appears to float free of any empirical anchor. And in the conservative 1990s, its intellectual currency appears to have waned. I suspect that this declining use had relatively little to do with the sense that it failed the scrutiny of sociological analysis. Rather, given the absence of any notable opposition at the elite level or otherwise, the concept just became less ideologically relevant. For as Robert Westbrook (1996: 69) has also noted, new-class theory was largely an instrument of intraclass warfare in which neoconservatives (and a few of their opponents) made a "play for the hearts and minds of the professional-managerial class." New-class theory, then, was born out of conservative anxieties about some political tumult (and some related radical hopes); its passing reflects the end of that tumult. After all, the conservative Clinton administrations have been rife with "new class" types.

McPROLETARIAT?

Just as the postindustrial economy is the alleged midwife of a new elite, it is also widely considered the source of a "new proletariat"—unskilled and poorly paid service sector employees. The reigning symbol is the McDonald's worker, decked out in the colors of the corporate chain, working near the minimum wage without basic benefits, repetitively performing carefully monitored simple tasks. These workers are "proletarian" in the sense that they do not own or control the means of production, have little responsibility or discretion on the job, and are poorly paid. What's alleged to be "new" about these workers is that they are enmeshed in a production process that substantially differs from that of blue-collar manufacturing work and that pays them worse.

Claiming that there are new distinctive work experiences at the bottom of the postindustrial hierarchy, Gosta Esping-Andersen writes,

> An unskilled factory worker and a fast-food counter worker occupy two distinct worlds; the former operates machines in subordination to a managerial hierarchy with a relatively clear productivity-reward nexus; the latter services persons in a setting with blurred hierarchies, usually a fair degree of autonomy and discretion, and only a vague link between productivity and rewards. (1993: 14)

That kind of sweeping generalization about the differences between manufacturing and service sector work is highly questionable. How many McDonald's workers get to value their autonomy and discretion? How many operators at a photocopy shop escape concerns about their productivity? And how many private guards are unaware of who supervises them? Moreover, increasing numbers of workers in the manufacturing sector don't fit the image of the cog on the assembly line—the so-called Fordist worker. Employed in establishments with flexible and specialized production techniques, these workers represent a "post-Fordist/post-Taylor" model with relatively flattened hierarchies and varied tasks.

Perhaps the more significant argument about the "new proletariat" is that it represents the dregs of the work force in the postindustrial economy—a group generally below the traditional working class. At least, so it is commonly claimed, many factory workers had some job security and the prospect of decent wages, especially in unionized "core" industries. By comparison, service-sector employment is portrayed as relatively insecure and poorly paid, providing the only opportunity for the unskilled in a "deindustrializing" economy. It's what racial minorities and women take because nothing better is available. They are consigned, it is also claimed, to an ongoing series of these dead-end positions with limited prospects of upward career mobility. The result: a new working class.

The role of sectorial transformations on the pattern of inequality is hotly debated (Bluestone 1995), though it is clear enough that the shift to increasing service-sector employment in itself is not some dominant cause of increasing disparities of income. Too often overlooked is the fact that both the secondary and tertiary sectors include many high- and low-paid positions, with even greater numbers at intermediary levels. The increasing income disparities, within both sectors, are partly linked to skill levels. In any event, sectorial transformations, with the accompanying emergence of new types of jobs, do not mean that new classes have emerged. Essential to study is the career fates of individuals.

Consistent with the structuration argument that I've advanced throughout this volume, Esping-Andersen also contends, "a class is hardly a class at all if it lacks membership stability" (1993: 14). So the key question is whether the hamburger servers typically spend their career in similar positions, or whether they more generally take these positions as stopgap work, usually early in their careers, and move on to other sorts of employment. Only if the former case is common can we meaningfully talk about a new service-based proletariat.

Before describing the careers of low-skilled service workers, it is worth clearing up the misconception that these workers represent some large and burgeoning share of the workforce. Crucial to keep in mind here is that only some of service *sector* employment is comprised of service *occupations*. About two-fifths of the labor force is in the service sector, which is more than the combined total of manufacturing, mining, and agriculture. However, based on the 1988 Current Population Survey, only 12.1 percent of the workforce has an unskilled service job (Jacobs 1993). In 1969 the comparative figure was just slightly lower, 11.8 percent. So for all the sectorial transformation, we haven't rushed to being a nation of hamburger flippers and the like.

Also counter to much popular commentary, unskilled service jobs have not become employment ghettos of the young, blacks, women, and the educationally deprived. Consider that in 1987

> the average age of the unskilled service worker was 36; in the total labor force, 37.6;
>
> 14 percent were black, compared to 8.4 percent of the total labor force;
>
> just over half (51 percent) were female, as were 47 percent of the total labor force;
>
> these workers, on average, fell just short of a high school degree (11.5 years), while the average in the labor force was 12.8 years.

To be sure, these numbers indicate some disproportionate concentrations, but the sociodemographic diversity within the ranks of unskilled service workers is still substantial. And the overrepresentations of women and blacks actually decreased from 1969 to 1987.

Jacob's analysis further indicates that these workers are not trapped in a service-based proletariat. Recent one-year "exit rates" into different types of jobs were about 12 percent. Among younger workers the rates were particularly high: 22 percent for those 16–24. These ex-service proletarians moved into sales and clerical occupations (about a third), manual jobs (about a third), skilled service jobs (about a sixth), and managerial, professional, technical jobs (another sixth). Moreover, the exit rates increased slightly in recent decades. Of course one-year exit rates do not give a complete picture of career trajectories, but high rates don't indicate the emergence of a socially closed service proletariat. So concludes Esping-Andersen, counter to his own initial supposition: "They [unskilled service workers] are structurally quite undetermined, fluid particles on the way to something else, be it careers, unemployment or mothering. They are not a class, but people temporarily willing or forced to take unpleasant jobs" (239). They may share an interest in leaving these lousy jobs behind, but their very success in doing so undermines their "classness" and their potential for collective political impact.

MORE GENERAL CONCERNS

The concept of postindustrialism points, vaguely to be sure, to a number of important transformations, prominently including the great significance of the service sector in the most developed countries, the role of sophisticated technological advances in spurring growth, the related prominence of well-educated elites in many sectors, and the general importance of skills in the labor market. In this setting, those favored by educational credentials/skills are best poised to take advantage of the most lucrative opportunities. If there's anything status attainment research tells us, it's that education is the key to success, and its impact appears to be looming ever larger. In recent years the income gap between the college-educated and the lesser educated has widened, and the relative payoff for advanced degrees is ever more pronounced.[1] Even if these education-based disparities have grown excessively in relation to the actual skill demands of the workplace, the rational choice from an individual's perspective is to invest in lots of schooling, especially geared to sophisticated technical training.

Yet the emergence of a postindustrial economy has not meant the concomitant emergence of a bifurcated society of high-skilled "winners" and low-skilled "losers." Recall, as detailed in Chapter 3, that the income distribution has become only slightly more unequal in recent years, not in any way taking on a dumbbell shape—people concentrated at the top and bottom. What's more, the extent of occupational transformation involving demands for high-level technical skills is often exaggerated.[2] Reflecting the results of many labor-force analyses, William Brock, former secretary of labor, has observed, "The good news is that there is no shortage of skilled workers in the United States. The bad news is that there is no shortage of skilled workers in the United States." In the contemporary economy, occupations don't divide into high-tech and low-tech categories. The demand for technical skills is highly variable. Even as skills are rewarded, they are rewarded in the context of finely gradated, complex hierarchies only partly defined by considerations of technical competence. Although some limited occupational solidarities rooted in the possession of particular skills may develop, these are a far cry from any meaningful sense of class (see Chapter 12).

Indeed, as postindustrial developments spur further economic differentiation, the likelihood of class structuration decreases (a point also developed in the concluding chapter). Here it can be said that the failed theories of the new class (supposedly knowledge-privileged "winners") and of the service proletariat (supposedly knowledge-deprived "losers") illustrate the general point. The economic circumstances of those so classified are diverse, and, predictably, they lack demographic and cultural cohesion. The general failure of class theory, then, can't be readily explained away by claiming that conventional class maps are outmoded products of an industrial society model that neglect the impact of contemporary economic changes. Evidence for the reality of new postindustrial classes is at least as sparse as evidence of older classes. It's hard to see how new maps can save class theory.

CHAPTER ELEVEN

American Unexceptionalism: A Comparative Perspective

De te fabula narratur! So Marx famously wrote in his 1867 preface to *Capital*. Addressing German readers, Marx meant that his analysis of England—the "classic ground" of capitalism—was intended to be the "chief illustration" of capitalism as a generic phenomenon. Germany should look to England as the "image of its own future," he thought.

Marx's bold claim raises a general issue: do capitalist societies follow a common trajectory so that the more advanced show the way to the less advanced? Marxists have been hardly alone in positing a regular developmental sequence. Modernization theorists point to various stages which all societies must go through to become a "developed" society, essentially an advanced capitalist society. So, if the logic of industrialism has social force, we should expect that other capitalist societies approximate, or are coming to approximate, the U.S. condition of classless inequality. That is, as the most "advanced" society, the United States may be considered the image of other countries' future.

Yet, there is a substantial, well-known counterargument: American exceptionalism. This view has been advanced in various ways by disparate yet influential thinkers, including Tocqueville, Sombart, Hartz, and Lipset—and even by Marx and Engels in some writings. A largely common theme is that the United States is distinctive in its low level of hereditary, castelike differences and its attendant high levels of mobility. America's unique historical circumstances, then, undercut the emergence of class structures. In this view, class has largely been a European phenomenon, and thus the American experience doesn't foretell the story of others.

So what can my analysis of the American "case" say about the *general* fate of classes in contemporary capitalist societies? Obviously, by itself, only a limited amount. Even so, it is essential to emphasize that the results presented in the preceding chapters indicate that substantial class structuration is not a *necessary* feature of contemporary capitalism. That is a fairly important claim, and the fact that the most powerful capitalist society lacks this structuration represents a significant limitation on the scope of any class theory. At the same time, a very plausible case can be made that American circumstances aren't notably distinctive—and, indeed, that in broad terms a low level of class structuration is the expectable outcome in all advanced capitalist societies. This argument follows from the fact that advanced economic development commonly means an increasingly complex division of labor and the increasing availability of technologies that break down local solidarities. As I'll argue in greater length in the concluding chapter, these factors increase the diversity of personal experiences, thus undercutting the potential for class structuration. But beyond appeals to the logic of development, the empirical record—limited as it may be—suggests good reason to believe the breakdown of class structuration is already a general development in advanced capitalist societies.

In this short comparative review I concentrate on mobility patterns and the connection between class and politics, both voting behavior and politically charged attitudes. This focus reflects the significance of these dimensions of structuration and the availability of relatively good, comparable data. By treating class structuration as a multidimensional variable, there's the possibility of ranking specific societies in their "classness." That I won't be able to do, as desirable as it may be. The necessary data aren't available. What I am able to do, however, is to show that there is a generally low level of structuration in a wide range of advanced capitalist societies, despite some modest cross-national differences in particular dimensions of structuration. To put the matter baldly, America is remarkably unexceptional.

MOBILITY

As many readers realize, the title of Robert Erikson and John Goldthorpe's influential study *The Constant Flux* invokes a passage from Marx. In *The Eighteenth Brumaire* Marx wrote that classes in America "have not become fixed but continually change and interchange their elements in constant flux." Marx's argument is that this high mobility—the constant flux— *undermined* the formation of classes. (Erikson and Goldthorpe seem to have chosen an odd title for a book that so vigorously argues the case *for* class analysis!)

Indeed, their comparative analyses, clearly still state-of-the-art, do establish the reality of the constant flux in many industrial societies. That is, intergenerational mobility is commonplace, not just in the United States (Chapter 4) but throughout the developed world. This high level of mobility means that the demographic identity of classes is generally limited.

Now, because this interpretation is so at odds with Erikson and Goldthorpe's own inferences, I'll briefly allude to some of their specific findings.[1] My intention here is not to relate the full set of findings that bear on the issue of class structuration or to systematically rank countries in terms of structuration. Rather, my more narrow and modest purpose is to show that the general contours of the mobility regime detailed in Chapter 4 for the United States are largely similar to those in other industrial societies—and to suggest that countries may have some modestly distinctive patterns within the overall mobility regime.

As before, I focus on absolute rates of mobility because, it bears repeating, these rates are most relevant to assessing class structuration. Much of recent comparative analysis of social mobility, by contrast, has focused on relative rates, the pattern of association between origins and destinations net of the effects of the marginal distributions of these categories. (These rates are essential to assessing the so-called Featherman-Jones-Hauser thesis that the pattern of relative mobility chances are basically similar in industrial societies.)[2] To repeat my argument in Chapter 4, absolute rates are what determine the social composition of classes and the connection between class background and life chances, the matters at issue in considering structuration.

Consider what inflow analyses using Goldthorpe's seven-category classification reveal. Table 11.1 shows the class self-recruitment rates (i.e., the percentage on the diagonal) for France, the Federal Republic of Germany, and the United States.[3] These three countries are frequently presumed to be different; their similarities illustrate the prevailing low levels of class self-recruitment.

In all three countries, within each of the nonfarm classes, a majority of the men—generally a substantial majority—had *different* class origins from their own eventual station in life. Indeed, in all three countries, among both the upper (I and II) and lower (IIIa and IIIb) middle classes, most men could look back to family roots in blue-collar or farming life. At the lower end of

TABLE 11.1

Class Self-Recruitment Rates (Inflows): France, Germany, and the U.S.

	Service Class (I, II)	Routine Nonmanual (IIIa, b)	Petty Bourgeoisie (IVa, b)	Farmers (IVc)	Skilled Workers (V, VI)	Nonskilled Workers (VIIa)	Agricultural Workers (VIIb)
France	33%	14%	39%	90%	31%	21%	30%
Germany	31	7	37	93	48	28	30
U.S.	26	13	23	80	24	32	22

SOURCE: CASMIN files; based on the seven-category version of Goldthorpe's class schema.

the class hierarchy, although relatively few of the unskilled manual workers (VIIa) were raised in the middle class, even this group is far from monolithic in occupational origins. Only the farmers had substantial self-recruitment.

The general similarity of inflow patterns leads to an obvious conclusion: classes, defined in Goldthorpe's terms, are *not* intergenerationally reproduced social groups. Social closure is minimal; the members of all classes, with the relatively inconsequential exception of farmers, have diverse origins. At the same time, some cross-national variations are notable.

To a modest extent, class reproduction tends to be lower in the United States than in France and Germany. The rates of self-recruitment are lowest in the United States for the following groups: upper white-collar, small owners (the largest deviation), farmers, skilled blue-collar workers, and farm workers. On the other hand, the rate of self-recruitment among unskilled blue-collar workers is highest in the United States.

The single most notable "deviant" class is German skilled blue-collar workers (VI). Just less than half of this class had origins in the class—by far the highest level of class self-recruitment among the nonfarm classes in any of the three countries. This exception probably reflects the impact of the distinctive German educational system with its strong emphasis on apprenticeships for skilled manual work. Structuration here appears fairly significant, but this group, representing more than a third of the German male work force, also stands out for its distinctiveness. Otherwise, the two European countries are remarkably alike.

It may be added here that, compared to other European societies, France and Germany don't have distinctly low levels of structuration. Indeed, France

TABLE 11.2
Summary Measures of Outflows, Twelve Countries

	Total Mobility Rate (2 classes)[1]	Total Mobility (7 classes)	Total Vertical[2]	Total Upward	Total Downward
Australia		70	52	39	13
England	33	65			
France	34	65			
Germany (FR)	32	62			
Hungary	33	76			
Ireland	30	58			
Japan		73	50	39	12
Northern Ireland	33	63			
Poland	32	60			
Scotland	32	64			
Sweden	37	73			
United States		73	50	40	15

NOTES: [1] Between manual and nonmanual for men of nonfarm origins in nonfarm distinctions.
[2] Total vertical mobility (column 3) is divided into upward and downward mobility.

SOURCE: Adapted from Erikson and Goldthorpe (1993): tables 6.1, 6.3, 9.4.

has the *highest* level of self-recruitment to the service class and to the petty bourgeoisie, Germany the *highest* to the farmer class and to skilled workers (Erikson and Goldthorpe 1993: 198–99, fig. 6.1). More generally, in all nine European countries included within the CASMIN Project, a majority of men in every class, with the exception of farmers, were raised in a family of a different class.

Moreover, Japan—the only non-Western society included within the CASMIN Project—is much like its European counterparts. Self-recruitment to the petty bourgeoisie in Japan is very slightly above the highest level in Europe; otherwise, class self-recruitment is within the rather restricted European ranges or, in the cases of skilled workers and nonskilled workers, is even lower (Erikson and Goldthorpe 1993: 356–57, fig. 10.1).

Now it is useful to consider the results of outflow analyses—indicators of the intergenerational continuity of class location. (See Table 11.2, which reports summary measures from Erikson and Goldthorpe 1993.) In all countries, a substantial majority ended up "belonging" to a different class from the one they were born into. In general, class inheritance is more unusual than the rule.

Total mobility, as well as the separate dimensions of mobility, is somewhat greater in the United States than typical in western Europe (though Erikson and Goldthorpe caution that some of the apparent mobility in the United States may be artifactual). However, a number of countries rival the level of mobility in the United States. If the American pattern is "exceptional," as is commonly supposed, then it is a very muted exception.

In all countries in the CASMIN Project mobility out of every class was common. The sons of service and skilled workers had the greatest class inheritance, but even so, the extent of intergenerational continuity hardly suggests social reproduction. At the extreme of class inheritance among the service class, six out of ten born to this class in France and Germany retained this status; but of course that also means that a substantial minority did not. Skilled blue-collar workers (VI) in Germany also had distinctly high class inheritance (49 percent), but the respective rates were much lower in other countries—for example, France, 39 percent; the United States, 30 percent.

The odds of attaining a higher class position clearly favor those advantaged by family circumstances, but their chances are just relatively good, never a matter that they can count on. Relatedly, in all countries substantial proportions of sons from the lower classes attained higher class positions. In eight European countries about a third were upwardly mobile; in Sweden, Australia, Japan, and the United States about 40 percent were so. Because most mobility was upward, reflecting the structural transformation of the workforce, many men could say that they did "better" than their father.

Much the same pattern emerges in analyses of mobility tables based on Wright's class schema. Table 11.3 shows (a) the extent of class self-recruitment among males for seven classes in Canada, Norway, Sweden, and the United States, and (b) the extent of class immobility for these countries (i.e., the percentage "on the diagonal" in an outflow table).[4]

Again, the United States doesn't appear especially exceptional. Not surprisingly, the overwhelming number of farmers were raised in farming families. More crucially, among all other classes in this schema, only the workers had even modest levels of self-recruitment, ranging from 38 percent

TABLE 11.3
Class Self-Recruitment Rates and Class Immobility Rates in Four Countries—
Wright's Class Schema

	Canada	Norway	Sweden	U.S.
A. *Inflow*[1]				
Employer	29%	26%	23%	18%
Petty Bourgeois	9	12	11	0
Farmer	94	75	67	67
Expert Manager	12	18	27	18
Manager	21	18	15	17
Expert	8	6	4	10
Worker	40	38	48	45
B. *Outflow*[2]				
Employer	14%	12%	26%	15%
Petty Bourgeois	12	8	5	0
Farmer	36	21	12	16
Expert Manager	18	16	40	27
Manager	21	15	18	13
Expert	20	23	22	22
Worker	51	49	53	52

NOTES: [1] Percentage of men in a class that were raised in that class (i.e., self-recruitment).
[2] Percentage of men raised in a class that stayed in that class themselves (i.e., class immobility).

SOURCE: Calculated from Western (1994): app. A.

in Norway to 48 percent in Sweden. This means that in all four cases Wright's expansively defined working class (including blue-collar and routine white-collar workers) is composed primarily of men with *non*-working-class backgrounds.

In these four countries the classes with productive/exploitive assets— either ownership, skills, or organizational position—are marked by even more social diversity. Within the employer class, self-recruitment rates range from a high of 29 percent in Canada to a low of 18 percent in the United States. With the exception of Swedish expert managers (27 percent), self-recruitment among the petty bourgeois, expert managers, managers, and nonmanagerial experts is generally even lower, often substantially so. And, indeed, in these four cases, more members of all the "exploiting" classes had working-class or farming origins than were "born into" their class.

The corresponding outflows show the great prevalence of class mobility. Overall, 70 percent of the U.S. men were mobile, as were 69 percent of the Canadians, 67 percent of the Swedes, and 72 percent of the Norwegians. How this gross rate is divided between upward and downward mobility is hard to say because the different bases of exploitation are not hierarchically ranked, but what is clear is that the exploiting classes do not typically, or even commonly, pass on their particular class advantage to their offspring.

Consider the fates of those raised in the employer class—supposedly the beneficiaries of the most fundamental asset in a capitalist society, ownership. About a quarter in Sweden became an employer themselves; the respective rates are much less in the other countries. Similarly, the offspring of expert managers, those presumably most advantaged by skill and organizational assets, did not generally "inherit" a like position. Again, Sweden is the outlier: 40 percent of the sons of expert managers acquired that type of position. The rates are much lower in the other countries—the United States, 27 percent; Canada, 18 percent; and Norway, 16 percent.

Nor was movement out of the working class some unusual accomplishment. About half born into the working class in each country became some kind of "exploiter" in their own work lives. Class origins are hardly destiny here. Working-class kids with occupational ambitions did not have unattainable fantasies.

So, in light of both Goldthorpe's and Wright's class schemas across a wide range of countries, the conclusion is the same: the class system is not even remotely marked by intergenerational class closure, nor are presumed class advantages commonly transmitted across generations. The cross-national similarities are striking, and the few instances of distinctive patterns represent limited deviations from a low baseline.

Cross-national similarities in work life mobility, Erikson and Goldthorpe document, are striking as well (see 1993: 331, table 9.5). Again, the United States does not stand out as an exception—and that means, as Chapter 4 of this book indicates, that many people change class locations in the course of their work lives.

Consider the trajectory of those who started out in skilled employment (V and VI). In the United States, 20 percent moved up to a service-class position; the comparable average for Austria, England, France, Scotland, and Sweden is 17.4 percent.

Start out in a semi- or unskilled position (VIIa) and chances of moving to the service class were 15 percent in the United States, 14 percent (on average) in these other countries. In short, in many societies a good number of men starting work in what is generally regarded as the working class ended up in the highest class.

Even if "owning my own business" is a distinctive part of the American dream, that accomplishment has been fairly common for men starting out in the working class in both the United States and all these countries. About a tenth of Americans starting in a skilled position became small owners later on; a slightly higher proportion in the European countries made this transition. A just slightly lower proportion of those starting in semi- or unskilled jobs, in both the United States and this comparison group, moved into the ranks of the self-employed.

Reflecting on the case for American exceptionalism (an argument that often extends to Australia, another "new nation") in terms of inter- and intra-generational mobility, Erikson and Goldthorpe write:

> No matter how distinctive the United States and Australia may be in the economic and social histories of their industrialization or in the ideas, beliefs, and values concerning mobility that are prevalent in their national cultures, it could not, on our evidence, be said that they differ more widely from European nations in their actual rates and patterns of mobility than do European nations among themselves. (337)

That means a *high* level of mobility—a constant flux—is common to all of these advanced societies. And the crucial implication is that class structuration is substantially dissolved in all of them.

POLITICS AND CONSCIOUSNESS

As noted in Chapter 6, in *Political Man* Lipset argued that class conflict had become institutionalized in the political arena, transformed into an electoral contest among competing political parties—what he called the democratic class struggle. This insight became the linchpin of a whole generation of political sociology. Parties of the left (primarily social democratic) pursued egalitarian expansion of the welfare state and were tightly aligned with the working class, often through the union movement. Parties of the right and center counted on the support of the middle classes as they resisted this expansion and sought to preserve business prerogatives. This struggle didn't involve fundamental issues of economic control. The disputes were more restrictedly about workplace conditions and provisions of government benefits. Nonetheless, these disputes reflected real divisions of interest. The organizational articulation of these interests through political parties and corporatist representation of labor and business seem to have promoted the formation of national classes, at least as imagined communities of fate. Pakulski and Waters encapsulate a complex development: "The welfare state was both the reproducer and the product of national classes" (1996: 98).

Now, at the turn of the century, the rhetoric of class generally has a subdued role in the organizational mobilization and ideological legitimation of political initiatives. Throughout the advanced industrial democracies, the political arena has been marked by retrenchment of the welfare state and free-market commitments to enhance global competitiveness. The voice of the left, with its long-standing egalitarian appeals to a working-class constituency, has become much less prominent in this arena. It's not that parties of the left and right have become totally indistinguishable in their programmatic vision, but their differences have become greatly reduced as they seek to capture some ill-defined "realistic center," and as numerous cultural issues have come to the fore.

Classes don't politically thrive, then, when political parties eschew class-based appeals and the political agenda is so ideologically restricted. To be sure, not all countries smoothly emulate the post-Reagan/Thatcher model. The nominally "socialist" government in France in the late nineties, for example, moved fitfully in attempting to simultaneously defend welfare-state provisions and cut government spending. Yet the "democratic class struggle" doesn't routinely animate political life at the institutional level in any advanced democracy.

Nor, crucially, is it reflected at the individual level in voting patterns. As I'll detail, the connection between class and vote is generally modest, notwithstanding some limited exceptions. Indeed, the decline of class-based political organizations and the decline of class voting are mutually reinforcing developments. The upshot is that classes, again with some limited exceptions, are not significantly unified by their political orientations.

To document this point, consider scores on the widely used Alford Index for party class voting in five countries that are widely perceived to have divergent political cultures. (This index is constructed by subtracting the percentage of nonmanual—"middle class"—voters who vote for the "left" party from the percentage of manual workers—"working class"—who do so.) In the 1980s these scores were: Britain, 21; France, 14; Germany (FR), 10; Sweden, 34; and the United States, 8 (Pakulski and Waters [1996], citing, as many others do, Lipset and Clark's work). Thus, confirming widespread impressions, the United States appears as the most lacking in class-rooted politics; at the other extreme, in Sweden, where the welfare state and corporatist organization are highly developed, class-based voting is relatively strong—and in absolute terms seems fairly considerable. These data valuably indicate that class voting varies cross-nationally, but they also suggest more of a Swedish "exceptionalism" in significant class voting than a "U.S. exceptionalism" in low rates.

Critics of the Alford Index raise some valid objections: (1) that its values are sensitive to the marginals; (2) that its dichotomous measure of class is too simplistic or misleading (e.g., some say that lower white-collar workers are "working class"); and (3) the complexity of multiparty politics is not adequately represented. True enough. Yet important implications of these scores should not be dismissed. The conventional vision of the democratic class conflict is a division between a left-oriented, blue-collar working class and a conservative, white-collar middle class (e.g., Parkin 1971). There's no reasonable way to construe the numbers underlying Alford Index scores to suggest that this view is generally accurate.

What's more, other analyses of class voting also point to generally low levels. Franklin, Mackie, and Valen (1992), writing under the auspices of the Committee on Political Sociology of the International Political Science Association, regressed "left vote" on a (roughly) standard set of sociodemographic variables, including working-class position, for sixteen countries. In the United States and Canada the class coefficients were trivial; in France the working class was about eleven points higher than others in left vote, in Germany about eighteen points higher. Overall, the full regression models ac-

TABLE 11.4
Percentage of Left-Wing Voters by Class

	Germany	Great Britain	Netherlands	United States
Service Class	37%	20%	26%	33%
Routine Non-Manual	40	32	32	38
Petty Bourgeois	16	19	15	35
Manual Workers	55	56	46	46
Farmers	8	9	8	35
Agricultural Workers	41	34	28	39
All	44	40	33	40

SOURCE: Adapted from De Graaf et al. (1995): table 2. Pooled data files, primarily 1970–90.

counted for so little variance that they concluded: "This breakdown of traditional linkages [i.e., between particular social groups and parties] involves
nothing less than the disintegration of cleavage politics."

Much of the recent debate about class voting seems to have become preoccupied with disputes about how best to analyze whether there's been a
decline in class voting, and whether any changes are attributable to changes
in absolute levels or relative levels of class voting. Amidst the concern for
model fitting and the development of new indices, however, important matters have been shunted aside. Most pertinent for the issue of class structuration: are classes *now* unified by distinctive political commitments?

An intuitively sensible way to address this issue is to simply look at the
actual class distribution of voting intention. It is one matter to say, for instance, that the working class is relatively inclined to the left; it is a related
but different matter to say that the working class is unified by a common
commitment to the left. See, then, Table 11.4, which shows the percentage
of "left wing" voters by class (a collapsed version of Goldthorpe's schema)
in four countries. In conducting this analysis, De Graaf, Nieuwbeerta, and
Heath (1995) aggregated the results for male respondents from many surveys for (roughly) the two decades prior to 1990.

In all four countries manual workers—the core of the working class in
most schemas—is the furthest left of all classes. That's the "natural" order
of things in the democratic class struggle. Yet this class is hardly unified as

a political force. The manual (male) working class in all cases was about equally likely to go to the right as to the left. Moreover, sizeable minorities of routine nonmanual workers (the lower middle class) were inclined to the left, so much so that they can't be represented as a political block.

On the other hand, the petty bourgeois in the European countries was overwhelmingly to the right, more so than the service class. Farmers in the European nations also were quite solidly to the right. American "exceptionalism" seems confined to these two smaller classes, which do have distinctive political orientations in Germany, Great Britain, and the Netherlands.

So if you conduct some further suitable multivariate analysis, you're likely to find in all countries that class has *some*, not much, predictive power for voting behavior. The U.S. and Canada will appear on the low side; most European countries will be higher, though not dramatically so. No one will think to exclude class from comprehensive statistical models of voting behavior, but its impact will be only assessed alongside other structural factors whose aggregate impact is low. Our low R^2's (and cognates) should tell us something: voting behavior has only weak social structural moorings.

Analyzing class voting has an obvious rationale because electoral outcomes can be so socially consequential. The answer to the question of whether classes make a difference is immediate and tangible. And, indeed, the class inclinations in party commitments can have electoral consequence even if the larger classes don't generally appear united by common party affiliations. Yet for the purposes of analyzing class structuration in a comparative light class voting may not be a sufficient indicator. As Geoff Evans, a British sociologist, argues, "The distinctiveness of party policies is a variable that is usually left unmeasured in studies of voting behaviour and therefore prevents the evaluation of just how distinct classes are in their political consciousness" (1993: 452).

In this light, it is instructive to consider Evans's analysis of political consciousness in Britain. As he notes, Britain has long been characterized as a class-conscious society, riven by political divisions between classes. Thus, if the conventional wisdom holds, it should be relatively easy to make a case for class in this country. Moreover, he analyzes the Essex Class Study, the same data set that Gordon Marshall and colleagues use, to mount a vigorous defense of class analysis. Their defense is adamant: "Our analysis suggests, then, that modern Britain is a society shaped predominantly by class rather

than other forms of social cleavage, no matter whether the phenomena under scrutiny are structural or cultural in nature" (1988: 183).

Marshall's defense critically hinges on an index of "class consciousness"
composed of six diverse items related to class identity, perceptions of ongoing class inequality, and views on an egalitarian incomes policy, the desirability of market principles, taxation to increase welfare benefits, and taxation of profits to create jobs. (Evans [1992] shows that this index simply
doesn't hang together as a valid unitary measure of consciousness.)[5] This
flawed index is modestly correlated (R^2 = 12 percent) with class position as
measured by the Goldthorpe schema, but this association is very largely accounted for by the correlation between class position and identity (Pseudo
R^2 = 18). Views on welfare benefits and the free market are unrelated to
class (including parental class), and class accounts for less than a tenth of the
variance in the other items. The association with class identity shows that
class is not without consequence for consciousness, but its impact on specifically political, policy-related concerns is negligible. Evans (1992) further
shows that egalitarian concerns, especially those that counter self-interest,
are unrelated to class position; later he (1993) demonstrates that an index
of political ideology is only weakly related to class (R^2 = .06 in both 1964
and 1987).

Taken together, these findings call into question a significant part of
Marshall and his colleagues' defense of class. True, the impacts of class may
not have declined and they may be more consequential than some other
structural cleavages. But the cited evidence shows that class consequences
have long been weak, and the regression-based competition between class
and other structural factors to account for political attitudes amounts to a
competition among rather puny competitors.

Defenders of class theory can find little more support in other analyses. To
cite one very prominent study that purports to make the case, consider the results from Wright's (1997) recent *Class Counts*. As I recounted in Chapter 5,
Wright has constructed an index of class consciousness that largely taps
respondents' attitudes toward the prerogatives of business and workers.[6]
These are explicitly class-related matters. If any measure were to pick up
class effects, this would seem to be it. In his most recent analyses he presents
the relationship between this measure and his twelve-class schema for Japan,
Sweden, and the United States.

As we've seen in other analyses, Sweden is the outlier. In that country Wright accounts for 16 percent of variance in "class consciousness," a pretty good amount against the standards of survey research on attitudes, though not suggesting major divisions. Indeed, recognize that on a *20-point* additive scale (-10 to 10) the range of average scores is from -3.4 for capitalists to 4.6 for skilled and unskilled workers. That's a fairly restricted range. Based on these average scores for classes, Wright sees three large "coalitions"—bourgeois, middle class, and working class—but their distinctiveness is fairly muted. The more procapitalist side of the large middle-class coalition is only about one point lower in procapitalist sentiments than those in the bourgeois coalition; in turn, the more pro-worker faction of the middle-class coalition is only about a point lower in pro-worker sentiments than those in the working-class coalition. Even in this most class-conscious society, class divisions don't demarcate competing worldviews.

Wright's class analysis fares much poorer in the other two countries. Class location accounts for 9 percent of the variance in "class consciousness" in the United States, 5 percent in Japan. Moreover, not only is the ideological range much narrower in these countries than Sweden, but "class coalitions" exist only if you attribute significance to very small differences, as Wright does. Perhaps class "counts," but it matters very little.

I will discuss one more study to make the point that findings about low class structuration in terms of politics and consciousness are quite robust—not affected by the sample of countries, the measures of class, or the measures of outcomes. Jonathan Kelley and M. D. R. Evans's (1995) study of "class conflict" in six Western democracies (the United States, Great Britain, Australia, Switzerland, Austria, and Germany) uses the 1987–88 "ideology of inequality" module of the International Social Survey Programme.

Recall from Chapter 5 that Kelley and Evans looked at subjective class consciousness in terms of how people placed themselves on a ten-point "scalometer." Americans clustered right in the middle; so did people in all the other countries. Moreover, "middle class" self-images prevailed at all levels of the objective economic hierarchy in all countries.

At the same time the general view in all societies was that class conflict was not absent but was far from intense. (Respondents were asked about the severity of conflicts—a four-point scale—between rich and poor and between the working and middle classes.) Overall, 84 percent saw no or not very strong conflict between the classes; between rich and poor the comparative figure was 54 percent. Ironically enough, the United States had the *highest* level of perceived conflict—ironic because a key aspect of the American exceptionalism thesis is the allegedly muted role of class in American politics compared to that in European politics.

While the results indicate only modest *general* levels of politically charged class consciousness, the further pertinent point for assessing structuration is that objective measures of class per se are at most weakly related to these attitudes. Kelley and Evans simultaneously measure class with a six-group categorization and continuous measures of education, income, and status, allowing comparison in multivariate models of the independent impact of each dimension.[7]

To the extent that "class" matters, the categorical measures of class fare badly. In all countries the multidimensional class model explains a decent amount of variance in class identification (the average is 18 percent, the level in the United States is slightly higher); but family income is generally by far the best predictor, and another continuous measure, education, is generally the next best predictor. The impact of the categorical dimensions of class are much lower: owners, the petty bourgeoisie, and supervisors just aren't very distinctive in their class identification. While some minor discrepancies are discernible between the Anglo-Celtic and Central European nations in the sources of class identification, the basic pattern is "similar," conclude Kelley and Evans.

Even less impressively, objective class, in all of its multidimensional meanings, accounts for little difference in people's perceptions of class conflict (average explained variance being 8.5 percent.) And in all six countries the categorical measures of class—the conceptualization that accords with the sense of class used throughout this volume—are essentially unrelated to perceptions of conflict.

Along with the prevalent "I'm in the middle" view, that condition hardly seems conducive to class-based politics. Indeed, Kelley and Evans show, like many others, that the impacts of class on vote are quite minor. Despite some marginal cross-national differences in the voting inclinations of particular classes, this conclusion holds across the six countries. What distinguishes the Anglo-Celtic nations from the Central European is that in the former *subjective* class and *perceived* class conflict have relatively large (though still modest) impact on voting, while in the latter religious factors are relatively consequential. The net impact of the continuous measures of class is generally irrelevant. In short, there's no sign of the democratic class struggle.

INEQUALITY AND CLASSLESSNESS

A recurrent theme in this volume is that inequality per se does not create classes. At issue is whether the inequalities in a society coalesce so that there are relatively discrete groupings—classes—with distinctive life chances, outlooks, and involvements. That is, inequality and class structuration are *analytically* distinct (see Chapter 3, especially).

A cross-national comparative perspective further suggests that these two dimensions of differentiation are not *empirically* related in any direct way. Inequality may be the ultimate seed bed for structuration, but greater inequality does not appear linked to greater structuration in a cross-sectional light.

The first point to recognize is that advanced capitalist societies do differ, significantly though not radically, in the extent of inequality. Different measures suggest more or less inequality within particular societies, thereby affecting the rank of countries in an international comparison. For our purposes here, however, the data in Table 11.5 are adequate to establish the range of inequality and to roughly place a number of countries within this range.

According to the Luxembourg Income Study (Smeeding, O'Higgins, and Rainwater 1990), family income inequality (gross and net) is relatively pronounced in the United States and Germany (then, only West Germany). Sweden stands out as the most egalitarian society in this seven-country comparison; Norway and the United Kingdom are relatively egalitarian.

Now consider the results of the preceding comparative analysis of class structuration. Although the general point was that a condition of classlessness was approached in all advanced societies (especially in light of the mobility data), some modest variations were apparent. While honoring my earlier commitment to avoid ranking the countries in terms of structuration, I think it's fair to say that on any reasonable index of overall structuration the United States (and Canada) would be on the low end. By comparison, Sweden, despite relatively high mobility, would be at the high end of this index.

TABLE 11.5

The Distribution of Income in Seven Countries

	Canada	United States	United Kingdom	West Germany	Sweden	Norway	Israel
QUINTILE SHARES (PERCENT) OF INCOME							
DISTRIBUTION OF FAMILY GROSS INCOME AMONG QUINTILES OF FAMILIES							
Lowest Quintile	4.6	3.8	4.9	4.4	6.6	4.9	4.5
Second Quintile	11.0	9.8	10.9	10.2	12.3	11.4	10.5
Third Quintile	17.7	16.6	18.2	15.9	17.2	18.4	16.5
Fourth Quintile	25.3	25.3	25.3	22.6	25.0	25.5	24.9
Top Quintile	41.4	44.5	40.8	46.9	38.9	39.8	43.6
Gini Coefficient	37.4	41.2	36.5	42.9	32.9	35.6	39.5
Revised West German Gini				41.4			
DISTRIBUTION OF FAMILY NET INCOME AMONG QUINTILES OF FAMILIES							
Lowest Quintiles	5.3	4.5	5.8	5.0	8.0	6.3	6.0
Second Quintiles	11.8	11.2	11.5	11.5	13.2	12.8	12.1
Third Quintile	18.1	17.7	18.2	15.9	17.4	18.9	17.9
Fourth Quintile	24.6	25.6	25.0	21.8	24.5	25.3	24.5
Top Quintile	39.7	41.0	39.5	45.8	36.9	36.7	39.5
Gini Coefficient	34.8	37.0	34.3	40.9	29.2	31.1	33.8
Revised West German Gini				38.9			

SOURCE: Smeeding et al. (1990): table 2.2. Adapted from Devine (1997): 249).

Recall its relatively high Alford Index score and the modest relationship between class and Wright's class-consciousness scale.

So, at the likely extremes, there's a relatively high inequality/low structuration case (the United States) and a relatively low inequality/high structuration case (Sweden). Does this comparison suggest (perhaps counterintuitively) a general relationship: the *greater* the inequality, the *lesser* the structuration? That question is hard to answer rigorously because the variance in structuration appears limited and is difficult to specify. Yet a number of cases seem to contradict this hypothesis. For one, Germany appears to be one of the more unequal nations, but in some regards structuration is at least relatively pronounced there (e.g., the sociodemographic identity of skilled workers and some relatively high indications of class voting). On the other hand, relatively egalitarian Japan appears to have low structuration, in some ways even lower than in the United States. And Canada, apparently low in structuration like the United States, is somewhat more equal than its southern neighbor.

Obviously this crude cross-sectional analysis doesn't fully consider the relationship between inequality and class structuration, but it should suffice to show that they can operate independently of each other. To understand the forces promoting one is not necessarily to understand the forces promoting the other. That said, however, within particular societies, some movement toward equality may be attributed to the successful political mobilization of the lower classes (notably in the Scandinavian countries). Conversely, the weakening or absence of class-based mobilization among the less well-off may remove a check on inequality-creating forces in the marketplace, thereby aggravating inequality. In any case, as I argue in the concluding chapter, differences in class structuration are unlikely to significantly account for future variations in the contours of inequality simply because the condition of classlessness is so widely approximated.

To suggest that the condition of classlessness has been widely *approximated* is a necessary qualification. My argument isn't absolutist—no signs whatsoever, anywhere, of classes. This brief review does point to some very modest indications of "classness" within a few countries for specific dimensions of structuration. And, perhaps, there's some structuration in the dimensions not considered here because of the unavailability of good comparable data.

Yet it is not essential to show the complete absence of class to undermine class theory. Whatever minor variations across countries may be detected, the overriding common condition cannot be ignored: in no advanced society does class represent an axial division—or even come close to being such a division. In that light, America is not exceptional.

CHAPTER TWELVE

Beyond Class

Here I first summarize this critique of class theory and then consider its implications for how we analyze inequality and for the politics of the future.

I justify this intensive "negative" endeavor on the grounds that we can progress in understanding contemporary inequalities and politics only if we have an arena of intellectual debate that is clear of debilitating ideas. We need a decisive break with the weighty intellectual and ideological baggage of class theory. Once we see that class theory represents a dead end, we won't waste time deciphering the meaning of classical texts, proposing ever more elaborate theoretical justifications of class analysis, or attempting to save it by definitional inflation or new measurement strategies. With this understanding, we can constructively proceed with the difficult task of comprehending our ever more complex social arrangements.

All the negative findings, detailed in the previous chapters, can be briefly summarized. Social science research, unusually so, delivers a quite unambiguous verdict. Considered together, analyses that bear on structuration significantly undermine the foundations of class theory. There's only little need to qualify conclusions, note important exceptions, or attempt to resolve discrepant findings.

This statement itself, though, must be issued with an important proviso. To accept the conclusions of this analysis you must accept four premises:

1. That class, at its core, is an *economically rooted* phenomenon, whether relations to the means of production or market capacities are stressed. As Erik Olin Wright has recently written, "the core of both the Marxist and Weberian traditions of class analysis revolves around the economic content of the concept" (1996: 701)." Class may have cultural or political components or ramifications, but economic roots are essential. Although this mean-

ing of class is consistent with conventional understanding, it is worth insisting upon because some recent analysts—most prominently, Bourdieu—have buried the economic essence of class, definitionally transforming cultural groupings (conventionally called status groups) and many other social groupings into classes. Class theory shouldn't be "saved" by definitional inflation; its distinctive claims, far-reaching but focused, should be assessed.

2. That a *realist* orientation to class analysis is necessary to assess it. That means classes exist only if you can empirically demonstrate that there are relatively discrete, hierarchically ordered social groups, each with distinctive common experiences.

3. That *methodological individualism* must underlie this realist assessment. That means if classes are real, you should be able to identify their "members" and show that these individuals tend to have distinctive experiences.

4. That the five dimensions of *structuration*—inter- and intragenerational mobility patterns, social interaction patterns, cultural orientations, class sentiment, and political action—represent the main features of social life that theorists have used to depict the reality of classes. I should reiterate here that I treat class structuration as a *multidimensional variable*, without according a priori primacy to any dimension, much less insisting that reality of class depends on strong structuration in each dimension. My argument is simply that classes are *more* real as social entities to the extent that structuration is apparent in each of these terms.

These premises are commonplace (though often only implicit), but I readily acknowledge that they aren't universally accepted by class analysts. I've tried to justify these premises at some length in Chapter 2 and won't repeat that discussion here. In any event, I suspect, staunch dissenters from this analytical approach are unlikely to have made it this far in the book. At the metatheoretical level of these premises, there simply aren't unambiguously decisive grounds for resolving differences. Fortunately, most social scientists should agree that the basic evidentiary rules used here are reasonable, providing legitimate grounds for the inquiry.

Here I recapitulate the findings in brief with a special concern for the United States:

1. Classes are not demographically well-formed groups. The "members" of all classes have diverse class origins—to the point, indeed, that substantial majorities of conventionally defined classes were raised in a different

class from their own. Individuals do not usually, much less routinely, inherit their class position: a large majority move out of their family's class, and a good part of this mobility is long-distance, crossing more than one class boundary. While the overall correlation between class origins and destinations is quite modest, intergenerational mobility may be somewhat more regular within both blue-collar and white-collar categories than across them. The analyses on this point are not fully consistent, however, and because this divide is so frequently traversed, it cannot be portrayed as a fundamental barrier delimiting life chances.

It bears repeating that all this mobility largely reflects structural changes in the economy and, concomitantly, the relative size of various classes. The fact that so-called social fluidity is modest speaks to the failure to realize egalitarian ideals, but it is total gross mobility that bears on class structuration. For whatever the *cause* of the mobility, the *result* is that the American class system is not marked by intergenerational social closure. This finding undermines a key tenet of class theory.

What is more, people are far from routinely stuck in the same type of job in their own career. Very often, they "belong" to different classes throughout their lives, a fact that undermines the meaning of "belonging." The professions and some skilled crafts are the partial exceptions, being more closed off than other occupational categories.

2. Class does not substantially shape patterns of social association. To the extent structuration occurs, it may be most evident among an upper middle class of professionals and managers, but because cross-class friendships and neighbors are generally so common, the class system is not socially reinforced as a set of distinct cultural groups.

3. There is little support for the reality of separate class cultures. Middle-class (i.e., white-collar) families may be slightly more inclined than working-class families to value self-direction in their children, but other important aspects of domestic life (including marital relations) appear remarkably similar from top to bottom in the class hierarchy. Moreover, class does not significantly affect a whole host of attitudes on social issues, values and lifestyle tastes, and communal attachments and socializing.

4. The connection between objective class position and class consciousness is weak. And if large numbers cannot place themselves in the "right" class, other indications of class members having common class consciousness are even less discernible.

5. As a predictive variable for political orientations, class position generally accounts for little, and in many respects verges on the irrelevant. At the individual level, class cleavages do not express political cleavages.

So, at least for the United States, it is not a matter of adjudicating among the merits of competing class maps. Goldthorpe, Wright, Giddens, Gilbert and Kahl, and so forth: it doesn't matter; all are deficient. None points to basic fissures that define the contours of social life. Although there are some very modest indications of structuration, they are all just that—modest. And the small cleavages that may mark one dimension of life do not consistently mark others. With such weak and inconsistent results, the reality of classes is elusive. And there is no reason to suspect that the class project can be saved by redrawing the maps, even to include the alleged new classes of the postindustrial order.

My limited comparative analysis suggests that this conclusion *generally* applies to other advanced societies as well, though the evidentiary basis for saying so is admittedly not fully adequate and should be augmented. The most notable (and best documented) indicator of low structuration relates to mobility: in all of these societies, classes are not demographically cohesive groups. Notwithstanding some minor exceptions, the common condition is that members of all classes have highly diverse origins—the result of the great structural mobility that all advanced societies experienced.

The comparative analysis indicates that countries do differ in their structuration for particular dimensions—for example, class effects on consciousness appear relatively pronounced (though modest) in Sweden, even as mobility patterns there point to relatively low structuration. Yet, at least for the dimensions of structuration that I considered, there are no signs of even modest, across-the-board class structuration in any society. Even if the United States and Canada may most closely approximate a condition of classlessness, any American "exceptionalism" seems very limited. Based on the available data, it's impossible to rank nations in terms of their structuration; in any case, it's likely to be an exercise in ordering minor differences. The larger point is that classes do not seem to vitally persist in any highly differentiated, technologically sophisticated economy.

Admittedly, this no-classes argument rests on a fairly strong test of what constitutes a class and a not fully complete evidentiary base. Not all "maps" were subject to an equally full battery of tests. Yet the central claim of class theory is itself strong, namely, that class is a fundamental stratifying force. If that is so, fairly consistent evidence for structuration should appear for at least some of its dimensions. Some studies that I'm unaware of may cloud the picture, but the accumulated weight of the many analyses reviewed here is a lot for class theorists to explain away.

Nor is it compelling to show that there are some minor "class effects" on a particular outcome and then claim validation of some modest version of class theory. That "validation" essentially demotes class to being just one variable—often a minor one—in a large set of "social location" variables that have some explanatory power. If that's the case, why do we need a distinctive *theory* of class? We don't elaborate separate theories for other aspects of social location—e.g., age, education, family structure, region, and so on—that have predictive ability, often greater than that of class. Such a defense of class theory "saves" it only by lowering the bar so low that virtually nothing is gained by retaining it.

My challenge to class theorists is this: what body of research suggests that class structuration in any dimension is substantial?

THE IDEOLOGY OF IT ALL

I've made my case on empirical grounds and my challenge invites rebuttals in kind. Yet because the conclusion is so ideologically charged, I don't and can't expect that empirical social science will be the sole arbitrator. The intersection of the empirical and the normative deserves further comment.

As this project entered its later phases, I increasingly wondered if this analysis could possibly persuade those predisposed to see a very different world—that is, a world structured and animated by class. Of course, I had doubts from the beginning of the project, and not primarily because I questioned whether the data were on my side as much as they initially appeared to be, or whether I could persuasively marshal the evidence to make the case. More fundamentally, I questioned whether those intellectually sympathetic to class theory, and its typically related political sentiments, were persuadable.

It's no news to say that class analysis is politically charged. As I noted in the introductory chapter, the Marxian legacy (including social democratic "reformism") looms large: a humane, just society is to be realized through the successful struggle of the exploited class(es). And, it's fair to say, class theorists generally see themselves as supporting the cause of underdogs. So, a no-class thesis seems to undermine the left's hopes for social transformation: the historically anointed agent of change has disappeared. The critique of class theory, then, implies more than a dispute about "facts," a matter of disinterested scholarly contention. Very often, it has implications for what people think the world *should* be like, their sense of social possibilities, and even their personal identity. In the face of such commitments on life-defining matters, the magnitudes of regression coefficients are unlikely to be a decisive concern.

Of course, those who believe in class theory are not distinctive in recognizing as Truth what they want to be so. I can readily imagine that conservative readers will be more readily persuaded by my "insight" than their counterparts on the left. After all, with few exceptions, conservatives don't defend the existence of classes. They want to deny the reality of classes, both to confirm to themselves the "goodness" of the arrangements they seek to conserve and to undercut challenges to these arrangements. In short, it may be comforting for conservatives to read my argument.

Now, perhaps I'm forced to say, so be it: there's no escaping the crucible of ideology on this issue. In some quarters, that might even be considered an admirable postmodernist response. Many postmodernists tell us that no account—no matter its claim to scientific procedures or evidence—is ultimately privileged over any other. All we can do is tell stories, relying on various rhetorical devices, that may or may not be deemed persuasive in different social circles. We may *want* to say "We're right and they're wrong," but we're pursuing an epistemological illusion if we do so.

I disagree, as I'm sure you would infer by now. I write as a social scientist with the belief that there is an objective reality to discern, that we can meaningfully though provisionally refer to facts, and that scientific procedures can more reliably lead us to these facts than any other method. The related faith is that people can be persuaded by evidence—even if it is somehow discomforting. Still, analysts don't and can't fully check their ideology and personal convictions at the door when they enter the hall of social science. Neither science nor scientists are inhuman. Yet the humanity of the scientific enterprise doesn't lead us into a relativistic abyss. What's critical to maintain is an intellectual space in which concerns for objective evidence have a *relatively* prominent role. For the analysis of class, that space can be promoted by at least partially decoupling empirical claims about class from political stances.

First, keep in mind that the absence of class doesn't mean we have an equal or just society. The distinction between inequality and class structuration, emphasized throughout this book, is critical here. Our inequalities of income and wealth translate into disparate experiences of almost unimaginable comfort and constant struggles for survival. Even if these inequalities are not structured in class terms, the reality in itself can surely provoke critical judgments about our social arrangements. And, by the same token, that reality provides a serious challenge to conservative defenses of these arrangements. Justice is still at stake.

Second, keep in mind that the absence of class doesn't mean the end of social conflict, even on distributional matters. Of course, without classes, it's impossible to have anything that could be meaningfully described as class conflict, but antagonisms between smaller and transitory economically rooted groups are likely to remain socially significant. Indeed, with the pressures of a hypercompetitive global economy and the emergence of technologies that make protest relatively easy, I expect these conflicts to be recurrent. I will postpone discussing the politics of our classless inequality until a later section of this chapter. Suffice it to say here, to the possible comfort of political "progressives," the grievances of underdog groups could temporarily coalesce into a larger agenda of egalitarian reform.

In brief, the left shouldn't emotionally reject the no-classes theses on the grounds that it implies, incorrectly, the realization of a just society or the end of political struggle with progressive potential. And the right shouldn't embrace the thesis as confirmation of their view that justice has arrived and that distributional politics have been transcended. All sides in the ideological struggles must recognize the reality of a highly unequal, classless society if they are to be politically successful in their own light.

WHAT IS TO BE DONE?

My task as critic of class theory is essentially complete. Yet, of course, critics face their own challenge: so, what's the alternative? My simple answer is that there is no alternative in the sense of some single unified conceptual perspective that makes sense of contemporary social hierarchies. That's what class theory purported to do, but it failed to account for the complexities of social life. These complexities must be matched by varied perspectives.

One of the defining themes of postmodern thought is that the Grand

Narratives are no longer compelling. Much of class theory, especially its Marxian variants, embodies some kind of grand narrative—suggesting, as an extreme example, that human emancipation will be realized through class conflict and by its eventual transcendence. But class theory doesn't fail just because its grand narratives haven't played out. (Nor do its failures at this level validate all the pronouncements of postmodernists.) As noted in the introductory chapter, not all class theory involves a theory of history, but all class theory does claim that class is the main axis (or at least one of the main axes) of differentiation. Its failures occur as well at this much more modest but still significant level: classes don't structure social life. Therefore, debates about their place in theories of history are largely moot. Class theory, as I've tested it in the preceding chapters, represents only a Great Simplification— summary statements about the substantially life-defining impact of a few economic distinctions.

At this point let me cite again Jencks's insight: "We use class labels precisely because we want to make the world tidier than it is." It's appealing to say something like "He's upper-middle-class" and presume, then, to have a good fix on his political orientations, cultural tastes, and likely social background. Such shorthand conveniently places the complexities of many lives in comprehensible terms. At the macro level, this shorthand also promises to explain the underlying foundations of political life—struggles among a few, relatively permanent and cohesive "blocs" of contestants. Yet however rhetorically convenient or ideologically appealing, this Great Simplification comes at the cost of fundamentally misrepresenting the world. To say, for instance, someone is upper-middle-class really doesn't mean that she has distinctive politics, cultural commitments, or the like. The shorthand doesn't work.

To be sure, parsimony is to be prized in the scientific enterprise; but as social scientists, our primary commitment must be to validity. If reality stubbornly resists being represented by some general principles, then theory must yield. We have reached that juncture with class theory.

In the introductory chapter I suggested that the major theoretical alternative to class theory is stratification theory. Recall that this perspective claims: (1) there are multiple dimensions of social hierarchy, (2) each of the hierarchies has many levels of rank (essentially a continuous distribution), and (3) rank on these different dimension of hierarchy is not tightly linked. The further presupposition is that ranks are socially consequential. This perspective surely provides no grand narrative, and its "simplifications" are less encompassing and analytically driven than class theory. Although continua of income, education, and occupational prestige hold central place in many analyses, they do so only because they often "work" as explanatory variables—and because they are readily measurable. There's no theoretical reason to focus on these three dimensions, nor not to expand the number of dimensions of hierarchy in the analysis.

Even so, we should give proper due to the fact that the stratification theory does "work" in the sense that its measures account for variance in many matters of social consequences. This conclusion partly emerges from many of the multivariate models that I've cited to assess the net impact of class. Just recall, for example, Locksley's findings (Chapter 7) that education, not class, is related to the nature of marital relations; Jackman and Jackman's demonstration (Chapter 5) that several continuous measures of status are substantially related to class identification and categorical measures of class are not; Robinson and Kelley's (Chapter 6) finding of the same for a host of political matters; and Kohn's research (Chapter 7) showing the notable connections among socioeconomic status (primarily education), a continuous measure of occupational self-direction, and parental valuation of self-direction for their children (also continuous).

This conclusion also emerges from other work that directly assesses the tenets of stratification theory, especially Richard Curtis and Elton Jackson's insufficiently appreciated *Inequality in American Communities* (1977). Considered together, this work points to an interesting pattern:

> ranks in the various dimensions of hierarchy are only modestly linked to each other;
>
> there's no "master" general dimension of rank; depending on the matter to be explained, the varying dimensions of rank differ in their relative explanatory power;
>
> the associations between measures of rank and a wide range of behaviors and attitudes are generally linear and additive;
>
> and (a matter that sociologists prefer not to acknowledge) while these associations are pervasive, they are rarely strong and commonly weak.

Such findings indicate that using composite measures of SES may well mask distinctive social processes. Parental education, for instance, seems to have greater effect on school performance than parental income; the reverse seems to hold for attendance at elite colleges. The multidimensionality of social hierarchy should be represented in statistical models. And given the typical linearity and additivity of "effects," regression-based models serve this purpose well, though we shouldn't automatically "default" to linear specifications without considering theoretically derived interactive formulations as well.

Substantively, these findings challenge analysts to develop an integrated understanding of social organization that reflects the impact of multiple hierarchies on diverse features of social life. Yet, if this general understanding of social organization is to be complete, it must incorporate more than continuous measures of economic hierarchy. Obviously the categorical distinctions based on gender, race, and citizenship must be taken into account, including their interaction with the hierarchies of money, prestige, and education. More than that, the minisolidarities of some work situations and localities, along with the identity-forming impact of many cultural groupings, command attention. Indeed, the significance of culturally based strata—formed by shifting configurations among those sharing common value commitments, aesthetic and consumption tastes, and cognitive orientations—seems likely to become ever greater.

My confident prediction is that any accurate depiction of this evolving structure will frustrate our desire for intellectual tidiness. We confront a social order marked by intersecting hierarchies of economic rank and fragmented, changing constellations of cultural strata. Pakulski and Waters vividly highlight the complexity:

> The stratification categories constitute a complex mosaic of taste subcultures, "new associations," civic initiatives, ethnic and religious revolutionary groups, generational cohorts, community action groups, new social movements, gangs, alternative production organizations, educational alumni, racial brotherhoods, gender sisterhoods, tax rebels, fundamentalist and revivalist religious movements, Internet discussion groups, purchasing co-ops, professional associations, and so on. (1996: 157)

Quite an eclectic brew! Their general account of historical transformation may overemphasize the self-created cultural dimension of the emerging stratification system and underemphasize the impact of economic factors, including their constraining impact on cultural commitments. Still, the crucial point remains that the social structure is complexly differentiated and that even the multidimensionality of stratification theory must be augmented by attention to cultural groupings.

THE PAST AND FUTURE

To this point, consistent with my announced intentions in the introductory chapter, my analysis has sidestepped the issue of whether classes *died*—that is, did we once have class structuration that has now essentially disappeared? To repeat, I'm inclined to say so, despite the fact that the necessary materials to make a convincing, full-fledged case on the matter aren't available. In *The Death of Class*, Pakulski and Waters plausibly argue that class died "somewhere between the beginning of the twentieth century and the end of the Great Depression" (26), even if a transformed sort of class remained through the first three-quarters of the century. That was the time of "organized-class society" in which the political sphere dominated. In this later stage of capitalism, they argue, classes were essentially economic entities organized by political forces. Their argument rests on the contention that class was the product of simple market-driven capitalism and died with the economic and political transformations within advanced capitalism. Though largely conjectural, this argument is supported by analyses of the two rounds of the Middletown studies. Comparison of Middletown in the 1920s and in the 1970s suggest, in an unusually rigorous way, the past significance of classes and their current insignificance (Lynd and Lynd 1929, 1937; and Caplow and Chadwick 1979). However, whatever the merits of this argument, you don't need to accept any judgment about a complex, disputed history to evaluate my analysis of current classlessness.

That said, this current condition is the expectable outcome of specific socioeconomic developments. Here I briefly highlight three developments that undermine class structuration: (1) economic differentiation, (2) high levels of inter- and intragenerational mobility, and (3) the widespread availability of transportation and information technologies that break down local solidarities. The crucial point to recognize here is that the formation of classes depends on *similarity* of experience—similarities in workplace and labor-market experiences, and similarities as well in related community-based experiences. The common significance of these three developments is that they increase the *diversity* of experiences, thus undermining class structuration.

Economic Differentiation

Admittedly, this often-invoked term has a vague quality about it, but it is a convenient way to allude to a set of specific transformations in the organization of work that bear directly on the issue of class. Concretely, differentiation means the great proliferation of occupations and work tasks in an economy producing ever more products and services, often involving technologies that require or at least encourage a complex division of labor. The upshot is wide intra- and cross-occupational variations in work conditions (authority, physical amenities, security of employment, skill demands, and prospects of advancement) and monetary rewards, including the provision of benefits. As I remarked before, the world of pin makers and owners of pin-making factories has long been eclipsed. The 1977 *Dictionary of Occupational Titles* lists more than 12,000 separate jobs; the Census Bureau in 1990 listed 503 detailed occupations.

To be sure, all the assembly-line workers at some factory or all the data enterers at a large file-processing unit may have common work experiences, as did Smith's pin makers; but more typically workers are employed at establishments which have a complex or flexible division of labor and many layers of responsibility. In contemporary workplaces, employees don't typically have authority *or* lack it; they have varying degrees of it. They don't exercise judgment and skill *or* not; they have highly varying opportunities to do so. Concomitantly, their pay is finely gradated, even within clusters of jobs that share the same occupational title. In other words, many dimensions of work that determine its presumed class-character are often more or less continuous, not categorical as presumed in class schemas.

While the trend is toward increasing complexity in the overall division of labor, it is also pertinent to note that work organizations themselves are increasingly variable. They vary in size, the extent of hierarchy, the operation of internal labor markets, and the distribution of rewards for particular types of work—among other matters that affect the work experience. As a result, all those people who work as, say, a midlevel manager—at Intel, the 7-Eleven outlet, the University of Virginia, and the local widget factory—seem almost more united by a label than common work experiences. And the same is often true for other occupational groupings that are deemed the backbone of specific classes.

In short, in wealthy societies like the United States the economy requires a complex division of labor, and this complexity generally undermines the widespread similarity of condition that promotes class structuration. Employees at all levels can often perceive many differences in work experiences and only limited commonalities with their coworkers—at their own workplace and at others. To the extent that workers can see common interests, it is with others in the same narrow occupational group—a phenomenon seemingly confined to some professions and skilled crafts (more on this below). Neither class sentiments nor political appeals to class interests are likely to resonate in this context.

Mobility

In Chapter 4, I detailed the high level of inter- and intragenerational occupational mobility. Recall again that most people, by a large margin, did not have a job within the same broad occupational category as their father. I argued that the mobility patterns were a key *indicator*, perhaps even the most significant, of low structuration. Yet as Goldthorpe and others have contended, some persisting sociodemographic coherence seems to be the bedrock condition for class formation in other respects. Social mobility is, then, both an indicator of structuration and a *causal* factor, affecting other dimensions of structuration. I made this point as well in Chapter 2, but it's worth reiterating here.

Because so many people themselves have been mobile, they've been unlikely to develop a sense of common fate with others in similar economic circumstances. What I've called class sentiment (Chapter 5) is likely to develop only if people in the same "class location" have lasting common experiences at work, and if they have sustained interaction with others in the same location. A strong sense of "we-ness" can't be forged if class location is commonly transient, a temporary station in life for people with varying backgrounds and varying prospects.

Mobility also undermines distinctive class-based cultural practices and political commitments. Both the reality of mobility in many lives and the perception that mobility is commonplace would seem to foster an outward-looking disposition—in effect, the sense that "my present isn't my destiny." The reference group for the mobile may not be their present intimates in the workplace or community. What's more, occupational mobility often means concrete changes that undermine group solidarity—for example, interacting with one set of people at work and different sorts of people in a neighborhood. With mobility, the occupation-based "message" about how to act and what to value is less consistent, less often reinforced—and hence less life-defining.

This is not to argue that we now have low structuration because we now have greater mobility than in the past. Judgments about the historical trajectory on mobility are open to question. Yet it seems fair to say that the extent of mobility has always been substantial. And because class solidarities depend on the persistence of conditions in people's lives, mobility has been and remains the great solvent of class structuration.

Technological Change

The widespread availability of informational and transportation technologies has had the cumulative effect of reducing the impact of localistic, face-to-face attachments in people's lives. Prior to television, one's source of "news" and awareness of the larger world was largely confined to the local newspaper and those in one's immediate personal network, primarily co-workers and neighbors. Prior to the telephone, one's social world was also largely confined to immediate contacts. And prior to the emergence of the car culture, many people were trapped in their own localities: their workplace, home, and local community circumscribed their world.

These technologies allowed people, more than ever before, to quite literally reach out and touch more people's lives, to have more diverse experiences, to cultivate different outlooks. To be sure, work experiences do still spill over into other aspects of people's lives. Yet work- and community-based networks became less necessarily definitive; people could readily experience more of the world. And because of that, work-based "messages" could only prove less compelling in defining one's social place, values, and commitments.

At the same time, the fact that these were *mass* technologies in itself broke down class distinctions. Everyone watched the same sitcoms and saw middle-class lives portrayed. Everyone could get on the highway and drive to the beach or the shopping center. And everyone could contemplate living far from work.

These developments promoting a diversity of experience, in the workplace and outside it, are unlikely to be reversed. Braverman's (1974) de-skilling argument hasn't withstood critical scrutiny; with the emergence of post-Fordist tendencies in work organization, marked by new technologies and more flexible organizational forms, the trend is toward a wider range of workplace experiences. Standardized production systems, which require many people to perform essentially the same job and hence are conducive to class structuration, will become an ever less prominent feature of the national economy.

Of course some people complain about the impersonality of digital communications, the ecological degradations occasioned by the car culture, the cultural barrenness of mass media, and the like. But the use of technologies that break down the dominance of localistic attachments continues unabated. We don't face the death of local community, but we have pervasively incorporated technologies into our lives that undermine the centrality of work-related community and create possibilities for communities being constructed on other bases.

The preceding argument draws, with a broad brush, the main developments that undermine class structuration. Yet, as I previously noted, group structure does not fully dissolve in the contemporary organization of work. Occupational solidarities, a notable instance of this countertrend, deserve attention now. And the very developments that break down many local work-connected solidarities also create or reinforce other local solidarities—a matter considered in the section "Postclass Politics."

OCCUPATIONAL SOLIDARITIES

Not only do some occupation-based solidarities persist in the highly differentiated contemporary economy, but new economic structures may actually promote some circumscribed solidarities in some particular sectors. The increasing professionalization of many economic tasks is an obvious case of this countertrend: economic groups with specific competencies consciously organize themselves, across work sites, to further their economic position. Credentialing and licensing are familiar, often successful strategies of exclusionary practices to achieve control over particular task niches—for example, prescribing drug treatments for illnesses (physicians); providing advice about how to realize unearned income (certified investment planners); wiring large manufacturing complexes (master electricians); and distributing economically valuable credentials (college faculty). The resulting "occupational closure" produces common economic interests and, perhaps, a sense of work-based identity.

Similarly, to the extent that post-Fordist developments incorporate a renewed role for artisan-like work, occupational solidarities may also increase. Like their predecessors, new-wave artisans have a collective incentive to promote their craft and cultivate appreciation of their distinctive skills. At the same time, some occupational solidarities seem to flourish for "old-fashioned" reasons: long, grueling training (the military); common tasks performed in geographically remote locales (fisherman and miners); and the self-selection of those with strong, unconventional tastes and access to related networks (actors and artists) (Grusky and Sorensen 1998).

At issue, however, is (1) how pervasive and life-defining any such occupational solidarities are, and (2) whether they represent even weak forms of *class* structuration.

The answer to the first question is that we really don't know. Impressionistically, it seems fair to say that the few very strong professions (e.g., physicians) have a relatively well developed sense of common economic interest and job identity; but even here, significant fractures appear (private practitioners/HMO employees, primary-care providers/specialists), and the extent to which job-related identities spill over to distinctive political commitments and cultural orientations is uncertain. Also, *most* professions can only hope to be strong; their occupational solidarity seems limited. Yes, occupational therapists may collectively strive to increase the market value and prestige of their services, but is there any reason to believe that they have substantial solidarities that go beyond their job-based concerns? The doubts that may apply to occupational therapists surely extend to most other professional groups.

The actual extent of a crafts revival in the post-Fordist economy is also questionable. What has occurred in the small businesses of north-central Italy—the most cited exemplar of new-wave artisanry—could possibly be a harbinger of more general developments. Yet proponents of this argument tend to be vague about the numbers involved at the national level, in the United States and elsewhere; there's no evidence that the new craftsmen represent more than a limited alternative form of work organization in the larger economy.

So, now consider the implications for class theory of the argument that, at the highly disaggregate level, some solidarities arise in the production process. Grusky and Sorensen argue that occupations have taken on "classlike" characteristics, especially insofar as they pursue exclusionary practices which in effect create the extraction of rent—and hence a collective economic interest. Occupations are involved, then, in processes of exploitation, as aggregate classes are often depicted.

Let's grant the argument that exclusionary practices do largely take place at the disaggregate level—among actuaries, say, and not among some larger grouping of professionals. That assumption seems sensible: after all, the material interests linking actuaries, social workers, and civil engineers are hard to discern. Let's also accept that the case for classlike occupations is strongest for the elite professions and skilled crafts, and that evidence of other classlike occupations is sparse at best. At the same time, let's keep in mind, as I just noted, that such classlike occupations represent only a small part of the workforce.

The upshot is a somewhat peculiar sense of the "class system": many, many classes exist *and* most people are classless. Of course, all the specific professions or occupational groups that pursue their narrow economic interests can be called classes, but that seems to depart from the conventional meaning. Class theories presuppose, as I argued in the introductory chapter, that the stratification system most fundamentally consists of a small set of distinct groups, defined and ordered by their economic position. That is, the fundamental units in the stratification system are relatively large aggregations. Class theory presumes that these aggregations fundamentally structure individual and collective life.

This is more than definitional quibble. Crucially, conventional class theory argues that a small number of economically based divisions are axial and broadly consequential; its analytical power rests on that claim, irrespective of its roots in Marxist or Weberian thought (Pakulski and Waters 1996). To see narrow occupational solidarities as classes is to envision a highly pluralistic economic structure with limited implications for social and political life. That extreme pluralism contradicts the reductionism inherent in class theory. Marx's famous exhortation to workers encompasses much more than "Trial lawyers of the country unite, you have nothing to lose but your contingency fees," or "Licensed clinical social workers of the state unite, you have nothing to lose but coverage in managed care plans."

Rather than becoming caught up in the metaphorical resonance of class language, then, it seems more sensible to directly recognize highly disaggregate economic solidarities for what they are—*occupation*-based solidarities. This is so even if occupations successfully pursue exploitive closure practices. By stressing that some solidarities may emerge from the organization of the workplace, Grusky and Sorensen valuably question unqualified assertions of the destructuring effects of contemporary work practices and the often related contention that all solidarities are now cultural. How pervasive and consequential these occupational groupings turn out to be is still a matter for empirical investigation. But no matter how many disaggregate occupations display solidarity, their existence "saves" class theory only by rather substantial definitional inflation.

WAITING FOR CLASS?

That classes are not now notably evident would seem to argue strongly against their emergence in the coming years. Yet class theorists might rejoin that the structural arrangements of capitalism embody the inherent *potential* for class formation, that its absence doesn't preclude its future. The distinction between class structure and class formation may be appealing in some political quarters because it offers hope that even if the presumed agents of progressive change have not appeared, they could emerge to fulfill this role.

Wright's exploitation-based class theory, at least in principle, sustains that hope. Underlying his class schema is the claim that each class "location" is embedded in a particular constellation of exploitive relations—and that people who are similarly situated thereby have a common objective interest in appropriating for themselves the losses they suffer because of the exploitation (see "A Discursus on Wright's Logic," Chapter 3). Presumably, at some point, those interests will generate class formation.

Of course the obvious question is this: why are we still waiting? If the structurally rooted exploitation is so fundamental, shouldn't we expect to see corresponding social divisions in the way people live? The case for the future of class must rest on the dubious claim that current socioeconomic trends are inhospitable but will be reversed.

Recall my prior argument that the formation of classes depends on similarity of experience—in the workplace, labor market, and community. This similarity is undermined in a society marked by increasing economic differentiation, high levels of occupational mobility, and widespread availability of technological and transportation technologies. The absence of class, then, is the predictable consequence of social conditions in advanced capitalism.

No one can plausibly argue that these conditions are likely to be reversed so that some greater similarity of experiences comes to be the rule. Yes, some narrow occupation-based solidarities may emerge, but the larger, general differentiation in economic organization continues apace. Ever more available information and transportation technologies provide an increasing diversity of experience. So, in effect, the very same general conditions that undermine class in the present also preclude its future.

More specifically, in the production process itself, future conditions would appear extremely unlikely to generate class formation. Wright created categorical divisions of skill and authority, with associated particular "interests," only by imposing crude and somewhat arbitrary distinctions on a complex reality. Pay, work conditions, future prospects—all of these vary greatly depending on the many levels of skill and authority that mark so many workplaces and occupations. Each of the boxes in Wright's schema that define "interests" include diverse sorts of workers; they also separate workers who are little different from each other.

Under these circumstances, consider workers who are "exploiters" by virtue of their high skill and are partially "exploited" by virtue of their limited authority (Wright calls them "expert supervisors"; see Table 3.1a). How probable is it that these workers could even perceive the complex "contradictory" nature of their position in terms of exploitive relations, much less be moved by it to bond with others who face the same contradictions? For people to rationally calculate their interests as Wright supposes, they must take on a very complex task, requiring abstract calculations about the "rents" they receive and the "appropriations" of their labor that they suffer. The world of Marxist game theory doesn't readily translate into everyday consciousness and action. Workers might sensibly calculate that their interest is to get more authority and skill themselves, and that their location in the production process is not life-defining in many social realms. Any theoretically created potential for class structuration loses force in the face of real-life conditions, in the workplace and outside it.

POSTCLASS POLITICS

Francis Fukuyama (1992) has famously proclaimed the end of history. Essentially he means that, with the triumph of liberal-democratic forms of market society throughout the world, ideological conflict has been resolved. Capitalism has won; communism is no longer an appealing alternative. At this very general level he is undoubtedly correct. Yet the end of general ideological conflict doesn't mean that distributional disputes have been transcended in a triumphant capitalist order or that all politics is now cultural. Such is the tempting conclusion in the absence of class: because the presumed agents of distributional politics no longer have a part on the historical stage, the related conflicts dissipate with their exit.

However, despite the absence of class, the politics of the future is likely to be conflictual, involving both distributional and cultural issues. It may not be a politics that promises fundamental challenge to the capitalist order, but the political future seems destined to be, at times, intense and strenuously contested, fought on multiple fronts, and organized on many social bases.

Surely cultural politics will have a prominent role, and these political divisions are no less conflictual than class struggles. As is readily evident, identities related to, *inter alia*, race, gender, sexual orientation, religious commitments, citizenship, lifestyle pursuits, artistic preference, and environmental attitudes have great political resonance. The gay-rights activist is often no less committed to political change than the union organizer, nor is the Latino community leader, the prolife/prochoice believer, the NRA member, or the fundamentalist Christian. Indeed, the passions of culture—rooted in visible identities like race and sex or chosen identities like religion that are reinforced by intense interaction—may frequently exceed those associated with economic interest. And they may be less amenable to compromise.

Because so many groups have the means—organizational, technological, and financial—to press their cause within an accommodating political structure, there are good prospects of an ever increasing number of cultural contestants and a continuing failure to resolve existing struggles. In effect, the result is contentious cultural gridlock. Ironically enough, some of the technologies that have undercut class solidarities have also been activated to mobilize nonclass, cultural solidarities. The culturally like-minded—animal rights activists or fundamentalist Christians, say—can readily travel to see each other, communicate electronically, build imagined communities through the media and mass mailings, and press their cause in many distant arenas with these same technologies.

However, the rise of cultural politics doesn't mean the corresponding end, or even decline, of economic struggles—the equivalent of a zero-sum game. This is so despite the fact that class divisions don't structure the political arena. Consider, for example, these distributional issues:

> Entitlement programs for the elderly. The division of interest here is significantly generational.

> Regulation of communications technologies. A significant part of the ensuing conflict is *intra*business: firms competing for access to publicly controlled resources such as television frequencies. Another part, however, represents a split between general consumer interests and the profit concerns of specific firms.

> Maternity policies for employed women. Matters such as protected and paid leaves involve direct costs and control over the terms of the labor contract. The presumed "business interest" here is to minimize labor costs and preserve flexibility. Yet both female and male workers and their families at all levels of the job hierarchy can benefit from accommodating policies. Neither class or gender clearly structure this issue; indeed, the division of interest here can't be reduced to any particular social fault line.

All of these distributional issues are overtly political in the direct sense that national legislative bodies and governmental agencies have been directly involved, but they have been propelled by economic divisions that aren't rooted in class. And as many cultural groups have done, the economic contestants can use all the new technologies to make their concerns part of the national agenda.

At the same time, localized economic disputes also have a political dimension—a group struggle for benefits—that can't be readily classified in class terms. Again, let me make the point through examples:

> Out-sourcing particular functions within an enterprise. Obviously the "losers" are all the workers (including managers) in a functional area who have their jobs exported to another firm; the "winners" are the management of the out-sourcing firm who presumably reduce costs *and* the workers and the managers at the firm that now provides the service. Perhaps in some abstract sense all employees, as a "class," have an interest in controlling their jobs, but the conflict here seems much more directly a matter of inter-firm competition than class conflict.

Providing benefits to adjunct faculty members. The interests of these professionals run up against administrators' cost-cutting concerns (and tenure-track faculty members' interests in maximizing their own allocation). Adjuncts' interests reflect the distressed condition of a segment of an occupation; they and part-timers in myriad other occupations don't constitute a class just because they are all poorly treated in benefits programs.

Securing professional recognition and access to employment opportunities. Health professionals like podiatrists and dentists lobby to have their services included within managed-care plans. They seek some of the rewards accruing to physicians; plan managers incorporate nonphysician services only insofar as doing so enhances their market position. These health professionals have an occupational interest, not a larger class interest.

What these few examples are meant to show is that distributional issues—fought out in the national political arena and many localities—don't disappear with the end of history in Fukuyama's sense or of classes. It should tax no one's imagination to multiply, almost endlessly, related instances. I risk stating the obvious here because the prominence of cultural matters in many fashionable postmodernist accounts seems to unduly downplay the continuing significance of economic concerns.

The politics of distributional matters, nonetheless, can become complexly intertwined with the politics of race and gender, among other matters. What has all the initial appearance of an economic dispute can be propelled by the dynamics of race or gender; and what has all the initial appearance of a cultural dispute may well turn on the pursuit of narrow economic interest.

Consider the following political controversies as illustrations of this general point.

The Politics of Work: A Case

As I write this section, so-called comp-time legislation has emerged as a controversial issue. It would allow workers to receive time off for overtime work rather than the now-mandated extra pay. However it becomes resolved, an economic distributional matter is clearly at stake, control over the terms of the labor contract with implications for the cost of labor.

Advocates argue that such legislation would provide an attractive choice to many time-pressed workers who would prefer opportunities for extra leisure and time with their families instead of a larger paycheck. It's promoted as family-friendly policy. Republicans initially pushed the idea, and

Democrats soon responded with their own proposal that preserved the core idea while tipping the terms of the choice to workers' advantage. Both parties clearly recognized that family-friendly policies can generate political goodwill, especially with female voters. Republicans are mindful that they have been on the wrong side of the gender gap; Democrats seek to maintain their advantage.

The revealing point is that neither business interests nor organized labor had called for such legislation. Gender politics has driven this distributional issue. Indeed, organized labor has to date opposed such legislation largely on the grounds that employers would pressure workers to accept time off in lieu of pay and that pay is generally preferable for workers. Perhaps so, but it seems likely that workers, as a group, have divided perspectives. Many salaried workers, especially women, want and can afford the luxury of time. A class-rooted workers' "interest," much less a unity of political preference, is hard to discern, even though many workers' lives would be significantly affected.

Business interests, predictably enough, have favored legislation allowing employers to choose whether employees get paid in time or money, but their involvement appears to be reactive, and their position appears to be politically untenable. Even if legislators seek to accommodate either the unions or business lobbyists (competing proposals tilt in expectable directions), they seem to recognize the gain of bypassing class politics in favor of gender politics.

A Vignette of Culture and Economics

"Politics and art and culture really don't mix very well," said Samuel Sachs II at the end of his service as director of the Detroit Institute of Arts (Bradesher 1997: B6). His museum and Detroit's new Museum of African-American History have been caught in the vortex of racial and cultural politics in that beleaguered city. The Institute of Arts, a public institution since 1919, has largely been supported by wealthy suburban white benefactors, though it has also received municipal support. It's now financially pressed and literally crumbling. However, the city floated large bonds to finance the Museum of African-American History—an impressive edifice by all accounts. Coleman Young, the black mayor for almost two decades, was a driving force behind this effort.

Yet this is not a simple tale of racial politics: politically victorious
African-Americans getting their "cultural spoils" after supplanting a white
establishment. The complication is that the traditional private benefactors of
the Institute of Art proposed to take on full responsibility for its daily management (with the city retaining ownership of the property), but the city
council rejected this financially attractive proposal. The council was strongly
influenced by union pressures. The museum's sixty-four unionized workers
(guards, janitors, maintenance personnel) strongly protested out of fear of
losing their civil-service status; however, they pressed their case by arguing
that a valuable cultural resource should not be given to white suburbanites.
Bret Ceriotti, Sr., the white union steward, said, "The race issue was made
the key role." Yet in an odd twist, Kay Everett, chair of city council at the
session, publicly pronounced, "I am for the proletariat, I am not for the
bourgeoisie." That is, the union invoked race on behalf of its members' economic interests, and the local politician invoked class even though matters
of race probably had broader resonance with her constituency.

Although Everett's Euro-class lingo is odd in an American municipal
hall, this case illustrates that local economic disputes of a classically distributional nature can become inseparably linked to racial-cultural politics.
Neither seems clearly decisive here, nor is either clearly derivative of the
other. Yet this dispute reminds us that all is not culture, even in the cultural
realm; economic divisions have consequence.

Postclass politics, then, is likely to be contentious, involving many cultural
and (often local) economic disputes. The demise of class politics doesn't
usher in an era of social harmony. What the absence of class means, however, is that political life loses any prospect of a central driving logic—large
groups consistently squared off against each other in struggles over fundamental matters like the largesse of the welfare state or general business prerogatives. This logic has collapsed with an increasing multitude of disputes
involving shifting constellations of social forces. Perhaps some general im-
pulse to the universal extension of personal rights may be considered the
logic of modernity, but even it collides with forces promoting the distinctiveness of particular social solidarities and group rights. As a result, the trajectory of political change appears unpredictable, though the arena of conflict appears ever more restricted to disputes *within* a capitalist order.

CAPITALISM TRIUMPHANT

Capitalism is now triumphant throughout the world. Loved or hated, it has no serious competitors. State-dominated economies have given way, in a dramatic global rush, to privatization and an increasing role for market-driven processes. This victory can be largely attributed to the fact that capitalist economics have delivered the goods better than any alternative. Although the argument that socialism has never been tried may have some scholarly meaning, it fails in the crucible of everyday lives.

As a socioeconomic order, capitalism appears ever more firmly entrenched partly *because* class structuration is so weak. With weak class structuration, the likelihood of a political challenge to the capitalist order is undercut. All history has never been the history of class conflict, but without some solidarity in their ranks, all the "losers" in capitalism pose a lesser political threat to the fundamental tenets of the system. This is not to argue that all the "losers" are somehow blind to their own "true interests" in radical change. Rather, it is simply to say that any challenge to capitalist tenets, however improbable, is most likely to emanate from the relatively disadvantaged and that this disparate group now lacks the social cohesion to take advantage of its numbers. Of course politics has rarely been a matter of direct mass participation—the dispossessed literally going to the barricades—but without some underlying solidarity to draw on, activist elites cannot effectively invoke a "class agenda" as a political resource.

The increasing economic inequalities in our classless era are a dramatic illustration of this general point. The very absence of class forces undermines an important check on the inequalities inevitably generated in the marketplace. Although the causes of rising inequality are multiple and hard to specify, they surely include the dissolution of organized labor and class-based parties as a counterweight to market forces. Without classes, capitalism operates in a relatively "pure" form, so that market forces alone can generate considerable inequalities.

Moreover, in a hypercompetitive global capitalist economy the room for political maneuver is structurally restricted. Our collective economic fates are linked to the ongoing health of capitalism, both locally and throughout the world. In effect, we have a huge sunk investment: if the system performs well, the benefits are widespread (though highly unequal); if it is disrupted, the negative consequences can reverberate widely. Investments flow to places that provide a hospitable environment for business. Just the implicit threat of capital mobility impedes political challenge. Indeed, political units frequently compete to provide the "best" environment for business—without business necessarily doing anything to promote their own cause. Our ability to debate the essential goodness of capitalism is severely constrained.

At the same time, as often recognized in the political arena, the "success" of capitalism has decidedly negative sides. It remains subject to reversals; the business cycle is hardly tamed. And with its dynamism, so-called dislocations are an inevitable by-product. Market operations may entail Creative Destruction, to use Schumpeter's famous phrase, but that often entails painful disruptions in individual lives and in the fates of large social groups and entire regions. These disruptions, as I previously suggested, are sure to induce ongoing political conflict. The pragmatic issue is, accordingly, how to reap the benefits of capitalistic dynamism while mitigating the social disruptions that it creates.

The United States may be the capitalist society par excellence, but not all countries equally endorse the "American model"—relatively unfettered business prerogatives and relatively minor public initiatives in response to market "failures." Advanced capitalist societies do not follow the American model in lockstep fashion; indeed, this model has been fitfully challenged, often because of electoral pressures (Phillips 1997). Countries' distinctive histories and institutional arrangements will surely affect responses to the inevitable dislocations that accompany capitalist operations. Yet with the general demise of class forces, differences in how societies accommodate these disruptions are unlikely to be significantly explained by differences in class-based political mobilization.

That reality and other features of triumphant capitalism may be either sobering or heartening; but whatever your reaction, class dynamics will not shape the future. In part, our ability to have a humane future depends on our willingness to set aside outmoded ideas and their related hopes. We should focus on the forms of inequality—some old, some new; some understood, some not—that are real and consequential. Class theory: RIP.

REFERENCE MATTER

Chapter 1: Framing the Issue

1. A distinction between "class theory" and "class analysis" has gained some currency. This essentially involves an attempt to distinguish arguments about class that (1) involve the central role of classes in macrolevel social dynamics (e.g., Marx's theory of history)—class theory; and (2) focus more narrowly on the reality of classes and their life-shaping impact (e.g., on voting behavior and cultural practices)—class analysis. A clear distinction along these lines is hard to make and doesn't seem too useful. Instead, in the subsection "But Differences . . ." that follows, I list *several* analytical dimensions along which theories about class may differ. The premises of class theory that I posit here represent the basic minimum claims of *any* argument that can be called class analysis or class theory. My point is that if classes don't exist at this level, any further discussion about their role as historical agents and the like is moot. For expository convenience, then, I interchange the terms class analysis and class theory.

Chapter 2: The Case for Realism

1. This approach is conceptually compatible with Landecker's (1981: 59) argument about class crystallization and boundaries: "classes exist to the extent that class crystallization or class boundaries exist." Classness is thus a variable. While Landecker focuses on positions within different ranks, the common implication is that classes are internally consistent to some nontrivial degree on theoretically relevant dimensions and are distinct from other classes also to a nontrivial degree.

2. To cite some examples: To test whether occupations generate distinct class cultures Davis (1982; see Chapter 7 of this volume) includes education as a control variable in multivariate models. He refers only to the lack of net effects of occupations in concluding that the class culture idea has little standing. Locksley (1982; see Chapter 5) dismisses the impact of class on marital behavior on the basis of multivariate models including education. Robinson and Kelley (1979; see Chapter 5) sought to test "class as conceived by Marx and Dahrendorf" by including categorical measures of class along with continuous stratification measures in their models.

Class theory was deemed convincing to the extent that the categorical measures had net effects. Indeed, the power of class theory seems to be most commonly tested in multivariate analyses.

Chapter 4: Mobility

1. This position is usually linked to particular structuralist strands within neo-Marxist thought (e.g., Poulantzas 1975, and Cardechi 1989), but has also been promoted by some prominent non-Marxists. Dahrendorf writes, "Social classes . . . are phenomena which at least potentially exist independent of the mode of recruitment and rate of fluctuation of their members. . . . Social mobility as such is irrelevant to the problem of the existence of classes." Schumpter expresses the matter with metaphorical flourish, writing "each class is like a hotel or an omnibus for the duration of its collective existence, which is always occupied, but always by other persons." Both are quoted in Mayer and Carroll (1987).

2. My analysis in this chapter could not be less methodologically sophisticated—just an examination of the distributions, expressed in percentage terms, in simple mobility tables. This is not to denigrate all the statistical sophistication that has been directed to the connection between origins and destinations. However, although loglinear models (e.g., Western's analysis showing relatively impermeable class boundaries) and regression-based analyses in the status attainment tradition are illuminating for some intellectually related concerns, they don't make clear the actual flows of people from particular origins to particular destinations. It is the pattern of these flows that allows us to judge the extent of structuration. I fear that many in the field have either become so mesmerized by technical adeptness or dismissive of numbers entirely that they miss the important message of simple numbers.

3. This table is constructed from the matrix of raw frequencies reported in Western (1994: 129–30, appendix A). Western uses Wright's data, *Comparative Project on Class Structure and Class Consciousness*. The frequency counts reflect weighted counts; the weights poststratify the sample to match Census Bureau estimates. This procedure yielded noninteger counts.

Western distinguishes between employers (at least one employee) and the petty bourgeoisie (self-employed, no employees) among those in nonfarm occupations. Farmers comprise all self-employed people in farming occupations. Excepting this nonfarm/farm distinction among owners, this categorization reflects Wright's "productive assets" (i.e., ownership, skills, organizational resources) schema.

4. The connection between quantitative data and verbal interpretation of them is often tenuous, inevitably subject to different "spins." But Western's claim that the "material circumstances of the capitalist and working classes make long-range mobility between them exceptionally rare" (122) seems difficult to sustain in light of these data. Thirty-seven percent of employers' sons became workers; and although only 6 percent of workers' sons became employers, so did only 15 percent

of employers' sons. If 6 percent represents an "exceptionally rare" pattern, what designation does 15 percent warrant?

5. This pattern of widespread fluctuations in family income is not an artifact of questionable or dated data or of Duncan's analytical procedure, which does raise concerns about "cut-off" effects. For example, estimates from the U.S. Bureau of the Census Survey of Income and Program Participation (1993) show that 23 percent of households experienced a 20 percent or more decline in income-to-poverty ratios between 1990 and 1991, and 17 percent increased 20 percent or more.

Chapter 5: Class Sentiment

1. In a later analysis Wright and Shin (1988) showed that a measure of "class salience" (spontaneous working-class identification, no class identity even when forced to choose, forced choice non-working-class identification, and spontaneous non-working-class identification) was weakly related to class location: $R^2 = .037$ for men, .009 for women.

Chapter 6: The Politics of Class

1. We also divided owners into two income categories in analyses not presented here. The results were largely similar, though the net effects for ownership were slightly more apt to be significant, not surprisingly so because we necessarily excluded family income as a control variable.

Chapter 7: Class Culture

1. Focusing on married couples with at least one spouse in the labor force, I used a subsample of the 1981 STU conducted by Juster, Stafford, Hill, and Parsons (as reported in Juster and Stafford 1985). They collected data in 1976 from a nationally representative sample of 1,519 adult Americans plus their spouses and children. In a 1981 follow-up, researchers contacted 620 of the 920 original panel numbers (and spouses and children, when present) who had participated in at least three waves of data collection. Four waves of interviews were spread approximately three months apart, two on weekdays, one on Saturday, and one on Sunday. In each wave respondents completed a detailed time diary by recalling for the interviewer all of their activities since the previous midnight. Respondents also indicated when each activity began and ended, where and with whom each activity occurred, and what else they were doing at the time. Particularly important for this analysis, both spouses furnished diaries and associated responses for the same days.

Diaries showing use of time are reasonably accurate. Robinson (1985) reports, for example, that when respondents told what they were doing when electronically "beeped," their answers corresponded closely to estimates derived from their diaries. Moreover, these reports seem substantially more accurate than "stylized" time-use estimates—a common approach asking respondents to report how much time they usually spend in a particular activity.

As noted in the text, I use a modified version of the Omnibus Measure of Class. I distinguished the elite (5) managers from the nonelite (4) with a fifty-thousand-dollar cutoff (instead of seventy-five thousand dollars) because the data came from an earlier era, thus making a higher cutoff too restrictive. I initially tried classifying by the joint occupational positions of the spouses, but because this procedure proved unwieldly, I simple analyzed a family's class position in terms of the husband's occupation (or the wife's if she was the single earner). Each procedure has conceptual drawbacks (see Chapter 8).

Chapter 9: Lives of the Rich and Poor

1. All figures in this paragraph from A. Hacker (1997).
2. All figures related to *Forbes* data are from Hacker (1997).
3. Didn't my introduction to *The High Status Track: Studies of Elite Schools and Stratification* (Kingston and Lewis 1990) indicate that elite private schools were an integral part of an interconnected set of academic institutions—also including the most prestigious undergraduate institutions and the top ranked schools of law and business—that "disproportionately channel their graduates into eventual positions of economic and cultural privilege" (p. xi)? Yes. And the argument remains valid, I believe. Recognize, however, that the focus there was on the *relatively* favorable odds of those on the track, not on the proportion of the economic elite with such credentials. The latter matter bears more directly on class structuration, and the extent to which these institutions "reproduce" an upper class.
4. A personal disclosure: in an early listing I was upper class by virtue of having graduated from a particular school, but because insufficient numbers of the well-born turned out to have done so, the school was dropped from the upper class list. I harbor no grudges for this social demotion, believe me.
5. I calculated this figure and the other figures cited in this paragraph from data presented in Pyle (1996). Obviously this group of listees in *Who's Who* isn't a representative sample of the corporate elite; it's biased in favor of the publicly influential and acclaimed.

Chapter 10: The Postindustrial Effect

1. This increasing income gap between the college- and high-school-educated reflects two developments: (1) the real wages of the less educated have dropped substantially, and (2) the real wages of the college-educated have increased very slightly.
2. See, for example, analyses of the skill content ratings of job types in the *Dictionary of Occupational Titles* (Teixeira and Mishel 1993); Department of Labor projections about the demand for college-educated labor (Shelley 1992; D. Hecker 1992); and surveys of skill demands reported by employers (Commission on the Skills of the American Workplace 1990).

Chapter 11: American Unexceptionalism

1. The data are from the Comparative Analysis of Social Mobility in Industrial Nations (CASMIN) Project, directed by Walter Muller and John Goldthorpe (see Erikson and Goldthorpe 1993).

2. The validity of this thesis seems to depend on deciding how similar countries must be in order to be considered basically similar. No one claims that relative rates are identical across countries; on the other hand, statistically significant deviations from the common patterns don't suggest substantively significant differences in social organization.

3. These rates were calculated by Heinz Herbert Noll using the CASMIN files.

4. These results were constructed from the matrix of raw frequencies reported in Western 1994, app. A.

5. No item in the index correlates higher than .24 with any other; the Cronbach's alpha is .42, well below conventionally acceptable levels of reliability.

6. In earlier analyses he used six items; in *Class Counts* he includes five.

7. The six categories are: owners who also supervise, supervisors, petty bourgeoisie (no employees), all other white-collar workers, blue-collar workers, and farmers.

REFERENCES

Abowitz, D. 1990. "Sociopolitical Participation and the Significance of Social Context: A Model of Competing Interests and Obligations." *Social Science Quarterly* 71: 543–66.

Acker, J. 1973. "Women and Social Stratification: A Case of Intellectual Sexism." *American Journal of Sociology* 78: 936–45.

Auletta, K. 1982. *The Underclass*. New York: Random House.

Baltzell, E. D. 1958. *Philadelphia Gentleman: The Making of a National Upper Class*. New York: Free Press.

———. 1964. *The Protestant Establishment: Aristocracy and Caste in America*. New York: Random House.

———. 1991. *The Protestant Establishment Revisited: The Collected Papers of E. Digby Baltzell*. Ed. H. Schneiderman. New Brunswick, N.J.: Transaction Publishers.

Berle, A., Jr., and G. Means. [1932] 1967. *The Modern Corporation and Private Property*. Reprint, New York: Harcourt, Brace, and World.

Blau, P. M., O. D. Duncan, and T. Andrea. 1967. *The American Occupational Structure*. New York: Wiley.

Bluestone, Barry. 1995. "The Inequality Express." *The American Prospect* 20: 81–93.

Bourdieu, P. 1984. *Distinction: A Social Critique of the Judgement of Taste*. Cambridge, Mass.: Harvard University Press.

———. 1987a. "What Makes a Social Class? On the Theoretical and Practical Existence of Groups." *Berkeley Journal of Sociology* 32: 1–17.

———. 1987b. "The Forms of Capital." In John Richardson, ed., *Handbook of Theory and Research for the Sociology of Education*. New York: Greenwood.

Bradesher, K. 1997. "A Rich Museum and Its Poor Cousin." *New York Times*, 28 May, pp. B1, 6.

Braverman, H. 1974. *Labor and Monopoly Capital*. New York: Monthly Review Press.

Breiger, R. L. 1981. "The Social Class Structure of Occupational Mobility." *American Journal of Sociology* 87: 578–611.

Brint, S. G. 1984. "New Class and Cumulative Trend Explanations of the Liberal
    Political Attitudes of Professionals." *American Journal of Sociology* 90: 30–71.
———. 1994. *In an Age of Experts: The Changing Role of Professionals in Politics
    and Professional Life.* Princeton, N.J.: Princeton University Press.
Brooks, C. 1994. "Class Consciousness and Politics in Comparative Perspective."
    Social Science Research 23: 167–95.
Caplow, T. Forthcoming. "Problems in the Comparative Charting of Trends in
    Social Stratification." In Y. Lemel and H. H. Noll, eds., *New Structure of
    Inequality.* Montreal: McGill-Queen's University Press.
Caplow, T., and B. Chadwick. 1979. "Inequality and Lifestyles in Middletown,
    1920–1978." *Social Science Quarterly* 60: 366–78.
Cardechi, G. 1989. *The Economic Identification of Social Classes.* London: Rout-
    ledge and Kegan Paul.
Centers, R. 1949. *The Psychology of Social Classes.* Princeton, N.J.: Princeton
    University Press.
Christopher, R. 1989. *Crashing the Gates: The De-Wasping of America's Power
    Elite.* New York: Simon and Schuster.
Clark, T., and S. M. Lipset. 1991. "Are Social Classes Dying?" *International Soci-
    ology* 6: 397–410.
Clark, T., S. M. Lipset, and M. Rempel. 1993. "The Declining Political Significance
    of Class." *International Sociology* 8: 293–316.
Clement, W., and J. Myles. 1994. *Relations of Ruling: Class and Gender in Post-
    industrial Societies.* Montreal: McGill-Queen's University Press.
Coleman, R., and L. Rainwater (with K. McClelland). 1978. *Social Standing in
    America: New Dimensions of Class.* New York: Basic.
Collins, R. 1977. *The Credential Society.* New York: Academic.
Commission on the Skills of the American Workplace. 1990. *America's Choice:
    High Skills or Low Wages!* Rochester, N.Y.: National Center on Education
    and the Economy.
Cookson, P. W., and C. H. Persell. 1985. *Preparing for Power: America's Elite
    Boarding Schools.* New York: Basic.
Curtis, R. F., and E. F. Jackson. 1977. *Inequality in American Communities.* New
    York: Academic.
Dahrendorf, R. 1959. *Class and Class Conflict in Industrial Society.* Stanford,
    Calif.: Stanford University Press.
Davis, J. A. 1982. "Achievement Variables and Class Cultures: Family, Schooling,
    Job, and Forty-nine Dependent Variables in the Cumulative G.S.S." *American
    Sociological Review* 47: 569–86.
Davis, N. J., and R. V. Robinson. 1988. "Class Identification of Men and Women
    in the 1970s and 1980s." *American Sociological Review* 53: 103–12.
De Graaf, N., P. Nieuwbeerta, and A. Heath. 1995. "Class Mobility and Political
    Preferences." *American Journal of Sociology* 100: 997–1027.

Devine, F. 1997. *Social Class in America and Britain*. Edinburgh: Edinburgh University Press.

Devine, J., and J. Wright. 1993. *The Greatest of Evils: Urban Poverty and the American Underclass*. New York: Aldine De Gruyter.

DiMaggio, P. 1994. "Social Stratification, Life-Style, and Social Cognition." In D. Grusky, ed., *Social Stratification*, pp. 458–65. Boulder, Colo.: Westview.

DiMaggio, P., and M. Useem. 1978. "The Origins and Consequences of Class Difference in Exposure to the Arts in America." *Theory and Society* 5: 141–61.

Domhoff, G. W. 1967. *Who Rules America?* Englewood Cliffs, N.J.: Prentice-Hall.

———. 1970. *The Higher Circles: The Governing Class in America*. New York: Vintage.

———. 1983. *Who Rules America Now? A View for the '80s*. Englewood Cliffs, N.J.: Prentice-Hall.

Duncan, G. J. 1984. *Years of Poverty, Years of Plenty*. Ann Arbor: University of Michigan, Institute for Social Research.

Dye, T. 1990. *Who's Running America? The Bush Era*. 5th ed. Englewood Cliffs, N.J.: Prentice-Hall.

Ehrenreich, J., and B. Ehrenreich. 1977. "The Professional-Managerial Class." *Radical America* 11: 7–31.

Erikson, R., and J. Goldthorpe. 1993. *The Constant Flux: A Study of Class Mobility in Industrial Societies*. New York: Oxford University Press.

Erlanger, H. S. 1974. "Class and Corporal Punishment in Childrearing." *American Sociological Review* 39: 68–85.

Esping-Andersen, G. 1993. "Post-industrial Class Structures: An Analytical Framework." In G. Esping-Andersen, ed., *Changing Classes: Stratification and Mobility in Post-Industrial Societies*. Newbury Park, Calif.: Sage.

Evans, G. 1992. "Is Britain a Class-Divided Society? A Re-analysis and Extension of Marshall et al.'s Study of Class Consciousness." *Sociology* 26: 233–58.

———. 1993. "The Decline of Class Divisions in Britain? Class and Ideological Preferences in the 1960s and 1980s." *British Journal of Sociology* 44: 449–571.

Fantasia, R. 1988. *Cultures of Solidarity: Consciousness, Action, and Contemporary American Workers*. Berkeley: University of California Press.

Featherman, D. L., and R. M. Hauser. 1978. *Opportunity and Change*. New York: Academic.

Form, W. H. 1985. *Divided We Stand: Working Class Stratification in America*. Urbana: University of Illinois Press.

Form, W. H., and C. Hanson. 1985. "The Consistency of Stratal Ideologies of Economic Justice." *Research in Social Stratification and Mobility* 4: 239–67.

Franklin, M., T. Mackie, and H. Valen. 1992. *Electoral Change: Responses to Evolving Social and Attitudinal Changes in Western Countries*. Cambridge, Eng.: Cambridge University Press.

Fukuyama, F. 1992. *The End of History and the Last Man*. New York: Free Press.

Fussell, P. 1983. *Class: A Guide Through the American Status System*. New York: Summit.

Giddens, A. 1973. *The Class Structure of the Advanced Societies*. New York: Harper and Row.

Gilbert, D., and J. Kahl. 1993. *The American Class Structure*. 4th ed. Belmont, Calif.: Wadsworth.

Goldthorpe, J. H. 1987. 2nd ed. *Social Mobility and Class Structure in Modern Britain*. Oxford: Clarendon.

Goldthorpe, J., and G. Marshall. 1992. "The Promising Future of Class Analysis: A Response to Recent Critiques." *Sociology* 26: 381–400.

Gouldner, A. 1979. *The Future of Intellectuals and the Rise of the New Class*. New York: Seabury.

Green, C., and R. M. Wilson. 1992. "Occupational Duration in the Careers of White Males." *Quarterly Review of Economics and Finance* 32: 118–31.

Grimes, M. 1991. *Class in Twentieth-Century American Sociology: An Analysis of Theories and Measurement Strategies*. New York: Praeger.

Grusky, D., and J. Sorensen. 1998. "Can Class Analysis Be Salvaged?" *American Journal of Sociology* 103: 1187–1234.

Hacker, A. 1997. *Money: Who Has How Much and Why*. New York: Scribner.

Halle, D. 1984. *America's Working Man: Work, Home, and Politics Among Blue-Collar Property-Home-Owners*. Chicago: University of Chicago Press.

———. 1993. *Inside Culture: Art and Class in the American Home*. Chicago: University of Chicago.

Halle, D., and F. Romo. 1991. "The Blue-Collar Working Class: Continuity and Change" in A. Wolfe, ed., *America at Century's End*. Berkeley: University of California Press.

Heaton, T. 1987. "Objective Status and Class Consciousness." *Social Science Quarterly* 68: 611–20.

Hecker, D. 1992. "Reconciling Conflicting Data on Jobs for College Graduates." *Monthly Labor Review* (July): 3–12.

Heilbroner, R. 1985. *The Nature and Logic of Capitalism*. New York: Norton.

Herman, E. S. 1981. *Corporate Control, Corporate Power*. New York: Cambridge University Press.

Higley, S. 1995. *Privilege, Power, and Place: The Geography of the American Upper Class*. Lantham, Md.: Rowan and Littlefield.

Hout, M. 1988. "More Universalism, Less Structural Mobility: The American Occupational Structure in the 1980s." *American Journal of Sociology* 93: 1358–1400.

Hout, M., C. Brooks, and J. Manza. 1993. "The Persistence of Class in Post-industrial Societies." *International Sociology* 8: 259–77.

———. 1995. "The Democratic Class Struggle in the United States, 1948–1992." *American Sociological Review* 60: 805–28.

Huckfeldt, R. R. 1983. "Social Contexts, Social Networks, and Urban Networks: Environmental Constraints on Friendship Choice." *American Journal of Sociology* 89: 651–69.

Hunter, J. D., and C. Bowman. 1996. *The State of Disunion: 1996 Survey of American Political Culture*. Ivy, Va.: In Media Res Educational Foundation.

Jackman, M. R., and R. W. Jackman. 1983. *Class Awareness in the United States*. Berkeley: University of California Press.

Jacobs, G. 1993. "Careers in the U.S. Service Economy." In G. Esping-Andersen, ed., *Changing Classes: Stratification and Mobility in Post-Industrial Societies*. Newbury Park, Calif.: Sage.

Jargowsky, P., and M. J. Bane. 1991. "Ghetto Poverty in the United States, 1970–1980." In C. Jencks and P. Peterson, eds., *The Urban Underclass*. Washington, D.C.: The Brookings Institution.

Jencks, C. 1991. "Is the American Underclass Growing?" In C. Jencks and P. Peterson, eds., *The Urban Underclass*. Washington, D.C.: The Brookings Institution.

Jencks, C., et al. 1979. *Who Gets Ahead? The Determinants of Economic Success in America*. New York: Basic.

Johnston, W. B., and M. D. Ornstein. 1985. "Social Class and Political Ideology in Canada." *The Canadian Review of Sociology and Anthropology* 22: 369–93.

Juster, F. T., and F. Stafford, eds. 1985. *Time, Goods, and Well-Being*. Ann Arbor, Mich.: Survey Research Center, Institute for Social Research, University of Michigan.

Kalleberg, A. L., and L. J. Griffin. 1980. "Class, Occupation and Inequality in Job Rewards." *American Journal of Sociology* 85: 731–68.

Kelley, J., and M. D. R. Evans. 1995. "Class and Class Conflict in Six Western Nations." *American Sociological Review* 60: 157–78.

Kerbo, H. R. 1996. *Social Stratification and Inequality: Class Conflict in the United States*. New York: McGraw Hill.

Kerckhoff, A. C., R. T. Campbell, and I. Winfield-Laird. 1985. "Social Mobility in Great Britain and the United States." *American Journal of Sociology* 91: 281–308.

Kingston, P. W., and J. Fries. 1994. "Having a Stake in the System: The Sociopolitical Ramifications of Business and Home Ownership." *Social Science Quarterly* 75: 679–86.

Kingston, P. W., and L. S. Lewis. 1990. *The High Status Track: Studies of Elite Schools and Stratification*. Albany: State University of New York Press.

Knoke, D., L. E. Raffalovich, and W. Erskine. 1987. "Class, Status and Economic Policy Preferences." *Research in Social Stratification and Mobility* 6: 141–58.

Knottnerus, J. D. 1987. "Status Attainment Research and Its Image of Society." *American Sociological Review* 52: 113–21.

Kohn, M. L. 1969. *Class and Conformity: A Study in Values*. Homewood, Ill.: Dorsey.

Kohn, M. L., and C. Schooler. 1983. *Work and Personality: An Inquiry into the Impact of Social Stratification.* Norwood, N.J.: Ablex.

Komarovsky, M. 1964. *Blue Collar Marriage.* New York: Random House.

Kristol, I. 1972. "About Equality." *Commentary* 54: 41–47.

Ladd, E. C., Jr. 1978. "The New Lines Are Drawn: Class and Ideology in America, Part 1." *Public Opinion* 3: 48–53.

Lamont, M. 1992. *Money, Morals, and Manners: The Culture of the French and American Upper-Middle Class.* Chicago: University of Chicago Press.

Lamont, M., and A. Lareau. 1988. "Cultural Capital: Allusions, Gaps, and Glissandos in Recent Theoretical Developments." *Sociological Theory* 6: 153–68.

Lamont, M., et al. 1994. "Cultural and Moral Boundaries in the United States: Inequality and Lifestyle Explanations." Paper presented at 1994 American Sociological Association Meeting, Los Angeles.

Landecker, W. 1981. *Class Crystallization.* New Brunswick, N.J.: Rutgers University Press.

Laumann, E. O. 1966. *Prestige and Association in an Urban Community.* Indianapolis: Bobbs-Merrill.

———. 1973. *Bonds of Pluralism: The Form and Substance of Urban Social Networks.* New York: Wiley.

Lemann, N. 1992. "Ruling by Degree: Why the Meritocracy is Bad for America." *The Washington Monthly* 24 (January–February): 41–46.

Lerner, R., A. Nagi, and S. Rothman. 1996. *American Elites.* New Haven, Conn.: Yale University Press.

Levy, Frank. 1995. "Incomes and Income Inequality." In R. Farley, ed., *State of the Union: America in the 1990s.* New York: Russell Sage Foundation.

Lindblom, C. 1978. "The Business of America Is Still Business." *New York Times,* 4 January, p. A19.

Lipset, S. M. 1959. *Political Man: The Social Bases of Politics.* Garden City, N.Y.: Doubleday.

———. 1981. *Political Man: The Social Bases of Politics.* Rev. ed. Baltimore: Johns Hopkins University Press.

Locksley, A. 1982. "Social Class and Marital Attitudes and Behavior." *Journal of Marriage and the Family* 44: 427–40.

Lucal, B. 1994. "Class Stratification in Introductory Textbooks: Relational and Distributional Models." *Teaching Sociology* 22: 139–50.

Lynd, R., and H. Lynd. 1929. *Middletown.* New York: Harcourt, Brace.

———. 1937. *Middletown in Transition.* New York: Harcourt, Brace.

Marshall, G., et al. 1988. *Social Class in Modern Britain.* London: Hutchinson.

———. 1995. "Class, Gender, and the Asymmetry Hypothesis." *European Sociological Review* 11: 1–15.

———. 1996. "Social Class and the Underclass in Britain and the U.S." *British Journal of Sociology* 47: 22–44.

Mayer, K., and A. Carroll. 1987. "Jobs and Classes: Structural Constraints on Career Mobility." *European Sociological Review* 3: 14–38.

Messner, S., and M. Krohn. 1990. "Class, Compliance Structures, and Delinquency: Assessing Integrated Structural Marxist Theory." *American Journal of Sociology* 96: 300–328.

Mills, C. W. 1951. *White Collar*. New York: Oxford University Press.

———. 1956. *The Power Elite*. New York: Oxford University Press.

Moore, G., and R. Alba. 1982. "Class and Prestige Origins in the American Elite." In P. Marsden and N. Lin, eds., *Social Structure and Network Analysis*. Beverly Hills, Calif.: Sage.

Muller, W. 1990. "Social Mobility in Industrial Nations." In J. Clark, C. Modgil, and S. Modgil, eds., *John H. Goldthorpe: Consensus and Controversy*. London: Falmer.

Murphy, R. 1988. *Social Closure: The Theory of Monopolization and Exclusion*. New York: Oxford University Press.

Nisbet, R. A. 1959. "The Decline and Fall of the Concept of Social Class." *Pacific Sociological Review* 2: 11–17.

Ostrander, S. 1984. *Women of the Upper Class*. Philadelphia: Temple University Press.

Ostrower, F. 1995. *Why the Wealthy Give: The Culture of Elite Philanthropy*. Princeton, N.J.: Princeton University Press.

Pakulski, J., and M. Waters. 1996. *The Death of Class*. Thousand Oaks, Calif.: Sage.

Parkin, F. 1971. *Class Inequality and Political Order: Social Stratification in Capitalist and Communist Societies*. New York: Praeger.

———. 1974. "Strategies of Social Closure in Class Formation." In Frank Parkin, ed., *The Social Analysis of the Class Structure*. London: Tavistock.

Peterson, R. 1992. "Understanding Audience Segmentation: From Elite and Mass to Omnivore and Univore." *Poetics* 21: 243–58.

Peterson, R., and A. Simkus. 1994. "How Musical Tastes Mark Occupational Status Groups." In Michele Lamont and Marcel Fournier, eds., *Cultivating Differences: Symbolic Boundaries and the Making of Inequality*. Chicago: University of Chicago Press.

Phillips, K. 1997. "European Conservatism Loses Steam." *Charlottesville (Virginia) Daily Progress*, 15 June, p. D1.

Poulantzas, N. 1975. *Classes in Contemporary Capitalism*. London: New Left.

Przeworski, A. 1977. "Proletariat into a Class: The Process of Class Formation from Karl Kautsky's 'The Class Struggle' to Recent Controversies." *Politics and Society* 7: 343–501.

Pyle, R. 1996. *Persistence and Change in the Protestant Establishment*. Westport, Conn.: Praeger.

Reed, J. 1988. "The Changing of the Old Guard." *U.S. News and World Report*, 8 February, pp. 38–40, 45–47.

Robinson, J. 1985. "The Validity and Reliability of Diaries versus Alternative Time Use Measures." In T. Juster and F. Stafford, eds., *Time, Goods, and Well-Being*. Ann Arbor: Survey Research Center, Institute for Social Research, University of Michigan.

Robinson, R. V., and J. Kelley. 1979. "Class As Conceived by Marx and Dahrendorf." *American Sociological Review* 44: 38–58.

Rossides, D. W. 1990. *Social Stratification: The American Class System in Comparative Perspective*. Englewood Cliffs, N.J.: Prentice-Hall.

Rothman, R. 1993. *Inequality and Stratification: Class, Color, and Gender*. Englewood Cliffs, N.J.: Prentice-Hall.

Rubin, L. B. 1976. *Worlds of Pain: Life in the Working-Class Family*. New York: Basic.

Schlozman, K. L., and S. Verba. 1979. *Injury to Insult: Unemployment, Class, and Political Response*. Cambridge, Mass.: Harvard University Press.

Shelley, K. 1992. "The Future of Jobs for College Graduates." *Monthly Labor Review*. July: 13–21.

Silvestri, G. 1991. "Who Are the Self-Employed? Employment Profiles and Recent Trends." *Occupational Outlook Quarterly* 35: 26–36.

Simkus, A. A. 1978. "Residential Segregation by Occupation and Race in Ten Urbanized Areas." *American Sociological Review* 43: 81–93.

Smeeding, T., M. O'Higgins, and L. Rainwater. 1990. *Poverty, Inequality, and Income Distribution in Comparative Perspective*. New York: Harvester/ Wheatsheaf.

Snipp, C. M. 1985. "Occupational Mobility and Social Class: Insights from Men's Career Mobility." *American Sociological Review* 50: 475–92.

Sombart, W. [1906, orig. German ed.] 1976. *Why Is There No Socialism in the United States?* Trans. P. Hocking and C. Husbands. White Plains, N.Y.: International Arts and Sciences Press.

Sorensen, A. 1994. "Women, Family, and Class." *Annual Review of Sociology* 20: 27–47.

Stanley, T., and W. Danko. 1996. *The Millionaire Next Door*. Atlanta: Longstreet.

Stier, H., and D. B. Grusky. 1990. "An Overlapping Persistence Model of Career Mobility." *American Sociological Review* 55: 736–56.

Stinchcombe, A. L. 1989. "Education, Exploitation, and Class Consciousness." In E. O. Wright, ed., *The Debate on Classes*. London: Verso.

Teixeira, R., and L. Mishel. 1993. "Whose Skills Shortage—Workers or Management?" *Issues in Science and Technology* (Summer): 69–74

Turner, J. 1984. *Social Stratification: A Theoretical Analysis*. New York: Columbia University Press.

U.S. Department of Labor. Bureau of Labor Statistics. 1980. *Occupational Mobility During 1977*. Special Labor Force Report, no. 231.

Useem, M. 1984. *The Inner Circle: Large Corporations and the Rise of Business Political Activity in the U.S. and the U.K.* New York: Oxford University Press.

Useem, M., and J. Karabel. 1990. In P. W. Kingston and L. Lewis, eds., "Pathways to Top Corporate Management," ch. 8. Albany: State University of New York Press.

Vanneman, R. 1977. "The Occupational Composition of American Classes." *American Journal of Sociology* 82: 783–807.

Wallace, M., and R. L. Jepperson. 1986. "Class Structure and Political Culture: Evaluations of Key Political Groups in Eight Western Capitalist Nations." *Research in Social Stratification and Mobility* 5: 321–61.

Warner, W. L., and P. Lunt. 1941. *The Social Life of a Modern Community*. New Haven, Conn.: Yale University Press.

Weiss, M. 1988. *The Clustering of America*. New York: Harper and Row.

Westbrook, R. 1996. "The Counter Intelligentsia: How Neoconservatism Lived and Died." *Lingua France* (November): 65–71.

Western, M. 1994. "Class Structure and Intergenerational Class Mobility: A Comparative Analysis of Nation and Gender." *Social Forces* 73: 101–34.

Wiley, N. 1967. "America's Unique Class Politics: The Interplay of the Labor, Credit, and Commodity Markets." *American Sociological Review* 32: 529–40.

Wilson, W. J. 1987. *The Truly Disadvantaged: The Inner City, the Underclass, and Public Policy*. Chicago: University of Chicago Press.

Wolff, E. N. 1995. "How the Pie is Sliced: America's Concentration of Wealth." *American Prospect* 22: 58–64.

Wright, E. O. 1985. *Classes*. London: Verso.

———. 1989. "Women in the Class Structure." *Politics and Society* 17: 35–66.

———. 1996. "The Continuing Relevance of Class Analysis—Comments." *Theory and Society* 25: 693–715.

———. 1997. *Class Counts: Comparative Studies in Class Analysis*. Cambridge, Eng.: Cambridge University Press.

Wright, E. O., and D. Cho. 1992. "The Relative Permeability of Class Boundaries to Cross-Class Friendships: A Comparative Study of the United States, Canada, Sweden, and Norway." *American Sociological Review* 57: 85–102.

Wright, E. O., and L. Perrone. 1977. "Marxist Class Categories and Income Inequality." *American Sociological Review* 47: 32–55.

Wright, E. O., and K. Shin. 1988. "Temporality and Class Analysis: A Comparative Analysis of Class Structure, Class Trajectory, and Class Consciousness in Sweden and the United States." *Sociological Theory* 6: 58–84.

Wright, E. O., C. Costello, D. Hachen, and J. Sprague. 1982. "The American Class Structure." *American Sociological Review* 47: 709–26.

Wright, E. O., et al. 1989. *The Debate on Classes*. London: Verso.

Wrong, D. 1988. "Social Inequality Without Social Stratification." In C. Heller, ed., *Structured Social Inequality: A Reader in Comparative Social Stratification*. New York: MacMillan.

Zipp, J. F. 1986. "Social Class and Social Liberalism." *Sociological Forum* 1: 301–29.

INDEX